GLOBALIZATION AND DEVELOPMENT STUDIES

Challenges for the 21st Century

Edited by

FRANS J. SCHUURMAN

SAGE Publications
London • Thousand Oaks • New Delhi

First published in 2001 by
THELA THESIS
Prinseneiland 305
1013 LR Amsterdam
The Netherlands

 SAGE Publications Ltd
6 Bonhill Street
London EC2A 4PU

SAGE Publications Inc
2455 Teller Road
Thousand Oaks, California 91320

SAGE Publications India Pvt Ltd
32, M-Block Market
Greater Kailash – I
New Delhi 110 048

British Library Cataloguing in Publication data

A catalogue record for this book is
available from the British Library

ISBN 0 7619 7266 8
ISBN 0 7619 7267 6   (pbk)

Library of Congress catalog record available

Typeset by Textcetera
Cover design by Lies Kindt
Cover photo by Octavio Tapia Lloret

TABLE OF CONTENTS

PREFACE

In 1991 the Nijmegen Institute of Comparative Development Studies (NICCOS) organized a workshop to take stock of what was known at the time as the impasse in development theories. From the mid-1980s onwards this impasse received attention in an increasing number of publications.

Now, nearly ten years later and with hindsight, it is clear that what in the beginning of the 1990s seemed a theoretical crisis or impasse, was in reality a crisis of paradigmatic proportions. This paradigmatic crisis continued to be fuelled by the growing popularity of the concept of globalization. At the same time development studies adopted globalization as a research topic. As such, development studies was forced to engage in a more rigorous paradigmatic introspection than ever before.

In November 1997 the Institute of Development Studies of the University of Nijmegen organized a workshop on the significance of globalization (as a concept, a theory, a discourse and/or as an ontological process) for development studies. The majority of the contributions presented at that workshop are included in the present anthology, some significantly revised. Other authors were invited to contribute in order to give this book a more balanced overview of the challenges for development studies of that polymorphous phenomenon called globalization. Some of the chapters have a common view of what globalization is supposed to be and what its significance is or could be for development studies. Other contributions reflect more divergent positions and as such represent neatly the heterogeneity of the impact of globalization within the discipline. Taken together, the contributions outline the challenges that globalization poses for development studies and what kind of paradigmatic changes loom on the horizon.

I would like to thank the following institutions for their financial support which enabled the organization of our 1997 workshop: NWO (Netherlands Foundation for Scientific Research), CERES (Research School for Resource Studies for Development), NICCOS (Nijmegen Institute for Comparative Studies in Development and Cultural Change) and the Faculty of Social Sciences of the University of Nijmegen. Thanks is due to Routledge for permission to use the chapter of Marchand and Runyan in a slightly different version. Thanks are also due to Sue Houston – who unfortunately passed away before this book was published – and Xavier la Crois for correcting the English drafts, and to Detlev Haude for initial support.

The editor

GLOBALIZATION AND DEVELOPMENT STUDIES: INTRODUCING THE CHALLENGES

Frans J. Schuurman

Introduction

In order to understand the challenges that globalization poses for development studies it is important to realize that the roots of social sciences, and as such also of the more recent discipline of development studies, are embedded in the 19th century. At that time social sciences attempted to understand the processes of social change in Western Europe which had started in the previous century with the Industrial Revolution and the French Revolution. The early social scientists, Auguste Comte, Alexis de Tocqueville and (especially) Herbert Spencer, greatly influenced by, on the one hand, the heritage of the Enlightenment and by Darwinian thinking on the other hand, tried to understand this change in terms of a transformation as part of a social evolutionary process. This was at least one reason why in due course much social theorizing developed progress-oriented, dichotomous thinking as so many variations on the mother of all social dichotomous thinking, i.e. tradition versus modernity.

In the course of the 19th century the social sciences developed further by studying, and sometimes also condemning, the effects of modernization (urbanization, the acceleration of industrialization, and increasing individualization). During that process the social sciences wrestled free from the humanities and from philosophy specifically under which paradigmatic tyranny it had resided for such a long time. As such it took refuge in natural science and opted for a nomothetic methodology in contrast to the idiographic methodology of the humanities. Separate disciplines came into being: sociology, economics, geography, political science, anthropology, followed in the second half of the 20th century by the newcomer; development studies.

All these branches of social science have their paradigmatic and methodological roots in the late 18th and 19th centuries which are currently labelled by an increasing number of scholars as counterproductive to understanding the so-called global age. In the 19th century, the rise of the social sciences took place in the context of accelerating military and economic colonization of the Third World, the process of nation-building in the First World, and, in general, the development of modernity. This context heavily influenced the rise of the social sciences with the nation-state as its referent. Economic theories, for example, concentrated upon the creation of national markets, political science on the creation of democratic states, and cultural sciences on the creation of new forms of collective identity (i.e. nationalism instead of traditional forms based on ethnicity or regionalism). The majority of theories that subsequently followed within each of these disciplines also carry overtones of the phenomenon of nation-states. Even when international comparisons were made, it was always with nation-states as the research units.

One of the consequences of taking spatial units (in this case the nation-state) as referents for social analysis was an essentialization of its inhabitants as homogeneous entities. As we will see later on, much post-World War II thinking concerning the Third World can be characterized by such an essentialization.

In short, and I limit myself to what is relevant in the context of this introduction: the social sciences' 19th century heritage bequeathed to its evolving theoretical framework an unconditional belief in the concept of progress and in the makeability of society, an essentialization of First and Third World inhabitants, and the importance of the (nation) state as a frame of reference.

It is clear that this 19th century heritage has significantly influenced thinking within development studies as it has evolved over the last fifty years. By the same token, it is also clear why globalization poses such a challenge for development studies. Without elaborating too much on what globalization is or is supposed to be, there is a general agreement among writers on globalization that economics is no longer about understanding national economic variables related to national markets and that political science is no longer about the state as *the* political actor. They also agree that the cultural sciences emphasize the increasing importance of other types of identity formation, even the existence of multiple types of identity, instead of only nationalism.

As was mentioned in the Preface to this anthology, development studies were thrown into a theoretical impasse from the mid 1980s onwards (Schuurman 1993). With the challenges that globalization poses to development studies we have landed with the impasse upon the paradigmatic level. In the next paragraphs I intend briefly to outline these challenges and introduce the contributions of the authors in Part I of this book.

Challenging the central paradigms in development studies

After World War II developmental paradigms shared at least three characteristics:

1 The essentialization of the Third World and its inhabitants as homogeneous entities.

2　The unconditional belief in the concept of progress and in the makeability of society.

3　The importance of the (nation) state as an analytical frame of reference and the political and scientific confidence in the role of the state to realize progress.

The first two characteristics of post-war development thinking (i.e. the Third World as a homogeneous entity and the unconditional belief in progress) form the core of what was termed developmentalism. This was evolutionary development thinking directed at the Third World that was unilinear and teleological, and as such could harbour two apparently contradictory clusters of development theories, i.e. modernization theories and Marxist development theories.

The third characteristic of post-war development thinking, the central role of the state in the development process, was a reflection of how, from its beginnings in the 19th century, the modern state increasingly took the initiative in the development process. This initiative found its highlight in the post-World War II phase of constructing the welfare state in the Western industrial world, an idea which was subsequently exported to the Third World.

History moves on, however. Social, economic, and political developments change the Zeitgeist. Thomas Kuhn had already noted that paradigms have a natural resistance to change, though some more than others. As such, the three paradigmatic characteristics of post-war development thinking have in time come under attack one by one. The critique of the first two paradigmatic characteristics came from post-modernist and post-development circles. I will limit myself here to a short introduction to this critique; elsewhere I have presented a more elaborate discussion (Schuurman 2000).

In the context of this introduction I especially want to concentrate on the third paradigmatic characteristic of development studies as this is specifically focussed on by the globalization discourse.

Ad. 1: The essentialization of the Third World
First of all there was a mounting critique on the idea of a homogeneous Third World. This critique was an extension of the critique on dependency theory, which in its most popular version could not explain the diversity of development experiences among Third World countries. The role of OPEC in the oil crisis at the beginning of the 1970s, the economic success of the Asian Tigers in relation to the continuation of extreme poverty in Africa, and the return of military dictatorships in several Latin American countries (which was seen as a sort of political regression), all these events, it was felt, made clear that the Third World was too heterogeneous a category to be covered by just one development theory that was itself drawn from a highly questionable dependency paradigm.

Towards the end of the 1980s, this critique on the alleged homogeneity of the Third World as a concept was strengthened by the post-modern critique on the essentialism of many concepts of the modernist discourse put forward by such postmodernist writers as Foucault and Derrida.

This led to a situation, within the realm of development studies, in which many researchers were reluctant to specify their field (studying the inequality in the Third World) to avoid being accused of essentialism. Instead they turned to the vague, but relatively safe, notion of 'diversity within Third World development experiences'. This led to the awkward situation in which, at a paradigmatic level, there was a change from an emphasis on inequality to diversity, but this never received further paradigmatic elaboration nor the necessary translation to the level of testable, workable development theories.

Ad. 2 The end of the belief in progress
In the 1990s the disappearance of the belief in progress was translated into the growth of, on the one hand, various versions of post-modern (non) development thinking, and on the other hand, of the idea of the global risk society.

In the 1980s development pessimism had already set in with the realization of the ever-widening gap between poor and rich countries. Where economic growth had occurred it had had a catastrophic effect on the environment and the end of existing socialism had removed socialist-inspired development trajectories from the academic and political agendas.

An early version of post-modern, in fact anti-modernist, (non) development thinking was introduced by Wolfgang Sachs (1992) "... development talk still pervades not only official declarations but *even the language of grassroots movements*. It is time to dismantle this mental structure" (Sachs, 1992: 1; my emphasis, FS).

Later versions of post-modern thinking also reflected similar anti-modernist ideas (e.g. Escobar 1995; Rahnema 1997), relegating progress and development to the dustbin of 20th century concepts better left behind before entering the third millennium. The Western notion of progress would only cause environmental pollution because it means industrialization. It would sever indigenous peoples from their cultural roots and expose them as helpless victims to a global, exploitative capitalism that through manipulation in the media urged them to consume the wrong things for the wrong reasons with money they do not have. Alternatives, though, put forward by post-development thinkers have a high New Age-like content clad in Third World clothes.

Two other variants of the loss in the belief of progress with a more *fin-de-siècle* air are embodied in the concept of the risk society, and in the suddenly popular publications of 'apocalypse' authors. Allow me to treat both briefly in order to complete the picture about the lost paradigm of progress.

Moving towards the 21st century and, more importantly, towards the next millennium has recently led to an array of philosophical treaties about the 'moral
consciousness' with which humankind has entered this century. These are not
merry publications; some even carry the notions of 'apocalypse' (Bull 1995) or
'betrayal' (Norgaard 1994) in their title. Samuel Huntington, Eric Hobsbawm,
and Robert Kaplan are well-known current authors embodying – to varying
degrees and for very different reasons – a *fin-de-siècle* pessimism. In his 1993 article *The Clash of Civilizations?* (later published as a book), Huntington urges the
West to give up its universal illusions and not to meddle in regional conflicts
elsewhere in the world. If the West, and more particularly the United States,
does not adhere to the principle of cultural relativism in international politics
then a 'clash of civilizations' will inevitably evolve.

Hobsbawm (1994) finds an explanation for the *fin-de-siècle* moral crisis in the
ultimate victory of individual materialism, which led to the degradation of traditional networks of human solidarity. This moral vacuum results in a chaos that is
completed by the onslaught of a global economy which leaves the nation-states
virtually defenceless. Huntington and Hobsbawm, however, are mildly optimis-
tic compared to Robert Kaplan. In his 1994 article *The Coming Anarchy* (elaborated and later published as a book), Kaplan takes the reader on a journey
through West Africa painting a picture of total political and social chaos. Para-
military warlords and organized bandits fight each other for the scarce
resources, while the urban centres are ruled by corruption, crime, disease, overpopulation, and phenomenal pollution. This regional criminal anarchy will
eventually reach global levels. According to Kaplan, the end of the Cold War did
not lead to 'the end of history', on the contrary, it ushered in a period in which
international relations will be dominated by chaos.

The *fin-de-siècle* studies of these authors are perhaps somewhat extreme but I do
not have the feeling that they are atypical. In any case, the recent *fin-de-siècle*
atmosphere was decidedly more pessimistic compared to the turn from the 19th
to the 20th century. Certainly, at the end of the 19th century there were also
doubts about what the twentieth century would bring but optimism, especially
faith in the wonders of technological progress, prevailed. At the end of the 20th
century, it is exactly this fear of the unintended consequences of technological
progress that has and is still having such a paralyzing effect on imagining positive future scenarios.

In 1986 the German sociologist Ulrich Beck (later joined by Anthony Giddens
and Scott Lash) had already introduced the term (global) risk society. This term
seems to imply a generalized feeling of *fin-de-siècle* pessimism, the feeling that it
is useless to look ahead, to plan, because of the increasing influence of unintended consequences which the technological growth machinery bestows upon
us. As a result, human agency – in spite of the reflexive modernity that would
enable human actors to cope with global risks – is apparently undervalued in

this approach, let alone concepts like progress and emancipation. In addition, global risk society seems to be a typical example of European ethnocentric thinking because many in the Third World have never known any another society than a risk society, but I will return to this later.

In the last two decades of the 20th century, progress, as one of the most central and omnipresent notions of modernity, finally met with serious opposition from anti-modernist, post-development quarters, from the *fin-de-siècle* 'riders of the apocalypse', and from the Anglo-German axis of the reflexive modernization theorists introducing the notion of global risk society.

Ad. 3 The end of the belief in the role of the state
It did not take long for the critique on the third common characteristic of post-war development thinking (the central role of the state in development theories) to take form. Postmodernism enjoyed its near hegemonic popularity for only a relatively short time because of the appearance of that other *fin-de-siècle* concept: globalization. As I mentioned earlier, in order to understand the impact that concept had on development studies it is important to realize the importance of the concept of the (nation) state for social science theories in general, and, by the same token, for development studies. The importance of the state became visible in modernization theories, dependency theories, and even in world-system theories.

Globalization changed all that. I will not tire the reader prematurely with an exposé of the many positions taken within the globalization debate. Elsewhere in this publication I have enumerated nine positions in the globalization debate, which range from (a) globalization indicates a new historical period (i.e. we don't know exactly how to describe it because we don't have the right vocabulary yet as our concepts are still steeped in the previous period of modernity) to the other extreme (b) that if there ever was anything like globalization then that is already over because we have now entered a period of increasing fragmentation and de-globalization.

In any case, many participants in the globalization debate seem to agree about the decreasing economic, political, and cultural importance of (nation) states. The central role of the state, it is said, is being hollowed out from above as well as from below. In a political sense one notices the increasing importance of international political organizations that interfere politically and militarily in particular states. They thereby relegate to the past the written and unwritten rules on the sovereignty of (nation) states and their using of institutionalized violence within their borders (which has always been the central element in the definition of states). The national state is hollowed out from below by the growing phenomenon of local government, which seems to have become *the* example of what good governance should be about. Economically, the state is seen disappearing as an economic actor through privatization supported by deregulation.

There is also the growing importance of the global financial markets, where daily about $US 1500 billion are shifted around the globe.

Culturally, the idea of a national identity as the central element in identity formation for individuals or groups is fast being eroded in favour of cosmopolitanism on the one hand and/or the fortification of ethnic, regional, and religious identities on the other hand.

As the state has always played a central role in development studies, it is not hard to imagine the impact that the globalization debate has had on development studies. The impasse in development theories, which was signalled in the mid 1980s, took on paradigmatic dimensions in the 1990s. What is more likely, however, is that the so-called impasse in development theories was a paradigmatic crisis right from the start. Within development studies it was always difficult to separate theories from paradigms because of its strong normative orientation.

From development studies to global studies?

Three paradigms of post-World War II development thinking have lost their hegemonic status within development studies. Should we regret this? Should we regret that development studies have moved from a theoretical crisis to a paradigmatic crisis, which has prompted some to replace development studies with something called 'global studies'? The answer depends to a large extent on whether the criticisms were justified in the first place, and if so, whether post-modernism, post-development, and globalization are capable of offering new exciting paradigms which cater to the explanandum of development studies.

I will address this question briefly for each one of the lost paradigms but emphasizing again the role of the nation-state.

Diversity vs. inequality

The very essence of development studies is a normative preoccupation with the poor, marginalized and exploited people in the South. In this sense, it should be in the first place *inequality* rather than *diversity* or *difference* that is the main focus for development studies: inequality of access to power, to resources, to a human existence – in short, inequality in emancipation. There is no doubt that there is a diversity in forms, experiences, and strategies for coping with inequality which deserves to be an integral part of the domain of development studies. There is also no doubt that globalization will contribute to new forms of inequality and new forms of resistance. However, it is inequality, as such, which should constitute the main focus within the explanandum of development studies. A universal, yet context-sensitive notion of justice is still far more attractive to reclaiming a normative and political progressive domain for development studies than any attempt inspired by either postmodernism or globalization in that direction.

Progress vs. risk management

The solution to underdevelopment as proposed by many of the authors in the post-modern/anti-modernist tradition is often astonishingly naïve in its simplicity, i.e. let the poor in the Third World forget about needs which resemble our own. Let them forget about wanting a standard of living like that in the North, let them forget about wanting a decent house, access to health care, employment, etc. These needs would draw them into the development process with all the implied negative connotations.

I have the strong impression, however, judging from the messages conveyed by many social movements in the Third World, that the majority of peasants and indigenous people in the South are really interested in getting the right price for their products, and having access to bilingual education, electricity, transportation, and adequate health care. In fact, many social movements and grassroots organizations in the South demand that their governments include them in the development process, no longer treating them as second-class citizens. Many NGOs in the South as well as in the North support these groups in their justified claims for full citizenship and political participation.

Hunger and high morbidity and mortality rates in the Third World do not just disappear by merely changing the subjective perspective of the people involved.

In addition the concept of global risk society is not uncontested with respect to its value for developed countries in the North, let alone its relevance for the poor in the South. Frank Füredi of the University of Kent is one of the concerned, progressive scholars who takes the concepts of reflexive modernization and risk-consciousness to task (Füredi 1996). Firstly, Füredi criticizes the idea that global risk is something new, that it is one of the side-effects or even one of the constituent characteristics of the Post-Fordist globalization phase. Füredi denounces this as a pretty ethnocentric and ahistorical view and points out the risks that colonized people forcibly had to endure because of the expansion of Western capitalism. As far as these indigenous peoples are concerned theirs has been a risk society ever since the penetration of colonialism.

Secondly, it seems very opportunistic to Füredi that a concept like global risk society emerged at a time when the risks that the North has always been able to export to the South now also began to threaten the industrialized nation-states. Füredi's third objection is that the concept of risk society evokes the image of the risks being evenly spread. Pointing out the global dimensions of risks does not detract from the fact that certain nations – or more specifically certain categories of people – are more risk-prone than others. Risk is unequally distributed geographically and sociologically, and thinking otherwise draws attention away from the necessity of emancipatory projects directed at the global underclasses.

Finally, the concept of risk society underrates the power of human agency and overrates the (apparent) autonomous dynamic of technology, which would lead us all unequivocally towards the apocalypse. In relation to the previous objection this means that collective social action to fight the unequal distribution of risk could be considered useless because social change can only be a consequence of technological developments. In a risk society, then, we are doomed to keep on running from one panic to the next. Collective emancipatory projects are relegated to the margin of the broader global picture.

A new morality based on self-restraint is put forward by the adherents of the risk society. However, it does not seem likely that risk management through self-restraint is an anymore powerful perspective for the poor in the Third World than the notion of progress.

Having entered the 21st century, the notion of progress seems to have lost much of its hegemonic status within development studies. Alternative views, however, have not been able, in a broadly accepted way, to reconstruct the paradigm-theory-practice chain in the same manner that the concept of progress did and incorporate it within development studies.

State vs. civil society
In the globalization debate the central role of the (nation) state has become de-emphasized in favour of either global governance or civil society, i.e. local government. The idea of civil society in particular plays an important role in current scientific and policy documents about development. It is often suggested that civil society has evolved from a rather indeterminate conglomerate of individual households and an inarticulate container of economic classes and disparate social movements to a fully-fledged, articulate actor with synergetic developmental potential. Where national governments in Third World countries have failed to institutionalize democracy and start a decent economic development, local government is now supposed to be able to do just that in a synergetic collaboration with actors from within civil society and with representatives of national and international capital. 'Good governance' nowadays is no longer associated with the old image of a welfare state but with new forms of local synergy between economic, political, and cultural actors. It is interesting to observe how developments within the economic, political, and cultural sciences reflect the move away from the central role of the nation-state. In the economic sciences we see the rapidly increasing interest in economic sociology, i.e. the idea that economic logic has more socio-cultural roots than was first thought. In the political sciences emphasis is increasingly put on local government, while cultural studies concentrates on new hybrid forms of identity construction. Many of these new developments come together in the study of civil society. National and international development projects also tend to concentrate ever more on fortifying the role of civil society.

I would like to comment briefly on three issues: the globalization notion concerning the retreat of the state, the potential emancipatory role of local government, and the significance of civil society.

In another contribution to this book I argue (see also Deepak Nayyar 1997) that it is naïve to write off nation-states as important players in the globalization game. This is in spite of the fact that in the imperial phase of globalization nation-states played a more important (economic and political) role than currently. I also agree with Jan-Aart Scholte (1995) that much of present-day capitalism is still bound up with national firms, national currencies, and national markets. Ethnic struggles and indigenous movements also tend to reproduce nationhood on a smaller scale. Scholte concludes that 'globalization also goes hand in hand with renationalisation'. Globalization is not about eliminating nations, only complicating the construction of collective identities leading to hybridization, and, as such, Scholte proclaims globalization a core feature of late modernity.

There is little reason to suppose that the role of the state came to an end because of globalization. By the same token, the issue of local government must be handled with care. It must be realized that the idea of local government is a decidedly Western notion that is intimately tied to the history of capitalism in the West, reaching its post-Fordist phase from the middle of the 1970s onwards. During this time the role of the state was increasingly seen as a hindrance to economic development. Now that many Third World countries are currently in a transition phase to democracy the notions of local government and local autonomy are fed into the national political rhetoric and are often used as such in façade politics. It is often conveniently forgotten, for example, that ideas like local government or local autonomy presuppose a phase of nation-building, during which time a civil society is firmly constructed. This was also a phase of welfare capitalism during which the state would provide a safety net for those who threatened to fall. Now, local governments in the Third World run the risk of falling prey to globally organized capitalism because their economic and political safety nets have not yet been constructed and their civil societies are weak because there was no initial phase of nation-building and welfare capitalism. It is tragic that at the moment as many Third World countries finally start to get rid of undemocratic regimes, the (nation) state is robbed of its importance.

So, can the responsibility for human emancipation, one of the key questions for the discipline of development studies, be moved from the state to civil society? Can the paradigmatic role of the state be replaced by that of civil society? Communitarians like Amitai Etzioni (1997) certainly seem to think so, at least for the developed world. An important comment to be made here is that the notion of civil society is highly reified. It is presented as an actor with enough agency to enter into in a synergetic relationship with local government. I do not want at this point to engage the reader in a discussion on the ins and outs of the concept of civil society. What is important to note is that in the context of development studies the concept of civil society is already politically translated into projects to support the transition to democracy in former war-torn countries like Guatemala, former non-democratic regimes like South Africa, and former Communist countries like Croatia. However, the enthusiasm with which civil society has been embraced as a new paradigm has not been matched by an elaboration of its theoretical dimensions. A focal point in the attempts to give civil society 'hands and feet' seems to be the notion of social capital. According to Robert Putnam (1993) and Francis Fukuyama (1996), the construction of a civil society with the 'right' kind (i.e. leading to democracy and economic development) of social capital is a highly (historic) path-dependent process. If these authors are correct then we can question current attempts to help Third World countries to construct a civil society with the 'right' kind of social capital. These exercises tend to carry, as an explanation of underdevelopment in terms of civil society and social capital, an implicit connotation of the victim-blaming approach. People are underdeveloped because they did not have the right kind of social capital. In any case, it would be highly premature for development studies to replace the paradigmatic importance of the state by that of the civil society.

Conclusion

All in all, then, development studies, as a typical post-World War II branch of the social sciences, has experienced its share of criticism of its central paradigms. To put it another way it has received more than its share because of its normative and interdisciplinary character. Some of these paradigms seemed to have been lost for good and, from the mid 1980s onwards, the contours of what became known as an impasse in development studies became clearly visible. When, in the following decade, the concept of globalization swept through academia and policy-making institutions it became clear that development studies would probably not make it as such into the next century. Its proposed replacement, global studies, already presented an enticing perspective. Nevertheless, development studies did cross the millennium threshold, though admittedly, not with a gracious jump. I have tried to show in this introduction where the criticisms on the central paradigms of development studies came from, what role has been played by the concept of globalization, and the relevance of alternative paradigms.

As the contributions in this book will show, the concept of globalization has influenced the various domains within development studies in various ways. Theories as well as policy-making in the fields of ecology, gender, urban life, ethics, and production are all influenced by globalization in its practical and theoretical dimensions. The space and time coordinates with which we used to understand societies have changed and this is reflected in the ways in which social scientists try to understand their specific objects of study. As the contributions in this book will show there is, however, no standardized way to fathom the influence of globalization on development studies.

The challenge for development studies is to re-establish its continued relevance to study and understand processes of exclusion, emancipation, and development. This cannot be achieved by clinging to its once treasured paradigms, but can be achieved by incorporating creatively the new Zeitgeist, without giving up its normative basis, i.e. the awareness that only with a universal morality of justice is there is a future for humanity.

References

Beck, U. et al. (1994) *Reflexive Modernization. Politics, Tradition and Aesthetics in the Modern Social Order*, Cambridge, Polity Press.

Bull, M. (1995) *Apocalypse Theory and the Ends of the World*, Oxford, Blackwell.

Escobar, A. (1996) *Encountering Development. The Making and Unmaking of the Third World*, Princeton, Princeton University Press.

Etzioni, Amitai (1997) "The End of Cross-Cultural Relativism", *Alternatives* 22, pp. 177-189.

Fukuyama, F. (1996) *Trust. The Social Virtues and the Creation of Prosperity*, New York, Free Press.

Füredi, F. (1996) *Risk-consciousness: the Escape from the Social*, Lecture at the Conference on The Direction of Contemporary Socialism, University of Sussex, 26-28 April.

Hobsbawm, E. (1994) *The Age of Extremes. The Short Twentieth Century 1914-1991*, London, Michael Joseph.

Huntington, S. (1993) "The Clash of Civilizations?", *Foreign Affairs* 73, pp. 22-49.

Huntington, S. (1996) *The Clash of Civilizations and the Remaking of the World Order*, New York, Simon & Schuster.

Kaplan, R. (1994) "The Coming Anarchy: How Scarcity, Crime, Overpopulation, Tribalism, and Disease are Rapidly Destroying the Social Fabric of Our Planet", *Atlantic Monthly* 273 (2), pp. 44-76.

Kaplan, R. (1996) *The Ends of the Earth. A Journey at the Dawn of the 21st Century*, New York, Random House.

Nayyar, Deepak (1997) "Globalization: the Past in Our Present", *Third World Economics* 168, pp. 7-15.

Norgaard, R. (1994) *Development Betrayed. The End of Progress and a Coevolutionary Revisioning of the Future*, London, Routledge.

Putnam. R. (1993) *Making Democracy Work: Civic Traditions in Modern Italy*, Princeton, Princeton University Press.

Rahnema, M. (ed.) (1997) *The Post-Development Reader*, London, Zed Books.

Sachs, W. (ed.) (1992) *The Development Dictionary. A Guide to Knowledge as Power*. London, Zed Books.

Scholte, Jan-Aart (1995) *Constructions of Collective Identity*, Paper for the Conference on The Organization Dimensions of Global Change: No Limits to Cooperation, Ohio, University of Cleveland.

Schuurman, F. (ed.) (1993) *Beyond the Impasse. New Directions in Development Theory*, London, Zed Books.

Schuurman, F. (2000) "Paradigms Lost, Paradigms Regained? Development Studies in the 21st Century", *Third World Quarterly* 21 (1), pp. 7-20.

PART I

THE CHALLENGES AND THEIR LIMITS

INTRODUCTION TO PART I

Frans J. Schuurman

In his contribution *Martin Albrow* emphasizes that globality is not the latest form of modernity. In contrast to the postmodern critique on modernity, which is still too far under the spell of modernity to recognize that it is simply a particular modern version of grand narratives, he stresses that we live in a Global Age. Globality is non-teleological and, in fact, consists of multiple globalizations without the totalizing character of the modern project, which neglected everything that resisted the advance of modernity. In Albrow's view there is a paradigmatic shift from modernity towards globality characterized, for example, by the displacement of the axial principles of modernity and the fact that the state has increasingly to compete with other agencies in the global field. He nevertheless finds the notion of the end of the nation-state too apocalyptic.

Albrow ties development studies to a particular historical period (the Cold War with its development aid programmes) and, as such, sees it as the product of an old and dated modernity which has collapsed in the Global Age. However, because of its interdisciplinary and international orientation development studies is well equipped to understand the realities of the Global Age. According to Albrow, development studies should renew itself under the heading of 'global studies'.

For *Arie de Ruijter*, too, the important issue in the globalization debate is whether we can describe and interpret an increasingly hybrid world in the 21st century using concepts and insights acquired at the end of the 19th century. This is a particularly pertinent question for development studies because its traditional modernization approach provides the basis for the social engineering in the developmental praxis. De Ruijter concentrates on the cultural content of hybridization, which in his view has provided social science with a more constructivist perspective, leading to a more fruitful balance between structure and process, between actor and system. At the same time, however, he warns against a too utilitarian vision of people playing fast and loose with their identity. In the case of development studies he agrees with Albrow that the object of study is no longer about drawing backward regions into a modernization process but about the co-existence of many worlds, each with its own logic. Nevertheless, De Ruijter warns against the risk of a too great emphasis on diversity, and an absence of mutually attuned interests and representations. Social scientists, and especially those dedicated to development studies, have a responsibility to take standpoints and to articulate possible solutions to alleviate the extreme unequal access to scarce resources in a global world.

John Tomlinson picks up the baton handed over by Arie de Ruijter. Tomlinson takes the British political philosopher John Gray to task for his interpretation of globalization as vicious universalism, as a masquerade of Western ethnocentrism. In his contribution Tomlinson separates vicious universalism (as the ugly face of free-market capitalism and neo-liberalism) from, what he calls, benign universalism, which is the project of universal emancipation in a cosmopolitan civilization. If globalization were to have the pretension to claim that one particular culture should become the only way of life then it is 'vicious', but if it can also be interpreted as a pursuit of consensual values, such as universal human rights, then it is certainly virtuous. Tomlinson condemns the 'new wars' (Bosnia, Rwanda, Kosovo) emerging from the political clefts between the politics of particularistic identity and the politics of cosmopolitan or humanist values. In his conclusion he stresses that we need sensitive analytical categories that allow us to make moral and political judgments. Although Tomlinson did not explicitly confront the question of whether, because of globalization, we would be in need of a new paradigm, his benign universalism seems firmly based on a combination of an Enlightenment-inspired idea about social justice and a modernity-based cosmopolitanism.

Although taking another route *Frans Schuurman*, in his contribution on emancipation and the role of the nation-state, essentially comes to the same conclusion as Tomlinson. For Schuurman the object of development studies, i.e. trajectories of human emancipation in the South, and the core feature of globalization (modernity and capitalism going transnational) concur in the nation-state as a central point of reference. Emancipatory struggles in the North, during the period of modernity, as well as in the South, in the period of gaining national independence and after, always had the nation-state as the political arena. In addition, the nation-state, as such, always was an important actor in those struggles, either as foe or as friend. Globalization seems to have changed that. The globalization discourse has it that, on the one hand, the state is (or has already been) hollowed out from above and from below. On the other hand, emancipatory struggles are increasingly transnationalizing and surpassing the nation-state as a political arena as well as bypassing the state as such as a central political referent. After presenting a taxonomy of positions in the globalization debate and pointing out some fallacies in 'glob-talk', Schuurman questions the often all-too-easy manner with which this view on the quickly declining role of the (nation) state has settled itself as a core feature of globalization. As such, he concludes that the nation-state is still important as a political arena for human emancipation, in the North and certainly in the South, although it has lost its historic primacy.

Taken together these contributions in Part I outline the contours of the challenges that globalization poses for development studies. These challenges do not limit themselves simply to incorporating new areas of research (like globalization itself for that matter) into the discipline of development studies. The challenge which globalization poses touches upon the central, paradigmatic features of development studies: its Enlightenment-inspired sense of social justice, the modernity-based issue of progress, and the role of the nation-state in the trajectories of emancipatory struggles. Some of the authors clearly herald the end of development studies as such, while others recognize the influence of globalization (as a process and as a discourse) on development studies but set limits to the challenges. In Part II the discussion continues on specific fields of study within the discipline.

GLOBALIZATION AFTER MODERNIZATION: A NEW PARADIGM FOR DEVELOPMENT STUDIES

Martin Albrow

Introduction

When did we become modern, or to put it another way, since Bruno Latour (1993) has challenged us to believe that we were never modern, when did people start to talk and write about being modern? The answer is, a long time ago, perhaps the fifth century AD, becoming more common in the fifteenth century and a dominant form of public discourse by the middle of the nineteenth. Modernization as a key term in this discourse dates only from the 1950s.

At any rate, the origins of discourses are shrouded in obscurity and it is rare indeed that we can find a single inventor of a term, or if we do, that we can attribute much importance to that person as opposed to the countless others who give it circulation and credibility. Who remembers the contributions to science by Destutt de Tracy, Vincent de Gournay, or come to that, apart from a few dedicated scholars, August Comte? Yet ideology, bureaucracy, and sociology are to this day terms safely lodged in social scientific vocabulary.

These observations are pertinent to the case of globalization. Already the origins of the term are lost to current consciousness, even though it has risen in the last decade to occupy a prominent place on the contemporary economic and political agenda of the great states, in the leader columns of the major daily newspapers, as well as in the grant lists of scientific funding agencies. If we argue that programmes for economic and social development have always had an intellectual axis then it is arguable that globalization has replaced modernization in the 1990s. If we claim this place for globalization it is no trivial matter. Indeed, it goes to the heart of the rationale of development programmes for poor countries and of the legitimacy of the strategies of international development and aid agencies. The idea that development meant incorporating hitherto excluded countries into a modernizing process along the course of which rich countries were already far advanced was axiomatic for both capitalist and socialist states in the 1960s and 1970s.

The fervent debates around modernization in this period were not about the core of the concept but about questions of national distribution and control, democracy and oligarchy, and personal freedom; issues which remain as salient today as they were then, and as they always have been. In other words debates and open conflicts about property, exploitation, entitlement, and freedom do not get to the core assumptions of modernity.

Both capitalist and state socialist countries took a range of assumptions for granted, including control over nature, the centrality of technological advance, the increasing power of productive processes, the importance of reliable administration, the need for a trained and disciplined workforce, and the desirability of growth and planning for it. These are the key factors which constitute the profile of modernity or the shape of what, in the context of the West, has often been called the Modern Project. In the West, modernity is normally equated with the Modern Project, rather than with modernization, because it is self- activated, conceived, and possessed by human agents who are in control of themselves and it. So modernity does not simply have a project. In the West modernity *is* the project. The factors we have listed cohere as a strategic programme for a collective agent. The West is in charge of itself. In respect of the rest of the world, on the other hand, modernity is called modernization. These subtle shifts of vocabulary are intriguing and revealing. Modernization is what happens to people when something is done to them. They are the recipients, beneficiaries, or victims of other people's projects. I think we are conscious of these nuances even though we rarely comment on them specifically. Consequently, in the West, if a political party does come to power, as sometimes happens, espousing modernization rather than simply claiming to be modern, then we will be alert to proposals for reform from above, to central direction, and to a determination to take charge.

This understanding of the semantics of the modern indicates why any suggestion that globalization has displaced modernization at the centre of public discourse is not just challenging, but may even be regarded as subversive. Any breach of that intimate association between control and modernity, where it directs the course of history with an everlasting self renewal, the Modern Age without end, appears to bring chaos. Hence modernity conjures up spectres of postmodern relativism or the end of history as the only alternatives to itself. Modernize or die is the implicit message. Of course, there can always be tactical reasons at particular historical moments for adopting a modernizing image. Whether right or wrong, likely to be successful or not, is a matter for judgement in the light of the circumstances at the time. However, as a generalization, it is very likely to go wrong quite quickly if its proponents believe their own rhetoric and imagine that there is no alternative to modernization, or that it is in any sense a sufficient programme for the development of their economy or society. Control, even control of nature, let alone of people, has to be for a purpose, not for its own sake, and, as I hinted above, modernization has no answers to problems of distribution, fairness, or personal freedom. These are variable and neutral in relation to the course of history, which means they have to be fought for afresh by every generation. There is a universalism of the problems of the human condition, even if only a limited universalism in their solution.

I do not want in this paper to explore the rhetoric of the political modernizers at any length, opportune though this may be in the current state of European politics. My reason for alluding to it here is because the reasoning, narrative devices, and imagery of contemporary social science parallels and sometimes even converges with the dominant discourse of public life. We live in a time when we have almost forgotten the theory of ideology because we live it so thoroughly. If we debate the place of globalization as a social scientific concept and research empirically processes in economy, culture, and society, which we define as globalization, then we rehearse and simultaneously criticize the intellectual basis of both political and business programmes all over the world today. We also find, however, that our problem setting is also largely derived from that public discourse. If our politicians get into difficulties, in all likelihood we find ourselves in the same boat.

II

For students of globalization our problem sometimes is that our work is just too live and close to the events of the time. This is why if we are to maintain the independence of judgement on which ultimately all academic work must depend, then we have to maintain strenuously the methods and approaches which give us at least a modicum of detachment.The rigour of natural scientific method is one way, transcendental philosophy another. My preferred approach is more like a comparative history, where one seeks to relativize the present and the modern against all that is past, and is non-modern.

I will try to show what this means by considering first some of the main responses by the modernizers to both the idea and the fact of globalization. For, let us make no mistake, the struggle has expanded. The idea of the modern has refused competitors now for centuries and it will not give in easily. The shift in vocabulary is a sign of the times and the pervasiveness of the global and terms derived from it, the diversity of meanings they take on and the breadth of the intellectual front on which the argument takes place across all disciplines, derive precisely from the claims of the modern to control contemporary discourse. This can be illustrated by listing some of the main variants of the idea of globalization. There are at least six which link it explicitly to modernity.

1 Globalization as the expansion of the world system (Wallerstein 1974, 1980, 1989).
2 Globalization as a necessary accompaniment of modernity (Robertson 1992).
3 Globalization as the creation of a single world market (Redwood 1993).
4 Globalization as the consequence of modernity (Giddens 1990).

5   Globalization as a modern myth (Hirst and Thompson 1996).
6   Globalization as a second modernity (Beck 1993).

All of these are essentially ways of accommodating the present to the immediate, the recent, and the distant past. They are all fundamentally developmental, even ones which see globalization as a discourse, or a myth, because either they subordinate it to a notion of unfolding modernity, which assumes self-renewal to be intrinsic to the modern, or else they make it the latest phase in a modern tale of progress. It is that unfolding modernity, controlled growth in the project, which gave us modernization and all the other process terms known by their -ization suffixes, like bureaucratization, urbanization, industrialization, and so on. Globalization is then the latest addition to the product range of the modern project, the most explicit venture yet to dominate the world market for visions of the future. It is the very transparency of this association between the global and the world and the grand claims which globalization discourse makes which invites postmodern critique. Lyotard (1984), Vattimo (1988), and Latour (1993) have cruelly exposed the pretensions of the discourse of the modern to provide a total account of the unfolding present. Revealing the inherent weaknesses of the assumptions which underpin modern accounts of our time at the same time does not in itself provide secure foundations for any alternative account. This may lead a rejoicing Baudrillard to dance away to where the intellectual fun is to be had, and I defy anyone not to enjoy the result, but more frequently there is a kind of anti-history of post-ism, a narrative of the fall, decline, collapse and chaos kind. This is actually the repressed side of modernity's self-image, what the project holds at bay, the danger to which it may succumb if it does not succeed. As a result many have seen the postmodern as the necessary accompaniment of the modern, rather than a period which comes later in time. For these and other reasons the postmodern as a concept is associated with the cultural contradictions of modernity. There is therefore a postmodern version of globalization as intensification of multicultural encounters and increased flows of global culture. In this account globalization is associated both with the diversification of culture and its accessibility anywhere in the world. We can then envisage equally global culture, globalization of local cultures, and the localization of the global, or as Robertson (1995) advocates, following the Japanese example, glocalization.

The importance of this strand of thinking about globalization for development studies is that it comes full circle to engage with the debate on Third World development, which had been generated within the Marxist and post-colonialist traditions. The idea of the development of underdevelopment was balanced always by a belief, sometimes wishful, that under the worst circumstances the cultural and spiritual resources of even the most oppressed could resist the encroachments of Western capitalism and rapacious indigenous elites. This was always something more than Marx's and Engels' belief that the forces which polarized classes, concentrated capital, and impoverished the proletariat, coupled with political organization, could secure revolution. It allowed for a residue of the human spirit which capitalism could not destroy and which always contained potential for resistance and autonomous development. Linked with the idea of globalization, as in Arjun Appadurai's work (1996), native peoples appropriate the products, ideals, and materials of the West and turn them to their own ends. Alternatively they may use the global means of communication to advance their own products and causes worldwide. It is a turn which Mike Featherstone, Scott Lash, and Roland Robertson (1995) effectively index as 'Global Modernities'. Modernity is pluralized and decentred simultaneously, but that really turns modernity inside out and upside down. Modernity could not allow competitors and it had to have a single core. Translated into the terms of old development studies how could there be many alternative developments in a non-Western world?

For me this suggests that you cannot save the notion of a singular course of world development by incorporating the idea of culture. This was always the dream of American theories of modernization, where economic development necessarily was linked with a secular nation-state, citizenship, religious tolerance, and so-called responsible parenthood. The cultural critique of world-system theory does not save the world for liberal democracy, rather it shows the exposure of capitalism to the autonomous influence of creativity without roots and the replacement of the Modern Age by new ages without end.

III

The importance of the postmodern side of, or response to, modernity is that it shows up the extreme difficulty of avoiding some kind of grand narrative of the present. While it distances itself from the modern in one respect, by appropriating the language of the global it takes the dominant contemporary narrative device for making sense of present change. The fact that it cannot find a direction in the present, that it can only register multiple modernities and alternative developments, makes it even more paradoxical that it embraces what so many theorists of modernity regard as its latest outcome, namely globalization. But these difficulties for the postmoderns in adopting the language of globalization even though they have long ceased to speak of bureaucratization, industrialization and the rest only suggests that the world as it is, contemporary social reality, intrudes on their vision and that they register the times, even as they tend to deny the possibility of rendering a true account.

Social scientists have to acknowledge that globalization, in common with the older modern social change terms, is not simply a technical term that they have invented for their own purposes. It inhabits the thoughtworld of the present, public discourse, not just as a slogan but as a rendering of experienced change where the distant has come near, where the globe as a place for humanity to exist has a threatened future, and where the stock exchanges of the world move in unison. These are not phantasms, and globalization as narrative is a story which millions of people live.

To this extent our accounts of globalization, as social scientists, are meta-narratives, none the worse for that, but equally they are not immune to correction. We are not rendering the experience of globalization adequately, even authentically, if we hold too hard to theories of a previous time. If we conceive of globalization as a facet of a unitary modernity then we fail to register multiple and contradictory globalizations. If we record these through the idea of global modernities we lose the sense of an overarching project which older modernity possessed without adequately expressing the profundity of the change. The very multiplicity of meanings of globalization in versions which associate it with modernity and in those accounts where it represents a postmodern challenge, or subterranean subversion of modernity, runs counter to any idea that modernity might be a unitary narrative for the present day. The idea of contemporaneous multiple modernities makes it possible to think of modernities coming and going. The contemporaneity of modernity is the constant passing of ephemeral presents. With that the very contrast of traditional and modern passes away, when the modern can become traditional and the preservation of the past becomes a present preoccupation. This fragmentation and transvaluation of modernities relaxes the hold of modernity on the imagination of the present. For Lyotard (1984) this was the end of the grand narrative altogether. My view is that this postmodern critique of modernity is still too much under the spell of modernity to recognize that it is simply a particular modern version of the grand narrative which has passed, rather than the grand narrative as such.

All our modern and postmodern accounts of globalization suggest that it is the global rather than the modern which provides the commonly understood markers of our time. We live in a Global Age, where there are multiple presents, differing time horizons, no common project, alternative developments, and a scepticism towards modernities of any kind. In spite of all this, however, it remains possible to characterize our time. Indeed, public discourse effectively designates it as an age of globalization, a formulation which is effectively a transitional one, masking the break from the modern by representing it as a continuation of modernity, for as we have seen, there are multiple globalizations, no single process. We can allow for this if we speak of orientations to the globe, rather than globalization and of the Global Age (Laszlo 1989, Albrow 1996) rather than an age of globalization. One of the conceits of modernity was to imagine that it had captured its own time. The Modern Age was for its proponents the triumph of the modern. They preferred to leave in its wake all those aspects of the time which resisted the advance of modernity, were premodern or represented non-modern aspects of the age.

By contrast with the Modern Age the Global Age is not the triumph of globality. Indeed the global inhabits the contemporary imagination in a quite different way from the modern. We do not control it, we relate to it, but it limits and threatens us at the same time. It frames our activities without totalizing them. It is therefore not composed of enabling and constraining institutions as structuration theory conceives of modern society (Giddens 1984). We accommodate each other through the global without requiring a necessary consensus of right-thinking rational people. The idea of society implied by the global field is fluid and only modestly structured. If the global takes on a universality, then it is material and pragmatic rather than ideal and logical. The systems which represent the development of modern technology have open future and ill-defined boundaries. The global is neither inherently structure nor system, the two favoured framing features for society which modernity sought to promote as universal necessities and which appealed so much to the modern nation-state. Indeed the global provides no preferred model of society at all and in that sense the social is emancipated from the straitjacket which modernity forced on it.

IV

Nothing illustrates the difference between the global and the modern better than the debates about the relation between the global and the local. From the standpoint of modernity the local is always relative to a wider instance, local is the neighbourhood in relation to the community, the community in relation to the nation-state, the nation-state in relation to the international system. Relations between localities are always determined by the higher instance of which they are a part, and that hierarchy of instances is an organization of territorial powers. By contrast, from the standpoint of globality, localities are always negotiating relative autonomy with each other and even with the globe. The global may be instantiated in the local, the local can become global. As compared with modernity the local/global relation ceases to be a mere territorial one and becomes a facet of the ontology of society, culture, and the agents of human history. The local ceases to be a land area and becomes a place in an imaginary field. The global becomes either the planet or a totality, without us ever being able to equate one with the other. We begin to see the country, the fatherland, the homeland as mythical entities, however necessary the myths appear to be for their adherents (Anderson 1986).

The idea that globalization requires a paradigm shift in the social sciences has been around now for a decade or so (Janos 1986). At the Roehampton Institute we (Albrow et al. 1994) sought to look at the consequences of globalization for sociological concepts and came to the conclusion that we had to be open to radical reformulations in such traditional areas as the study of community and culture. When we turned to describing social process in an area of London (Eade 1997) which we researched then we had to begin to work with new ideas like socioscapes and sociospheres (Albrow 1997) to capture new realities beyond old community. Our starting point then was not the paradigm shift that occurred as a result of new theoretical discoveries, rather that it was the transformation in the world that required us to look at it with spectacles which went beyond the modern era. In turn that requires us to review the means by which we account for social life and to generate a narrative which is not impelled by the particular dynamic of modernity; by the assumption that the epoch, the project, and its agents make up a single coherent system which takes humanity into the future. If we centre our new accounts of the present on globalization as an extension of modernity then we miss the transformation which is precisely the delinkage of the epoch from any organizing principle and the release of communities and individuals from overarching control. It is the displacement of the axial principles of modernity. Often this is expressed as the end of the nation-state. This is far too apocalyptic, but what is certain is that nation-states, even the most powerful ones, no longer have the same degree of control on the future and on their citizens which was taken for granted in the high modern period. That does not mean that it is not still a key collective actor in the contemporary world, only that it has to compete with other agencies, economic, religious, and ethnic, as well as movements and media which move more freely in a global field.

The novelty of this perception should, however, not be overstated. In fact the theory of the Global Age sets both paradigm shift and the idea of the decline of the nation-state in the context of an older kind of narrative which modernity sought to suppress, namely the idea of human history as a succession of unmotivated changes, where epochs are marked off from each other not by processes governed by scientific laws, nor by a series of necessary stages of development, but by an overall shift in ways of life and of looking at the world which occur without any necessary predetermined direction. The shift to the Global Age has been marked by consequences of human actions and by events which could not reasonably be foretold. The various events, which we can call paradigmatic, which signalled the beginning of the Global Age, such as the Hiroshima bomb, the landing on the Moon, the invention of the silicon chip, the collapse of the Soviet Union, or climate change, render it impossible (as in principle it always was except in the self-deception of modernity) to find any single direction in human history. At the same time they each contribute to the exposure of humanity to globality in an unprecedented way. We do not have to look within the theories of the social sciences for a theory of history. What we have to do is to theorize the historical narrative which we call the present, and one of my purposes in invoking the Global Age is to encourage historians to free the theory of their discipline from its long servitude to the social sciences.

V

Where does this leave development studies? The origins of development studies, the interdisciplinary models of development linking economic growth with social and political institutions, and then the immanent critiques from Marxist and indigenous standpoints all mark it out as a transitional field of studies tied to a particular historical period. Essentially it is based on the aid and development programmes of the 1960s and 1970s and the Cold War. In other words it is a product of an old and dated modernity which, as such, has collapsed in the Global Age. These would be bold judgements indeed if they were not reinforced by writings from within development studies which acknowledged the theoretical impasse in the discipline and called for the exploration of avenues in contemporary sociology and in globalization theory in particular (cf. Schuurman 1994).

This is a relevant direction but I would go further. I do not think that a theoretical rehabilitation of development studies as such is possible. The theory has moved on and so has the world and this suggests new disciplinary configurations or paradigms. Schuurman also mentioned the middle-range theories and the normative domain of development studies. These are not unrelated and survive the demise of an integrated theory. Indeed the present anthology itself proves that the contributions of scholars in the field of development studies to our understanding of contemporary global realities are not confined by an outdated theoretical framework. Indeed the contrary is the case. It seems to me that there are few other modern fields of study that are better equipped to understand the realities of the Global Age, for in a global field poverty is not modern it is global and it is, above all, diverse. Development studies as a discipline faces not global modernities but global poverties, exploitations, and rights abuses, as well as global population management, the power of transnational corporations, and global cities. We know that the fate of child prostitutes in Thailand is linked directly with the sex trade in Europe and that the career of the heroin addict in the urban slums of the West is linked to opium cultivation in South East Asia. Development studies no longer confronts three worlds or even two, but many worlds inhabiting an endangered globe. Its topic is no longer generic development, but developments of all kinds which call the survival of humanity and human values into question.

Moreover we can discern no necessary and easy harmony of these multiple developments. Sustainable development in the Brundtland sense is not, as we have long known, easily compatible with economic development and the greening of development is not necessarily compatible with local democracy. But these are already old observations for students of development, and because they, above all, are aware of the contradictions of old modernity, it seems to me that they are better prepared than students of Western modernity to work within and meet the demands for understanding the new global field. If globalization theory proves a fruitful direction for their work then that is because it matches their perceptions of a changed world. But it will not revive development theory, rather it signals its end. What this suggests is that over time the term development studies will give way to something more appropriate to the field. Current researchers are likely to adopt a variety of names for their schools, centres, departments, and institutes in the future. For my part, as well-wishing outsider may I suggest that perhaps only 'Global Studies' will convey the scope of the agenda which 'Development Studies' has unavoidably both raised and left unfinished on the table for its heirs and successors.

References

Albrow, Martin (1996) *The Global Age: State and Society beyond Modernity*, Cambridge, Polity.

Albrow, Martin (1997) "Travelling beyond Local Culture: Socioscapes in a Global City". In: John Eade (ed.) (1997) pp. 37-55.

Albrow, Martin, Eade, John, Washbourne, Neil, and Durrschmidt, Jorg (1994) "The Impact of Globalization on Sociological Concepts: Community, Culture and Milieu". In: *Innovation 7*, pp. 371-89 and in John Eade (ed.) (1997) pp. 20-36.

Anderson, Benedict (1986) *Imagined Communities: Reflections on the Origins and Spread of Nationalism*, London, Verso.

Appadurai, Arjun (1996) *Modernity at Large: Cultural Dimensions of Globalization*, Minneapolis, University of Minnesota Press.

Beck, Ulrich (1993*) Die Erfindung des Politischen*, Frankfurt, Suhrkamp.

Eade, John (ed.) (1997) *Living the Global City: Globalization as a Local Process*, London, Routledge.

Featherstone, Mike, (et al.) (eds) (1995) *Global Modernities*, London, Sage.

Giddens, Anthony (1984) *The Constitution of Society*, Cambridge, Polity.

Giddens, Anthony (1990) *The Consequences of Modernity*, Stanford, Stanford University Press.

Hirst, Paul, and Thompson, Grahame (1996) *Globalization in Question*, Cambridge, Polity.

Janos, Andrew C. (1986) *Politics and Paradigms: Changing Theories of Change in Social Science*, Stanford, Stanford University Press.

Laszlo, E. (l989) *The Inner Limits of Mankind*, London, Oneworld.

Latour, Bruno (1993) *We Have Never Been Modern*, Hemel Hempstead, Harvester Wheatsheaf.

Lyotard, Jean Francois (1984) *The Postmodern Condition*, Minneapolis, University of Minneapolis Press.

Redwood, John (1993) *The Global Marketplace: Capitalism and its Future*, London, Harper Collins.

Robertson, Roland (1992) *Globalization*, Newbury Park, CA, Sage.

Robertson, Roland (1995) "Glocalization: Time-Space and Homogeneity and Heterogeneity". In: Featherstone, Lash, and Robertson (eds),(1995), pp. 25-44.

Schuurman, Frans J. (1994) *Current Issues in Development Studies*. Nijmegen Studies in Development and Cultural Change, no 21, Saarbruecken, Verlag fuer Entwicklungspolitik Breitenbach.

Vattimo, Gianni (1988) *The End of Modernity*, Cambridge, Polity.

Wallerstein, Immanuel (1974, 1980, 1989) *The Modern World-System*, 3 Vols, New York and San Diego, Academic Press.

GLOBALIZATION:
A CHALLENGE TO THE SOCIAL SCIENCES

Arie de Ruijter

Introduction

Our daily lives are governed by products and images originating from all the corners of the world. We can justifiably and reasonably speak of globalization. This concerns not only the incorporation of more and more people in an encompassing politico-economic system; globalization also refers to sociocultural encapsulation processes. We see the world turning into a global village (McLuhan 1964:93). Although this process has been going on at least since the end of the Middle Ages, we have to acknowledge that the current wave of globalization is unique in scope and impact. This is usually interpreted positively. Perhaps we can sense a crack in the trend now, at the beginning of the 21st century. We are asking more and more questions. We ask ourselves, with references to the increase in diversity, whether this 'uniformization' of the world is actually a fact now or not. We ask ourselves, furthermore, whether we view homogenization as an ideal or a nightmare. Some of us applaud the increase in diversity as a source of alternative behaviours or as empowerment of indigenous peoples and marginalized groups. Others regret this diversity. They refer to the growing complexity and uncertainty of our existence. I admit that it is difficult to evaluate this 'diversity'. We cannot, however, escape it. We must, after all, live in this reality and this reality is characterized by just such diversity. The complexity connected to the diversity is inevitable. Perhaps this will increase. The twofold action between the processes which constitute and feed each other, i.e. globalization and localization, is responsible for this. The end product of the interaction between these two extremes can be described as 'glocalisation' (Robertson 1995), 'creolisation' (Hannerz 1992), or 'hybridization' (Latour 1994).

We have to ask ourselves what the impact of 'glocalisation' is on our conceptualizing of 'our world'. Can we analyze this phenomenon using the traditional modernization approach or are we in need of a paradigm shift? To formulate a provisional answer to this question I will begin with a sketch of globalization. Next I will outline three perspectives on the future development of globalization to indicate whether or not the 'dialectics' between globalization and localization is of a transitory nature. Finally I will discuss some core concepts – in particular 'culture' – in the context of 'glocalisation'.

Globalization and localization

Globalization can be seen as a transformation of a world system with its own laws and rules (Wallerstein 1974, 1980, 1989) into a transnational global system. This development goes hand in hand with growth of mutual dependencies and a condensation of relationships and interactions between an increasing number of actors (a.o. Appadurai 1990). In this context multinationals become global concerns. Standardized time, money, and expert systems are introduced everywhere. A massive, global exchange of people, goods, services, and images takes place by means of telecommunication and transport technology. Apart from the more rapid increase, the long-distance migration is also characterized by a wider distribution: more and more countries and regions becoming involved in networks spanning the globe. Lifestyles, consumption patterns, and other forms of cultural expression are exchanged more rapidly between more and more locations. Developments of a political, ideological, religious, or cultural nature, which originally appear to be connected with a specific region, culture, or period, are being echoed in large parts of the world. "The most obvious reasons for this change were the growing capital-intensity of manufacture; the accelerating momentum of technologies; the emergence of a growing body of universal users; and the spreading of neoprotectionist pressures" (Brenner 1996:19). This globalization, by the way, refers not only to processes; the world as a whole is adopting systemic properties in which characteristics of each particular entity have to be understood within the framework of the world as a whole (e.g. Robertson 1992, Friedman 1995). "In short, a world wide web of interdependencies has been spun, and not just on the Internet" (de Ruijter 1997:382).

What is interesting is that, at the same time, increasing globalization creates favourable conditions for all forms of particularization, localization, and even fragmentation (a.o. Featherstone 1990; Friedman 1995; Giddens 1990; Hannerz 1992; Latour 1994; Robertson 1992, 1995). Apparently the emergence of a transnational system implies the rebirth of nationalism, regionalism, and ethnicity (Anderson 1992). Here we touch the other extreme, the localization. It appears that globalization cannot exist without its corollary, i.e. the processes of localization (Hannerz 1992). Apparently they constitute and feed each other. In this era of time-space compression, distant localities are linked in such a way that local happenings are shaped by events occurring many miles away and *vice versa* (Giddens 1990:64). For instance, we see that transmigrants act, take decisions, and develop identities while embedded in networks of relationships which bind them with two or more nation-states simultaneously. They develop new spheres of experiences and new kinds of social relations because of this, a situation of 'in-betweenness' is created.

Bound up with this, we see a transformation of the nation-state with the shifting of accents to above or below-state arrangements. There is, thus, a transfer of formal state powers to continental 'power blocks', with, at the same time, a steady increase in regulations and effects on regional and local levels. There are also increasing gaps between sectors of society. In a period of 'open borders', of advanced specialization and division of labour, and of continually increasing physical and sociocultural mobility, society is being pulled apart more than ever before (Salet 1996:7). The social agents (people, organizations, governments) can rely less and less on the power of what already exists. They must find their own way, the result of which is the hybridization of institutions, as well as the particularization, sometimes even fragmentation, of world views and moral frames of reference (Bauman 1991). As a consequence, individuals and groups, confronted with the uprooting of many existing local identities, feel an increasing need to construe or 'invent' new identities. Although the geographical bond of identities has become less 'natural' because of globalization processes – it is a case of 'deterritorialisation of identities' (Malkki 1992) – people cling to a geographical grid for the construction and experiencing of a cultural or ethnic identity. These 're-inventions of tradition' (e.g. Roosens 1989) can partly be interpreted as a new defensive orthodoxy, in which – paradoxically – modern communication technology is intensively used (e.g. Appadurai 1996). As a result of this some group borders are fading but others are articulated and defended more strongly. Various (corporate) agents, with their divergent histories, views, and interests, are thus engaged in ongoing negations to define reality and to access scarce resources. In the course of these 'exchanges and negotiations of meaning', the various identities are expressed, affirmed, commented on, and externally imposed and adjusted in their mutual relations. Individuals and groups thus have multiple identities. This leads to diversity and ambiguity. It results in a drop in the acceptability of the certainties offered by local or national communities with their concomitant moral orientations. The resulting plurality of 'representations' and 'voices' gives rise to conflicts, controversies, and variations, but also to attempts to live peacefully together, to co-ordinate activities, and to balance interests. In short, present-day society is nothing but 'a never-ending story' of antagonistic cooperation. As such, it embodies the ongoing dialectical processes of globalization and localization.

Diversity and new patterns of inequality

Let me rephrase my argument. The rise of liberalism, deregulation and privatization, the development of post-industrial employment structures in the West and the industrialization of the so-called Third World countries, the restructuring of European welfare states, the growth of multiple identities, the rise of interethnic conflicts, the growing importance of regional and organizational networks, the fascination with regional identity, to name just a few, are in all

respects at the same time causes and consequences of globalization and localization. We are confronted thus with a tautology, an effect of our lack of detailed
knowledge of the chain of interdependencies between the above mentioned
processes (see also Schuurman's contribution to this volume). As a result, we
have to envisage a world in which variety of and diversity in core-institutions
will probably increase. These will partly follow classic boundaries of region,
socio-economic class, age, gender, and religion, but will also run along new lines
of ethnicity and lifestyle. Because the disadvantages of this variety – lack of consensus, increasing strife over scarce provisions – can often rely on more public
interest than the advantages, increasing demands for integration and decreasing
tolerance for variety will become significant social powers. This creates a new
paradox: the growing variety calls up powers which hinder the pursuit of integration. Differences between nations and groups are great and their number
sizeable, so that a common global or national culture is an illusion. People will
have to learn to live with diversity. Because a worldwide, common set of values,
standards, and repertoires of actions is, in my opinion, illusory, we can only
strive towards the functional co-ordination of differences on the basis of a limited number of rules of the game. The realization of this functional co-ordination
will be extremely difficult. The social fabric is built up of groups with different
visions and interests. Societies at almost every level will be split but also connected via processes and structures whereby distinction is continually made
between inside and outside, between us and them. What about the classical split
between the haves and the have nots which forces itself on us in the wake of globalization and reassessment of the nation-state in various forms? It is highly
likely that specific groups will fall economically, socioculturally, or technologically even further behind. Drop-out symptoms will increase. Large groups are in
danger of ending up on the sidelines of social life. We have to remember that
opportunities for mobility and the availability of resources are highly differentiated. While these new processes of transnationalization hold out new opportunities for some groups of the world population, the same processes are
disadvantageous for other groups. We have to acknowledge that knowledge,
social practices, and identities are construed in a context of inequality of power
and unequal access to scarce resources (Mohanty 1990). We see that globalization
is accompanied by new patterns of inequality and polarization. We have to
acknowledge that the global restructuring of production that is taking place
favours a number of countries and ethnic groups but bypasses or even harms a
considerably larger number. Poorer segments of the world population are
increasingly pushed towards degraded areas and are forced to overexploit natural resources, straining the adaptability of local cultures. The commercialization
of agricultural production and the processes of migration accompanying industrialization have had all kinds of 'gender-effects' and have deepened the interactive patterns between rural and urban areas. The labour markets are
characterized by numerous forms of fragmentation. Attempts at macro-eco-

nomic stabilization are accompanied by institutional reforms that emphasize liberalization, deregulation, and privatization, all implying a withdrawal of the state in favour of the private sector. In a number of countries the 'separation' of state institutions from the internal dynamics of society has resulted in a complete collapse of the state and an absorption of the state functions by an intricate network of legal and illegal transactions between patrons and clients. Sometimes this leads to the complete marginalization of a growing number of groups, who increasingly resort to the informal sector as a means of survival. The related risk of social isolation is a fertile breeding-ground for racism, religious fundamentalism, and ethnocentrism, with all the disastrous consequences that entails, as ethnic violence in so many parts of the world clearly demonstrates.

It must be clear that it is not just about the making of difference, drawing boundaries, creating a specific order, but also about the realization of an inequality, even marginalization of specific groups by means of categorizing groups of people and situations in specific ways. After all, categorization has an intrinsic power dimension and is in many cases constitutive for the interpretation of the reality and the positions of different groups within it (Tajfel and Turner 1986). Bourdieu (1991:221) described this as follows: "What is at stake here is the power of imposing a vision of the social world through principles of di-vision", including the unequal access to and control of scarce resources which is connected to it. It is difficult to get a grip on this process. Society – as a layered configuration of arenas in which changing groups try to realize their often conflicting objectives and to satisfy their needs according to changing procedures and rules of the game – demands a powerful government. Here it is lacking. This applies regionally and nationally, but also at global level. Despite the coining of terms such as 'the new global order', there are serious problems because of a lack or rather weakness of global governance.

Globalization and localization: future perspectives

An important question in this context is whether or not the interaction between globalization and localization is of a transitory nature. We have a choice of three perspectives: (1) convergence, (2) divergence, (3) hybridization. Each of these perspectives involves different views of our future (see Nederveen Pieterse 1996, on which I base my description).

The first perspective is that of cultural convergence or growing sameness: this perspective represents the classic vision of modernization as a steamroller denying and eliminating the cultural differences in its path. Adherents of this 'MacDonaldization' thesis believe that growing global interdependence and interconnection will lead to an increase in cultural standardization and uniformity. The 'almighty transnational corporations' will erase the differences through rationalization in the Weberian sense, i.e. through formal rationality laid down in rules and regulations. It combines efficiency, calculability, predictability, and controllability. MacDonaldization represents at the same time the theme of modernization and the theme of cultural imperialism.

In the second perspective, the accent is laid precisely on that which is ignored in the homogenization thesis: the difference. In addition, the notion of cultural difference is, in particular, connected with identity politics and policies, with gender issues, with rights of minorities and indigenous peoples.

As we know, both a harmony and a conflict variant can be distinguished within this perspective. Supporters of both variants underline both sociocultural or ethnic differences between various groups in their empirical studies, as the lasting and immutable nature hereof, implying or articulating the problems which will occur if and when these differences are denied or suppressed. They only differ in their evaluation and interpretation of these differences. In the harmony variant, stamping out cultural variety is seen as a 'form of disenchantment with the world': alienation and displacement become apparent (Nederveen Pieterse 1996:1389). In the harmony variant, it is stressed that the presence of cultural differences and cultural collectivities should not merely be tolerated, but rather acknowledged as permanent and valuable, it should actively be protected and promoted in law and public policy (Taylor 1992). In the conflict variant, difference is seen as generating rivalry and conflict. Theoretically, difference is disruptive. A well-known proponent of this rivalry and conflict view is Samuel Huntington who argued that "a crucial... aspect of what global politics is likely to be in the coming years... will be the clash of civilisations" (Huntington 1993:38). It should come as no surprise that this variant tends towards racism, nationalism, or religious or ethnic fundamentalism with the associated apartheid philosophy and ethnic cleansing. The difference between both variants must not be exaggerated though, at least not as regards actual everyday practices. For although multiculturalism as a form of state-sanctioned cultural pluralism is "based on an ideology which holds that cultural diversity is tolerated, valued and accommodated in society, within a set of overarching principles based on the values normally associated with a liberal democracy – e.g. the civic unity and equality of all people within the state, and individual rights" (McAllister 1997:2), we know that the practice of multiculturalism effectively reinforces domination by one specific ethnic group. Diversity is domesticated, shaped, and harnessed to the yoke of the dominant sociocultural order and economy.

The third perspective stresses that the current hybridization is structural. This hybridization thesis, also known as syncretization or creolization, "springs from the taboo zones of nationalism and racialism because it refers to that which the doctrines of racial, national and ethnic purity could not even bear to acknowledge the existence of: the half-caste, mixed-breed, metis", or in other terms, the between and betwixt, because it starts out from the fuzziness of boundaries, from boundary crossing, from 'cut'n'mix', because it represents in Foucauldian terms "a resurrection of subjugated knowledges" (Nederveen

Pieterse 1996:1392). Hybridization emphasizes the idea that the global powers are – and will always be – quite vulnerable to very small-scale and local resistances. Hybridization acknowledges that "communities are always in flux, divided, contested; people are perpetually escaping them as well as mobilizing to enforce them" (Kalb 1997:5). Hybridization refers to a worldview "which is not frozen by global images and metaphors, but which refers to the multi-localized (in the geographical and institutional sense) resistances, to the vulnerabilities and tensions, in short to the contradictions, of the ongoing struggle about living and working conditions" (Maier 1996). This formulation reminds us of the inherent tension between an imagined ideal world and the actual practices of the existing social order. The dilemma we have to face in dealing with multiculturalism can be formulated in a nutshell: "Multiculturalism conveys the idea of 'many cultures', each distinct from each other, implying boundaries rather than continuities; logically followed by separateness and distinctiveness. This contrasts with the conscious mixing of language, race and culture in much of contemporary societies. This implies that the boundaries between groups must not be formalized and institutionalized" (McAllister 1997:20). That, however, provokes penetrative questions. For instance, will formal multiculturalism with its institutionalized boundaries lead to a categorization, polarization, or pillarization of people with greater ethnic stereotyping and mobilization along ethnic lines? Is a formal recognition of cultural difference required to facilitate reconciliation, redistribution of resources and the elimination of disadvantage? I do not know.

Hybridization: a new view on culture

Whatever the answers to these questions may be, an issue we cannot evade is whether a hybrid world in the 21st century can be described and interpreted using concepts and insights acquired at the end of the 19th century. Does hybridization force us to reassess established concepts? For instance, what about the overarching concept of 'culture' in anthropology? Until the 1960s the culturalism paradigm was dominant. This perspective – that fits the above-mentioned difference or divergence thesis very well – is characterized by essentialism, primordialism, and reductionism (Tempelman 1997). Essentialism refers to the tendency to reify culture. Culture is presented as a unified entity that has a definite substance and assumes the status of a 'thing' that people 'have', 'belong to', or 'are members of'(Baumann 1997:211). This essentialism is accompanied by the habit of equating cultural content and cultural communities. In this way the world is imagined as made up of discrete cultural collectivities, each based on a homogeneous culture that distinguishes it from others. These views merge through the notion of community. Cultural values and practices are supposed to be embedded in communal relationships, while collective identities are validated as referring to actual communities. This slips into the idea that cultural collectivities, by the very nature of their communal bond, share a common cultural content. The essentialist, content-cum-community notion is subsequently defined along primordialist lines. Cultural forms and features, such as ethnic origin, language and customs, are seen as objective and inevitable, as if given by nature. Finally, the culturalist discourse adopts a reductionist approach to issues concerning cultural identity. Cultural consciousness, mobilization, and conflict are explained as arising out of the existence of common origins, religious convictions, language, or even biological 'facts'. In short, in the culturalism perspective, culture consists of four related characteristics, which are supposed to co-exist harmoniously. Firstly, culture is learned, acquired in social interaction. Secondly, culture is somehow integrated, neatly fitting together. Thirdly, culture is something which comes in varying packages, distinctive to human collectivities. Fourthly, as a rule, these collectivities belong in or have territories (Hannerz 1996:8).

It is clear that the last two characteristics, in particular, cultures as packages of meanings and meaningful forms, distinctive as regards collectivities and territories, are most obviously affected by the changing conditions of mankind. In fact, only the first characteristic remains: culture as shaped and acquired in social interaction. With regard to the other "the strategy now should be to reformulate them as core problematics in our thinking comparatively about culture, its variations and its historical shifts. How, and to what degree, do people arrange culture into coherent patterns as they go about their lives? How, as they involve themselves with the interconnectedness of the world, does culture sometimes in some ways, become organized into the more or less tidy packages we have called 'cultures'" (Hannerz 1996:8).

We see that hybridization has made room for the articulation of another view on culture. We may call it a constructivist approach. From this perspective, culture and the accompanying cultural identity are defined as situational, instrumental, and political (Tempelman 1997). This perspective stresses the fluidity and malleability of cultures and cultural identities (Barth 1969, 1994, Eisenstadt & Giesen 1995). Cultures are not things, they are the flexible, changeable, and adaptive products of ongoing processes of social interaction and definition. Collective identities are construed by the drawing of boundaries that separate the collectivity from the outside world, determining what belongs to the collectivity and what does not, distinguishing insiders from strangers. Cultural groups are seen as a form of social organization rather than as an expression of culture. From this situationalist vantage point, cultural pluralism becomes contingent and circumstantial. The distinctive cultural features can be fabricated and manipulated in processes labelled variously as 'invention of tradition' (Hobsbawn & Ranger 1988), 'ethnogenesis' (Roosens 1989), 'ethnurgy' (Hanf 1995) and 'imagined communities' (Anderson 1983). In sharp contrast to the primordialism of the culturalist approach, constructivism is based on an instrumentalist view of cultures and cultural identity. Cultural identity is not seen as representing 'already existing' and persistent things that are 'natural' or 'spiritual', but as an ideology to legitimize power and privilege and to vent frustration (Hanf 1995:47), as a resource that individuals and groups employ to maximize their rational preferences (Hechter 1986) or as a strategy for different interest and status groups involved in elite competition (Cohen 1969). In the words of Daniel Bell "ethnicity is best understood not as a primordial phenomenon in which deeply held identities have to emerge, but as a strategic choice by individuals who, in other circumstances, would choose other group memberships as means of gaining some power and privilege" (Bell 1975:146). Or as Crawford Young puts it "The heart of the matter, then, was to perceive ethnicity as manufactured, rather than as given, an innovative act of creative imagination... The process of social construction proceeds at an individual as well as group level; in the innumerable transactions of daily life, individuals are engaged in a constant process of defining and redefining themselves; identity thus understood is not a 'fixed essence' but a 'strategic assertion'" (Young 1993:24). It may be clear that attention shifts from the study of ways of life – a classical definition of culture – to the study of culture as politics, stressing processes of identification (Balibar 1995) why do people identify themselves and others in particular ways? How are these cultural identifications created and reproduced? Which cultural features become important as markers of identity? How are these employed to foster internal cohesion and to sustain the separateness of the group?

The constructivist approach has the definitive advantage over the culturalist view that it allows, indeed compels, us to problematize culture and cultural identity. Each definition or form of cultural identity is the highly-situated product of continuous construction, often strategically chosen and manipulated and related to political and social conditions rather than to 'authentic' cultural needs. This insight opens the way for all kinds of empirical and normative questions: How are cultural boundaries legitimized and how are these legitimations accepted? How can boundaries be contested and revised? What are the consequences of the processes of inclusion and exclusion that accompany the construction of cultural identity. On what grounds can we distinguish the different cultural collectivities. We cannot fall back on definitions of these collectivities beforehand. After all, the actual definition of the group involved in recognition itself provides particular possibilities and problems. In Canada, for instance, the question of whether indigenous people are distinct nations or ethnic groups that may be put on a par with immigrant minorities is the subject of heated debate. The form that 'cultural identity' takes in this instance is not simply given by the objective features of the group, it is the result of political struggles and decisions that confer particular benefits and costs (Boldt & Long 1984).

However, we have to be careful in applying a constructivist perspective. We have to admit that there is the danger that a definition of culture in terms of the 'politics of recognition' overemphasizes the fabricated and instrumental nature of culture and cultural identity. Let us not forget that the freedom of people to 'play' with identities is limited. Although cultures and identities are never definitely fixed, this does not mean that they can always be adopted, put aside, fabricated, or revised at whim. Identification processes cannot be converted to suit the strategic promotion of interests. Identities may be 'invented' but these inventions are not always the result of intended construction nor do conscious efforts at construction always have their intended results. One has to guard against seeing human interactions exclusively in terms of transactions (Epstein 1978, De Vos 1975). People also have an elementary need to belong. Affections and emotions are intrinsically interwoven with arguments and interests (Friedman 1995). People are, furthermore, only partly able to be objective with regard to their imposed identity, even although they have the capacity to look at themselves, even although they realize that they are playing a role (Procee 1991), even although they can put on masks (Goffman 1959). Furthermore, they also have to take others into account in the social arenas in which the identities are formed. In other words, the construction of identities is the result of ascription and subscription. People are, after all, not accountants who repeatedly take on a new identity according to the costs-benefits balance. In addition to this, the reality is not transparent and cannot be caught in unequivocal 'utility values'.

This constructivist vision of culture also leads to the over-accentuation of the situational and dynamic character of cultures and identities. Finally, the emphasis on boundaries and differences does not necessarily imply a pre-occupation with the other (Benda-Beckman & Verkuyten 1995:17). Members may be entirely concerned with their own group and their life in it, and have only a vague notion of those who do not belong to it (Roosens 1994, Parekh 1995).

In short, hybridization processes have provided anthropologists with opportunities to reconceptualize their core concept. This has resulted in a whole new set of research-questions, in a more fruitful balance between structure and process, in a better insight into the relationship between communality or the sharing of mental maps and co-ordinated actions between individuals and groups.

New narratives for development studies

Hybridization also demands the renewed thinking through of 'development studies'. The recognition of the complexity of the interwovenness between components of a reality which we do not know sufficiently well has far-reaching consequences for the basing of our interventions, as institutionalized in development studies, a branch of the applied sciences in which the ideology of social engineering is strongly anchored. "Both capitalist and state socialist countries took a range of assumptions for granted including control over nature, the centrality of technological advance, the increasing power of productive processes, the importance of reliable administration, the need for a trained and disciplined workforce, the desirability of growth and planning for it. These are the key factors which constitute the profile of modernity or the shape of what in the context of the West has often been called the Modern Project" (Albrow, this volume).

However, social engineering, representing at the same time the Enlightenment idea of governance through knowledge, operationalized in functional, rational, bureaucratic procedures and the ideal of sociocultural consensus, is under strong pressure. The same goes for the idea that development means incorporating hitherto excluded 'backward' regions and groups into a modernization process along the path of which rich postindustrial countries were already far advanced (e.g. Albrow, this volume). Nowadays, the topic of development studies is no longer modernization. Development studies refers to the co-existence of many worlds, each with its own 'logic'. A new narrative has emerged in which multiplicity, diversity, specificity, ambiguity, and ambivalence are key-terms. Paradoxically, "there is a growing need for consensus as a basis for meaningful social action between a growing number of mutually related actors, while the possibility of doing so is diminishing, no matter what the mass media say. There is a risk of the absence of common or mutually attuned interests and representations, as well as of too much diversity" (De Ruijter 1996:7). All the same, this 'absence' has become a genuine problem for the making and implementing of policy measures. After all, the paradox of the growing need for 'consensus' and the diminishing prospects of its realization raises major questions about our ability to deal with 'development issues'. We do not yet know what is necessary to increase our insight and to strengthen our capacity for managing these problems, let alone solving them. We no longer even know whether this is within our power. Perhaps the problems are too great, perhaps they have too great a resistance to policy, but even though we do not have a sufficient knowledge of the conditions for the successful or fruitful scientific founding of policy measures, a minimal necessary condition is the development of an integrative approach, in which classical dichotomies as structure-agency have been surpassed.

However, it is not just a matter of adapting our conceptual apparatus to a changing object of research, we also have to participate in rethinking or even reshaping our social policies. As researchers and citizens we have to accept our responsibilities. We ourselves must make choices and take standpoints. We have to articulate possible solutions to alleviate the extreme unequal access to scarce resources. We have to take action to restore the balance of power. We have to be aware of possible consequences of these actions, e.g. advocating affirmative, targeted programs. We have to realize that the basic political problem with a non-existent or minimal welfare state (by far the majority of existing states) is that numerous targeted programmes are required for specific groups. These targeted programmes invite a permanent public discussion about the groups deserving it. This public debate constitutes a threat to civic solidarity and integration. However, "instead of a retreat from all sorts of politics in the name of globalization and individualization, I think what is needed is a civic movement, a popular front, or whatever, that reminds our politicians that they should not beg away from regulating the markets, in particular the financial markets that foster so much turbulence and stepped-up competition in the international system" (Kalb

1997:12), in view of the far-reaching consequences for the quality of life of large groups of people.

References

Anderson, B. (1983) *Imagined Communities: Reflection on the Origin and Spread of Nationalism*, London and New York, Verso.

Anderson, B. (1992) *Long-Distance Nationalism: World Capitalism and the Rise of Identity Politics*, Centre for Asian Studies, Amsterdam.

Appadurai, A. (1990) *Disjuncture and Difference in the Global Cultural Economy*. In Featherstone, M. (ed.), *Global Culture: Nationalism, Globalization and Modernity*, London, Sage, pp. 295-310.

Appadurai, A. (1996) *Modernity at Large: Cultural Dimensions of Globalization*, Minneapolis, University of Minnesota Press.

Balibar, E. (1995) *Cultural and Identity*. In: Rajchman, J. (ed.), *The Identity in Question*, London, Routledge.

Barth, F. (ed.) (1969) *Ethnic Groups and Boundaries. The Social Organization of Culture Difference*, Boston, Little, Brown.

Barth, F. (1994) *Enduring and Emerging Issues in the Analysis of Ethnicity*. In: Vermeulen, H., and Govers, C. (eds.), *The Anthropology of Ethnicity. Beyond 'Ethnic Groups and Boundaries'*, Amsterdam, Het Spinhuis.

Bauman, Z. (1991) *Modernity and Ambivalence*, Polity Press, Cambridge.

Baumann, G. (1997) *Dominant and Demotic Discourses of Culture: Their Relevance to Multi-ethnic Alliances*. In: Baumann, G., *Debating Cultural Hybridity*.

Bell, D. (1975) *Ethnicity and Social Change*. In: Glazer, N., and Moynihan, D.P. (eds.), *Ethnicity: Theory and Experience*, Cambridge, Mass., Harvard University Press, pp. 141-177.

Benda-Beckmann, K. von, and Verkuyten, M. (eds.) (1994) "Introduction: cultural identity and development in Europe", in: Benda-Beckmann, K. von, and Verkutyen, M. (eds.), *Cultural Identity and Development in Europe*, London, London University Press, pp. 1-30.

Boldt, M., and Long, J.A. (1984) "Tribal Traditions and European-Western Political Ideologies: The Dilemma of Canada's Native Indians", *Canadian Journal of Political Science*, XVII, 3, pp. 537-554.

Bourdieu, P. (1991) *Language and Symbolic Power*, Cambridge, Polity Press.

Brenner, Y.S. (1996) *Looking Back*, Utrecht.

Breuer, S. (1992) *Die Gesellschaft des Verschwindens*, Hamburg, Junius Verlag.

Cohen, A. (1969) *Customs and Politics in Urban Africa: A Study of Hausa Migrants in Yoruba Towns*, Berkeley, University of California Press.

De Vos, G. (1975)*Ethnic Pluralism. Conflict and Accommodation*. In De Vos, G., and Romanucci-Ross, L. (eds.). *Ethnic Identity: Cultural Continuities and Change*, Mayfield, Palo Alto, pp. 5-41.

Eisenstadt, S.N., and Giesen, B. (1995) "The Construction of Collective Identity", *Arch. Europ. Sociol.*, XXXVI, pp. 72-102.

Epstein, A. (1978) *Ethos and Identity*, London, Tavistock.

Featherstone, M. (1990) *Global Culture, Nationality, Globalization and Modernity*, London, Sage.

Friedman, J. (1995) *Cultural Identity and Global Process*, London, Sage.

Giddens, A. (1984) *The Constitution of Society. Outline of a Theory of Structuration*, London, Polity Press.

Giddens, A. (1990) *The Consequences of Modernity*, London, Polity Press.

Goffman, E. (1959) *The Presentation of Self in Everyday Life*. New York, Doubleday.

Gunsteren, H. van (1993) Eenvoud in veelvoud, *Beleid en Maatschappij*, jaargang XX, pp. 3-8.

Hammar, T. (1990) *Democracy and the Nation State. Aliens, Denizens and Citizens in a World of International Migration*, Aldershot, Avebury.

Hannerz, U. (1992) *Cultural Complexity: Studies in the Social Organization of Meaning*, New York, Columbia University Press.

Hannerz, U. (1996) *Transnational Connections. Culture, People, Places*, London, Routledge.

Hechter, M. (1986) *A Rational Choice Approach to Race and Ethnic Relations*. In: Mason, D. and Rex, J. (eds.), *Theories of Race and Ethnic Relations*, Cambridge, Cambridge University Press.

Hobsbawm, E.J., and Ranger, T. (eds.) (1983) *The Invention of Tradition*, Cambridge, Cambridge University Press.

Huntington, S. (1993) "The Clash of Civilisations", *Foreign Affairs*, 72 (3), pp. 22-49.

Kalb, D. (1997) *The Ghost of Milton Friedman; Dissident Remarks on the new Social Orthodoxy* (unpublished paper).

Latour, B. (1994) *Wij zijn nooit modern geweest. Pleidooi voor een symmetrische antropologie*, Rotterdam, van Gennep.

Lévi-Strauss, Cl. (1962) *La Pensee Sauvage*, Paris, Plon.

Maier, R. (1996) *Globalization: Fact or Fiction* (unpublished paper).

Malkki, L. (1992) "National Geographic: the Rooting of Peoples and the Territorialization of National Identity among Scholars and Refugees", *Cultural Anthropology* 7 (1), pp. 24-44.

McAllister, P.A. (1997) "Cultural Diversity and Public policy in Australia and South-Africa. The Implication of 'Multiculturalism'", *African Sociological Review* 1, (in press).

McLuhan, M. (1964) *Understanding Media*, New York, McGraw-Hill.

Mingione, E. (1996) *Urban Poverty in the Advanced Industrial World: Concepts, Analysis and Debates*. In: Mingione, E. (ed.), *Urban Poverty and the Underclass*, Oxford, Blackwell.

Mohanty, Ch. (1990) "On Race and Voice: Challenges for Liberal Education in the 1990's", *Cultural Critique*, Winter Issue.

Nederveen Pieterse, J. (1996) "Globalization and Culture. Three Paradigms", *Economic and Political Weekly*, vol. XXXI, no. 23, 8 June, pp. 1389-1393.

Parekh, B. (1995) "The Concept of National Identity", *New Community*, 21, 2, pp. 255-268.

Procee, H. (1991) *Over de grenzen van culturen. Voorbij universalisme en relativisme*, Meppel.

Reitsma, H.A., and Kleinpenning, J.M.G. (1989) *The Third World in Perspective* (sec. ed.), van Gorcum, Assen.

Robertson, R. (1992) *Globalization: Social Theory and Global Culture*, London, Sage,.

Robertson, R. (1995) Glocalization': Time-Space and Homogeneity-Heterogeneity. In: Featherstone, M., Lash, S., and Robertson, R. (eds.), *Global Modernities*, London, Sage, pp. 25-44.

Roosens, E.A. (1989) *Creating Ethnicity. The Process of Ethnogenesis*, London, Sage.

Roosens, E. (1994) *Ethnicity as a Creation: Some Theoretical Reflections*. In: Benda-Beckmann, K. von, and Verkutyen, M. (eds.), *Cultural Identity and Development in Europe*, London, London University Press, pp. 30-40.

Ruijter, A. de (1996) *Hybridization and Governance*, Den Haag. ISS.

Ruijter, A. de (1997) *The Era of Glocalisation*. In: Naerssen, T. van, Rutten, N., and Zoomers, A.(eds.), *The Diversity of Development*, Assen, Van Gorkum, pp. 381-391.

Salet, W. (1996) *De conditie van stedelijkheid en het vraagstuk van maatschappelijk integratie*, Den Haag, Vuga.

Tajfel, H., and Turner, J.C. (1986) *The Social Identity Theory of Intergroup Behaviour*. In: Worchel, S. and Austin, W.G. (eds.), *Psychology of Intergroup Relations*. Chicago: Nelson-Hall.

Taylor, C. (1992) *Multiculturalism and The Politics of Recognition*, Princeton N.J., Princeton University Press.

Tempelman, S. (1997) *Cultural Identity: A cautious Constructivist Approach* (unpublished paper).

Wallerstein, I. (1974, 1980, 1989) *The Modern World System*, New York, Academic Press.

Young, C. (1993) *The Dialectics of Cultural Pluralism: Concept and Reality*. In Young, C., *The Kissing Tide of Cultural Pluralism: The Nation-State at Bay?*, Madison Wisconsin: The University of Wisconsin Press.

VICIOUS AND BENIGN UNIVERSALISM

John Tomlinson

The critique of globalization as the critique of universalism

As we all know, there are plenty of reasons to be critical of globalization. Some of these are very familiar – often straightforward extensions of Marxist or other leftist critiques of global capitalism, which emphasize the political-economic 'unevenness' (a strangely euphemistic term) of the process. Equally familiar are those critiques that portray globalization as the latest phase in the long story of an expanding Western cultural hegemony. It would fly in the face of a great deal of evidence to argue with the political-economic critiques of globalization and this is certainly not my intention here. It would be less foolish to pick a fight with the criticisms of cultural hegemony since these often tend to attack the complex and still evolving cultural politics set in train by globalization with the rather blunt-edged concepts of 'Westernization' or cultural imperialism (Latouche 1996; Petras, 1993; Schiller 1995). Globalization is frequently taken in this tradition of thought to imply a trend towards a simple 'globality' – a cultural homogenization which, whilst rhetorically persuasive, remains anthropologically implausible.

This does not, of course, imply that the critique of globalization in the cultural sphere is either inappropriate or unimportant – merely that it is a more complicated business. One of its many complications lies in the fact that cultural practices and processes are not neatly separable from economic ones.

For example, one target deserving of a cultural critique of globalization might be the Panglossian discourse of the global techno-enthusiasts: those who see in the technological modalities of globalization (computer-mediated communication- the Internet- is an obvious example) everything working together for good. This sort of celebration of the cultural benefits of time-space compression (for the communications-affluent sectors of communications-affluent nations) attracts criticism not just on account of its wide-eyed naïveté, but because it has a putative ideological function. As Armand Mattelart has pointed out, this techno-Utopianism encourages us to accept the cultural, political, and economic *terms* of globalization as a *fait accompli* – a simple entailment of the fruits of technological progress which it seems difficult to oppose. Such conjuring of inevitability,

Mattelart argues, conceals questions of agency and locus of control, allowing the traditional centres of capitalist concentration to continue as globalization 'winners'. In Carlos Monsivais's apt formulation, "Globalization means never having to say you're sorry." (quoted, Mattelart 1999:3).

Given that there is a significant political link between culture and economy, however, this still proves very difficult to analyse in a way that does justice to the cultural dimension. The problem is most commonly seen in accounts that enlist either a reductive logic of market determinations to account for cultural experiences, or a functionalist logic of cultural practices to account for growth in the capitalist system. These twin reductionisms – typical features of the critical discourse of cultural imperialism – aim to grasp the elusive connection between culture and economy but always fail. They fail because the causal connections they attempt to identify – driven by an entirely laudatory emancipatory politics – are nonetheless too simple and direct to do justice to the existentially complex domain of experience that we describe as 'culture'.

In the following contribution I would like to take a more oblique approach to these problems by focusing on a concept which is arguably at such a level of abstraction as to provide a bridge between the economic and the cultural, avoiding the more obvious reductionisms. This is the principle of universalism.

Universalism has an intuitive connection with globalization, which could easily lead us back to simplistic notions of the threat of global homogeneity. However, the concept is a much richer one, pertaining more to claims to the general applicability of social, political, and cultural understandings and values, than to simple notions of the drab uniformity of commodified cultural experience supposed in the fears of 'coca-colonization' and so forth. The relationship between universalism and globalization then, is not one of identity – two names for the same material cultural-economic condition. Rather, universalism has been regarded as a cultural-political *principle* informing (perhaps legitimating) the process of globalization.

A good example of a critique of globalization which puts the cultural-political principle of universalism at the forefront is found in the work of the British political philosopher John Gray, and it is on his account that I shall focus in the first part of this paper.[1] For Gray, both the social process of globalization and the cultural/political principle of universalism are unambiguously negative.

Globalization, Gray says, is "only a perverse and atavistic form of modernity – that, roughly, of nineteenth-century English and twentieth century American economic individualism – projected worldwide" (Gray 1997:183), and he

---

1. An earlier version of the sections of this chapter which deal with Gray's arguments appeared in Tomlinson 1999.

describes universalism as: "one of the least useful and indeed most dangerous aspects of the western intellectual tradition.... the metaphysical faith that local western values are authoritative for all cultures and peoples". This 'foundational' principle of universalism, he argues, is to be seen in "the Socratic project of the examined life, in the Christian commitment to a redemption for all humankind and in the Enlightenment project of progress towards a universal human civilization" (p. 158).

Both of these definitions express important aspects of globalization and universalism, but both are very particular, *partial* understandings. In the case of globalization, Gray grasps it primarily – indeed almost exclusively – as an economic phenomenon – as the global extension of the capitalist free market. This is, as we have noticed, a very common understanding amongst critics of globalization – as for instance in Paul Hirst and Grahame Thompson's celebrated sceptical analysis, *Globalization in Question* (1996), and it is, I believe, a mistaken view. Although I shall not elaborate the argument here,[2] I believe that the reduction of globalization to merely the operation of the global capitalist market is one of the most tempting but misleading moves in the critical discourse established around globalization. Rather, globalization has to be understood as a general process of *complex connectivity*, that is as a multi-dimensional process proceeding simultaneously in the economic, political, cultural, and technological spheres. The global capitalist market is hugely important for all these spheres, but rather than trying to read off consequences from this one dimension of globalization – the economic – it is precisely the complexity of interactions between these fields that we need to grasp.

This is however, in a curious sense, precisely what Gray turns out to be attempting in connecting globalization with the principle of universalism. For him it is the principle of universalism that is the real underlying target – a principle with deep roots in the Western tradition embracing both economic and cultural practices.

Vicious universalism 1: universalism as masquerade

Gray's understanding of universalism is also, however, a partial one – at least at this point in his argument. For in a way that is familiar from the discourse of cultural imperialism, he sees universalism as the illegitimate projection of Western values onto all other global cultures. The universalism he objects to here is actually a case of the particular disguising itself – *masquerading* – as the universal. This is indeed an important aspect of universalism as an ideology: we see it most dramatically in critiques of the imperialist mind-set – in the bluff ethnocentri-

---

2. For further discussion of the inherent multidimensionality of globalization and a critique of the unidimensionality of Hirst and Thompson's analysis see Tomlinson 1999, chapter one.)

cism of, for example, the Pax Britannica which was the cultural bedrock of 19th century colonial domination. Universalism as masquerade, however, is also familiar as a more directly political-economic ideology, for instance, in Marx's ideology-critique, where he exposes the mystification involved in the particular interests of the bourgeoisie within the production relationship passing themselves off as universal interests.

Now we can see more clearly what ties together economic globalization and cultural universalism in Gray's account. Globalization – specifically the global 'free market' – is the institutional mechanism by which Western capitalism is globally distributed – with, it has to be allowed, spectacular 'success'. At the same time, though, it is, for Gray, the prime agency via which particular Western values and intellectual traditions – for example, possessive individualism – become 'universalized'. An intimate relationship is proposed between the cultural/political principle of universalism – seen here as the sustaining ideology of Western (Enlightenment) modernity – and the narrowly defined process of (free-market capitalist) globalization. Here then is the link between globalization as culture and as economy articulated through the 'vicious' category of universalism.

It has to be said that Gray's critique has a certain purchase on contemporary ideology, for clearly there is still plenty of universalism as masquerade present in the world today. To academics, inhabiting a liberal intellectual culture pervaded by cultural relativism, pluralism, and anxieties over epistemological foundations, this might not be immediately obvious. As Timothy Brennan points out, though, arrogant strains of old-fashioned ethnocentric projection are alive and well in the popular political consciousness of powerful countries like the United States. Brennan cites as an example Ben Wattenberg's (1991) book *The First Universal Nation*:

> "We are the first universal nation. "First" as in the first one, "first" as in "number one". And "universal" within our borders and globally. In America, we now come from everywhere, becoming one people...vastly enriched by our pluralism... We don't much read, watch or listen to their [Europe's and the third world's] stuff. Is it that Americans are provincial, insular, parochial boors? More likely it is that we have a taste for just what the rest of the world now enjoys.... In the future the No. 1 country will be the one that is most successful in shaping the global democratic culture... Only Americans have the sense of mission – and gall – to engage in benign but energetic global advocacy. Hence the doctrine of "neo-manifest destinarianism", to help form a world that is user-friendly to American values." (Wattenberg, quoted Brennan 1997:60)

As Brennan suggests, the fact that such gross ethnocentricism is easy meat for informed academic critique is beside the point. It is the immediate popular emotional appeal of such rhetoric (Wattenberg's book was adapted and screened as a television documentary with support from right-wing bodies like the Heritage Foundation) that makes it significant. In the face of this sort of sentiment, linked to the undeniable economic and strategic power of countries like the United States, Gray's argument that universalism is, "one of the most dangerous aspects of the western intellectual tradition" appears compelling.

But is it? Does the ideological inflection given to the principle in the case of nationalist agendas mean that universalism is irrevocably vicious? One reason to doubt this is the extraordinarily wide *scope* of Gray's critique, for we must realize that Gray is not articulating a standard leftist critique of global capitalism. He indeed comes from a *conservative* tradition in political thought, albeit one which is vehemently opposed to the neo-liberal wing of conservative politics. The wide-ranging critique of Enlightenment modernity from which he approaches globalization bundles it together not only with free-market capitalism and neo-liberalism, but with humanism and, indeed, with "the left project of universal emancipation in a cosmopolitan civilization" (Gray, 1997:160). All of these are, for Gray, equally the follies of a universalizing cultural imagination.

However, it will be obvious that this sweeping critical embrace will not appeal to many on the political left. These latter may cheer Gray's critique of the universalizing of the capitalist market, yet remain committed to a broader ideal of internationalism, which has definite underpinnings in the universalizing thrust of the Enlightenment project. Do these people want to have their cake and eat it; to oppose universalism where it serves the cause of capitalist expansion but to cling to it as part of their own particular 'local' political dogma? Or is it rather the case that Gray is too totalizing in his view of the inherent viciousness of universalism as a principle? Is it a matter of being more discriminating in a critique of the various *forms* that universalism can take?

One obvious rejoinder to Gray might be that the issue of universalism is in fact a relatively minor one in relation to the overall critique of the global capitalist market. A typical left critique would point, for example, to the manifest ills that attend the capitalist system, particularly as it is unevenly globalized. It would highlight the inequitable and indiscriminate distribution of economic advantage, the indifference of the free market to the general meeting of human needs, the commodification of social and cultural experience, the amplification of waste, pollution, and environmental damage, and so on. Gray is right to say that the capitalist free market, as opposed to the general, ubiquitous notion of market exchange, is a product of the recent history of the West and that its global spread is therefore a case of the particular passing off as the universal. What this reminds us is that the free market system is not an inevitable destiny for all human societies. Though valid, this might be viewed as simply an additional point to add to the already strong range of reasons for resisting the spread of the global free market. Left critics may therefore feel they can get along quite well without resorting to the broad attack on a package of Enlightenment ideas – including open-ended 'progress', humanism, cosmopolitanism, the conquest and control of the natural world, and so on – that Gray proposes.

Before deciding that they can, we ought to explore another aspect of Gray's critique.

Vicious universalism 2: antipathy to cultural difference

Indeed, Gray has another reason for objecting to universalism – other, that is, than its appearance as masquerade. He objects to the very principle of Enlightenment universalizing thought and practice because he sees the 'modern notion of a universal civilization' as in inherent tension with the sustenance of human *cultural* life and the political practices this cultural life necessarily entails.

> "The disposition to constitute for itself different cultures or ways of life appears to be universal and primordial in the human animal. Yet the idea of a human universal civilization, as we find it in Condorcet, J.S. Mill, Marx and Rorty, is compelled to treat cultural difference as transitory or epiphenomi-nal, a passing stage in the history of the species. Modern thinkers have been led accordingly to misconceive the telos of political life. The end of politics is not the construction of institutions that are universally rationally authorita-tive. It is the pursuit of a *modus vivendi* among cultures and communities." (Gray, 1997:177)

Universalism as a political principle is now deplored because of its supposed opposition to 'culture' itself – which is understood here as centred on *difference*. Gray understands 'culture' essentially in the plural, as 'cultures' – local, particu-lar ways of life tied to and expressive of time and place; and universalism is the mistaken political aspiration of transcending this 'natural' plurality of different ways of being. Here we see Gray's rather convoluted conservatism emerge more clearly in the paradoxical appeal to a 'universal and primordial' disposition towards constituting cultural difference. The universality invoked here is not so much a simple contradiction as an indication of a fundamentally pessimistic view of the human condition that is a familiar theme in conservative thought. Gray sees humanity as 'an earthbound species' whose common experience of 'finitude, scarcity and mortality'... sets a limit to human hope" (p.177). More par-ticularly and fatally for Enlightenment aspiration, his 'tragic' conservatism asserts, "the truth that there is no common measure of improvement for all societies" (p. 176).

The key political issue, then, is whether universalizing projects *as such* – within which we would have to number socialism, the liberalism of human rights politics, some forms of environmentalism and feminism, and many other emancipatory movements – are in fact in tension with the supposed 'primordial' cultural dispositions of human beings. Gray's position is, as we have seen, a slightly idiosyncratic one. Nevertheless it chimes with a more general opposition to universalizing thought (for instance in postmodernism and postcolonialism), which rests on the assertion of cultural difference as a more or less self-evident good, the preservation of which is in inherent tension with universalizing projects associated with Enlightenment modernity. This tension however, exists *only* if, as Gray suggests, culture is intrinsically and essentially about difference.

Culture, difference, and universals

I shall argue that this is by no means self-evidently true and, indeed, that culture is associated with difference only contingently and not necessarily. If we can speak of cultural practices having any intrinsic function it would seem much more plausible that this lies in the *constitution of meaning* that the human species seems to require, rather than in the establishment and maintenance of patterns of difference. Cultural practices, in so far as they are distinguishable from the economic and the political, provide resources of meaning through collective symbolization woven into a set of material practices that sustain a viable way of life.

How does the idea of culture become so intuitively connected with the idea of difference? Well, setting aside for the moment structuralist anthropological notions of binary opposition, it seems to me that, for the most part, the connection is simply in the work of history. That is to say, human beings collectively pursue cultural practices with the aim of making their lives meaningful, and different local circumstances, combined with the sedimenting of particular practices as 'traditions' over time, result in the rich array of cultural difference that we see in the world. The important point here is that this difference does not arise as the *telos* of cultural practices, but simply as its consequence. Cultural work may produce difference but this is not the same as saying that culture is founded in difference.

This is not to deny that, once established and institutionalized, cultural differences *themselves* have a force in individual and collective meaning construction – as in the obvious case of the 'us-them'/ 'in group-out group' binarism often associated with national or ethnic cultural identity construction. I think, however, that it is a mistake to take the rather specific case of in-group/out-group identification as typical of the totality of cultural practice and experience. In the first place, as Benedict Anderson (1991) has shown, the construction of national identity has much deeper sources in the cultural-existential needs of communities than is accountable in terms of mere binarism. In the second place, significant expressions of national identity are known for their tendency to 'surge and decline' (Giddens, 1981) in relation to the political stability of societies. It could therefore be argued that – except in unusual circumstances of social instability or crisis – identifications based on difference are generally grounded in everyday lived experience. People are constantly engaged in cultural practices but they are only periodically, or in particular circumstances of cultural stress or oppression, preoccupied with cultural difference.

If this is true, and culture is not wedded essentially to difference, it also follows that it is not intrinsically antithetical to universals. In fact culture is arguably *built* on universals: on at least two sets of 'universal' human needs.

The first of these is that set of basic material needs – for food, shelter, physical comfort, sexuality, and so on, which all human beings share as a part of their existence as embodied creatures. Culture in its broadest anthropological sense is always established and elaborated around the satisfaction of these needs, though not always, importantly, in a direct functional relation to their satisfaction.

The second of these universals is the peculiar 'existential need' of human beings to generate satisfying collective narratives of meaning and orientation. This need, which derives from the human condition of embodied and finite reflexive consciousness, may be historically and geographically variable in its mode of expression. There is evidence of this, for example, in the global variety of aesthetic or religious practices – but, as Peter Berger amongst others has argued, (1974:195) it remains, 'a historical and cross cultural universal'.

It seems to me that cultural practices can best be understood in terms of the complex interplay between these two sets of needs. In many instances they seem to run together so that there is an interactive parallel between the pursuit of material needs and the pursuit of meaning. A form of life then most usually involves the elaboration of a narrative that co-exists subtly with the routine practices of satisfying material needs – this is one reason why culture and political economy are so closely connected. They can, of course, also be in tension. For example, the need for nourishment does not always sit in a comfortable 'functional' relationship with the narratives of self-identity or of life-purpose that people construct for themselves. This can be clearly seen in such phenomena as religious fasting, hunger strikes, slimming and dieting, or in such identity-related eating disorders as anorexia nervosa. Nonetheless, in the vast majority of cases there is a close (if in some instances contradictory) relationship between the generation of meaning and the mundane business of keeping oneself alive. This is one way of interpreting Raymond Williams's famous materialist-cultural dictum that 'culture is ordinary'.

Given this view of the significance of culture, how shall we formulate the threat that globalization poses to it? It is not, I shall argue, primarily a threat of the universal overwhelming the particular, but a more complicated story of the penetration and transformation of local cultural-material practices. To help to explore this, I shall use the example of the collective response to globalizing forces of a group of Zapotec Indians living in the state of Oaxaca in southern Mexico, who describe themselves as the Grupo Solidario de Quiatoni.

In 1997 the Grupo Solidario de Quiatoni produced a video documenting their attempts over a number of years to respond as a community to transformations in their way of life that can be attributed to the incursions of global modernity. What globalization has meant for them has been a complex process of the penetration of their local circumstances by a range of distant forces. One of these is undoubtedly the global free market that John Gray rightly deplores. In fact the Mexican government's neo-liberal structural adjustment policies of the 1980s and 1990s are prime examples of the – often brutal – marginalizing effects on local rural communities that the pursuit of national 'success' in the global market produces. This was of course most famously highlighted by the 1994 Zapatista uprising in the neighbouring state of Chiapas, but for the people who made this video it is clear that the global market was not the only, nor perhaps the most immediate, penetration of their locality. One of the main things they were trying to respond to was a dramatic climatic change. This was part of a broader pattern of global environmental change associated with the 'El Niño' phenomenon that had been affecting them: the failure of rains over a number of years and the threat this presented to the viability of their agriculture.

The video describes the way in which the community experimented with different farming methods and economic practices to meet the changed material conditions they were experiencing. In the process they rediscovered some of the very effective traditional methods employed by their ancestors and recontextualized these within a modern market system. More than this, however, the video represents what we could call a project of 're-embedding' of cultural identity.

One of the intriguing things about the video is the title: in Spanish, 'Buscando el Bienestar' – roughly translated as 'In Search of Well-being'. This also describes the collective project of the community – they refer to themselves as 'people searching for well-being'. This is not just a tactic of mere survival or 'getting by' in a world that is dramatically changing around them, but a rather sophisticated and deliberate holistic economic-cultural *project*. 'Well-being' suggests a way of life that is not only economically viable, but dignified, existentially satisfying, and which allows their culture, their identity, and their collective self-understanding to flourish. Most importantly for our present discussion, it is not a nostalgic, retrospective or 'reactionary' project. They are not seeking simply to hold doggedly on to, or to reinstate, a lost set of traditions, but actively to select those traditional practices that seem to work well in a changing context. To use Anthony Giddens's (1990) term, this could be seen as a process of 're-embedding' a set of material-cultural practices in the space left by the 'disembedding' of social life produced by globalization.

The video then does not document a *refusal* of modernity. The attitude of these people, it seems to me, is an intensely pragmatic one, making use of whatever material, technological, and 'cultural' resources are available. In doing this they seem to make a complex, pragmatic 'bargain' with modernity (Giddens, 1990). They are not overwhelmed by it or passive in the face of its advance, but neither do they reject modern technologies and patterns of thought in principle. Their rediscovery of traditional agricultural practices is thoroughly 'modern' in its empirical, experimental, spirit. They approach the practices of their forefathers in the spirit of sceptical, heuristic enquiry – seeing which seem to work and which don't. They make use of any available technologies – most obviously the video technology itself. Furthermore, the cultural act of documenting, recording, and 're-presenting' that the production of the video represents is an entirely modern, reflexive cultural one. What this pragmatic bargain with modernity also demonstrates is an aspect of the dialectical character of globalization. The complex set of penetrations of locality that disrupted the Zapotec way of life in the first place also provides some of the resources with which they are re-embedding. Most notable is, of course, the communications technology (here one is also reminded of Subcomandante Marcos' famous exploitation of the Internet in the Zapatista struggle). Other important resources that were made available were the market for their organic produce, the regional government assistance for the indigenous video projects, and even the audience for the video provided by the international media studies conference in Oaxaca City at which the film makers made their presentation.

If the cultural-economic response of the Grupo Solidario de Quiatoni is not crudely anti-modernizing there is even less sense in their project of a resistance to the principle of universalism. Pursuing 'well-being' does indeed involve the articulation of a distinctive cultural identity, but this is quite clearly approached in terms of the holistic project of making their communal life viable and convivial, not of maintaining cultural difference as an end in itself. These people want to remember their history and 'heritage' as part of their 'well-being', but there is no evidence of the robust assertion of difference here. Indeed I think it would strike them as rather curious if their project were described to them as a resistance of the universalizing tendencies of the European Enlightenment. To interpret what they are doing in this way might seem to be the sort of inexplicable mistake only European intellectuals could make.

One obvious way of reading this example then would be to say that, for cultures threatened by globalizing forces, anxieties over the abstract principles of universalism and difference are scarcely the most pressing concern. However, this is not really the main point I want to make. Rather it is that the (re)-construction of a viable culture is not noticeably here dependent on the assertion or rigorous preservation of cultural difference; but it is very much bound up with the two material 'universals' I mentioned earlier as underlying cultural practices. We are all in this sense, however our cultural situation varies, people 'in search of well-being'.

Benign universalism?

What I have tried to argue so far is that universalism as a political-cultural principle is not necessarily the enemy of flourishing particular local cultures.

However there clearly remains a whole raft of both theoretical and moral/political problems associated with universalizing thought. These have been highlighted in recent years, particularly in the field of identity politics. Here hostility towards the universalizing project of the Enlightenment has arisen – explicitly or implicitly – from all manner of marginalized groups in the West, who point, quite correctly, to the tendency to subsume the cultural difference that matters to them in broader categories like 'humanity'. Within any universal category it seems can be found a suppressed voice of difference: women within humanity; black women within the women's movement; lesbian black women, and so on. The struggle of these particular identities to find voice and to press their political agendas has combined with a suspicion, prompted by postmodernist thought, of the 'totalitarian' tendencies of European Enlightenment modernity to account in large part for the pervasive anti-universalizing intellectual tenor of the times.

Universalism, I have already conceded, is deeply prone to the ideological masquerade that passes off one powerful but particular way of life as the only way that life can or should be lived. Indeed the idea that the 'one true way of life' is probably always going to be prone to such ideological distortions, not only in the obvious case where it is used as a tacit legitimating ideology for a shallow global commercial culture ('a world of Coke'), but even in the most high-minded visions of a unified, pacified global culture. In these forms, critics like Gray are absolutely right to oppose it.

However universalism seen as the recognition that there are *some* common underlying conditions of existence that hold true for all human beings on the planet, irrespective of cultural particularities, and that there may be consensual values to be constructed in respect of this commonality is not so obviously wrong. The pursuit of such consensual values – for instance in the politico-legal discourse of universal human rights – is certainly virtuous, and does not, so far as I can see, have to entail a suppression of difference.[3] Furthermore, I think the complex connectivity, the compressions and the forced proximity of globalization is making this sort of universalism increasingly relevant, so we have to avoid throwing away the baby with the bathwater.

To conclude, then, I offer two reasons why we should hold on to a 'benign' form of universalism in constructing an appropriate cultural politics of globalization.

The first is the very practical reason that universal thinking in some form and degree seems to be pretty much inevitable in a globalized world which is rapidly creating mutual problems and risks. I am thinking here, for example, of the need for common consensual politics on the global environmental problems that beset us all. The problem of global warming, for instance, that exacerbated the effects of El Niño in Oaxaca, and also produced the devastating floods in China and Korea in 1999. The smoke haze that once again this year (2000) is spreading from the forest fires in Sumatra and Borneo to other parts of South-East Asia. Now there are, of course, particular and antagonistic constituencies of interest involved even in these 'global' problems. One only has to think of the different perspectives that have arisen in the attempt to regulate the production of ozone-destructive CFC gases under the 'Montreal Protocol': differences between producer and consumer nations and between the developed and the developing world (Yearley 1996). These genuine and thorny political problems are surely not going to be solved by a facile 'one worldism'. However, the point is that *no* solution to this sort of global problem can ever arise unless the universal interest is placed seriously alongside more immediate particular interests. With globalization we live in a world in which there are, politically and culturally speaking, many others, but, as Ulrich Beck has put it (1992), we also live in a world in which, in respect of global environmental threats, there are *no* others. What is needed therefore is a broadly diffused cultural/political sensibility that lifts us out of the immediate and proximate demands of the local and the particular to at least a *recognition* that there is a legitimate constituency of interest of 'humanity as a whole'. Furthermore, that this interest is not an abstraction, but is materially instantiated in all particular local experiences. The argument is not that the uni-

---

3. Even that most vigorous pragmatist critic of universalizing philosophies, Richard Rorty, concedes that a discourse of (universal) human rights can be legitimately constructed even if not upon a foundation of claims about a universal human nature (Rorty 1993). In this regard see also Norman Geras's elegant unpacking of the contortions of Rorty's position (Geras 1995).

versal human interest immediately 'trumps' all other particular local interests, but simply that it is reckoned seriously in the negotiations.

My second reason for defending a benign universalism is that it is a principle which grounds an attractive inclusivist ethics and politics. In its formulation in liberal and radical thought from Kant, Thomas Paine, and Marx onwards, universalizing thought points us away from the chauvinism that can arise in the institutionalizing of national or ethnic difference – made all too familiar in the bloody ethnic conflicts of the 1990s – Bosnia, Rwanda, Kosovo – towards a cosmopolitan disposition that is, I think, certainly politically progressive.

Of direct relevance here is the unabashed universalism adopted by Mary Kaldor (1999) in her advocacy of a form of 'cosmopolitan governance'. Kaldor's concern is with the 'new wars', which mark out organized violence in the era of late-modern globalization from the large-scale 'old wars' fought between nation-states from the 18th century onwards. 'New wars' – like that in Bosnia-Herzogovina – are linked, for Kaldor, to the interconnectivity of globalization in several ways, but in particular they express a violent manifestation of the cultural fragmentation that globalization produces. These are wars fought around 'identity politics' rather than over the ideological and geo-political goals of nation-state 'old wars'. For Kaldor, though, the particularism they involve – 'the claim to power on the basis of a particular identity' – be it national, clan, religious or linguistic' – is not generally a straightforward expression of the emancipatory struggle of repressed cultural groups. Rather these wars frequently involve the violent struggle for dominance of particularlistic interests within a locality which generally involves both the suppression of other cultural identities and deliberate terror against civilian populations: they are "a mixture of war, crime and human rights violations" (Kaldor 1999:11). In the phenomenon of new wars then we can see the sort of 'bad particularism' – identity politics based on often spurious cultural 'labels', division and exclusivity – that is emerging in the uneven wake of globalization.

Kaldor therefore interprets the politics of new wars in terms not of a simple 'localism vs. globalism perspective', but rather as "the emerging political cleavage between the politics of particularistic identity and the politics of cosmopolitan or humanist values" (p. 70). Her response is decidedly universalizing. She is on the side of "those who support cosmopolitan civic values, who favour openness, toleration and participation" as against, "those who are tied to particularist, exclusivist, often collectivist political positions" (p. 147). What this comes down to in direct policy terms is the advocacy of international intervention – 'cosmopolitan peacekeeping' – in wars like those fought in the Balkans. Kaldor sees such intervention, directed specifically towards, and legitimated by, the pro-

tection of universal human rights, as the responsibility of a global community[4] –
perhaps organized along the sort of federal lines envisaged in Kant's famous
cosmopolitan politics (Kant 1991).

Kaldor anticipates the obvious criticism of the cosmopolitanism she adopts: that
it has not learnt from the failure of earlier modernist projects of Enlightenment
universalism. Her answer is that it is perfectly possible to espouse universalist
principles with respect to specific human rights, whilst applying these principles
reflexively and with a sensitivity towards cultural difference. Cosmopolitanism
she maintains, following Appiah (1998), is not the necessary enemy of cultural
diversity.

Zygmunt Bauman develops this last point in terms of a more general notion of
open-ended inclusivist political discourse:

> "The pursuit of universality does not involve the smothering of cultural poly-
> valence or the pressure to reach cultural consensus. Universality means no
> more, yet no less either, than the across-the-species ability to communicate
> and reach mutual understanding.... Such universality reaching beyond the
> confines of sovereign or quasi-sovereign communities is a *conditio sine qua
> non* of a republic reaching beyond the confines of sovereign or quasi-sover-
> eign states: and the republic doing just that is the sole alternative to blind, ele-
> mental, erratic, uncontrolled, divisive and polarizing forces of globalization."
> (Bauman 1999:202)

Bauman is at least as stern a critic of the costs of globalization as Gray (Bauman
1998). Yet for him, as for Kaldor and others (Giddens 1994; Beck 1998), a benign
form of universalism employed in the service of a cosmopolitan politics, far from
being the cardinal sin of globalization, is an essential aspect of a progressive
political response to it. Finally what seems important is to overcome the sort of
polarizing thought – an unfortunate feature of contemporary intellectual habit
not helped by the fusion of postmodernism with the politics of identity – which
pits the ideas of universalism and difference against each other as mutually hostile iron principles. In an ever more complex situation of global political and cultural proximity, what we need above all is to develop supple and sensitive
analytical categories that allow us to make nuanced moral and political judgments. Such ideas should be judged in terms of how they speak to people's
material-cultural condition in today's complexly connected world, not in the

---

4. This whilst always recognizing the danger Ulrich Beck (1998:29) points to that, "a 'cosmopolitan
   façade' arises which legitimizes western military intervention" in such situations. Such an outcome –
   'power strategies disguised as humanitarian intervention' – would of course be an instance of universalism as masquerade, not of universalism as principle.

terms of the specific cultural baggage – of the European Enlightenment – they are assumed necessarily to trail behind them.

References

Appiah, K.A. (1998) "Cosmopolitan Patriots". In: Pheng Cheah and Robbins, Bruce (eds) *Cosmopolitics*, Minneapolis, University of Minnesota Press, pp. 91-114.

Anderson, B. (1991) *Imagined Communities: Reflections on the origin and spread of nationalism* (Revised 2nd Edition), London, Verso.

Bauman, Z. (1998) *Globalization: The Human Consequences*, Cambridge, Polity Press.

Bauman, Z. (1999) *In Search of Politics*, Cambridge, Polity Press.

Beck, U. (1992) *Risk Society: Towards a New Modernity*, London, Sage.

Berger, P. (1974) *Pyramids of Sacrifice*, Harmondsworth, Allen Lane.

Brennan, T. (1997) *At Home in the World: Cosmopolitanism Now*, Cambridge Mass., Harvard University Press.

Geras, N. (1995) *Solidarity in the Conversation of Humankind*, London, Verso.

Giddens, A. (1981) *A Contemporary Critique of Historical Materialism*, Vol. 1, *Power, Property and the State*, London, Macmillan.

Giddens, A. (1990) *The Consequences of Modernity*, Cambridge, Polity Press.

Giddens, A. (1994) *Beyond Left and Right*, Cambridge, Polity Press.

Gray, J. (1997) *Endgames: Questions in Late Modern Political Thought*, Cambridge, Polity Press.

Hirst, P. and Thompson, G. (1996) *Globalization in Question*, Cambridge, Polity Press.

Kaldor, M. (1999) *New and Old Wars*, Cambridge, Polity Press.

Kant, I. (1991) "Perpetual Peace: A Philosophical Sketch". In: Reiss, H. (ed.), *Kant: Political Writing*, Cambridge, Cambridge University Press, pp. 93-130.

Latouche, S. (1996) *The Westernization of the World*, Cambridge, Polity Press.

Mattelart, A. (1999) "Against Global Inevitability". In: *Media Development*, XLVI, pp. 2, 3-6.

Petras, J. (1993) "Cultural Imperialism in the Late 20th Century". In: *Journal of Contemporary Asia*, 23, 2, pp. 139-148.

Rorty, R. (1993) "Human Rights, Rationality and Sentimentality". In: Hurley, Susan and Shute, Stephen (eds) *On Human Rights: The Oxford Amnesty Lectures 1993*, New York, Basic Books, pp.111-134.

Schiller, H. I. (1995) "The Global Information Highway: Project for an Ungovernable World". In: Brook, J.and Boal, I.A. (eds.) *Resisting the Virtual Life*, San Francisco, City Lights, pp. 17-33.

Tomlinson, J. (1999) *Globalization and Culture*, Cambridge, Polity Press.

Wattenberg, B. J. (1991) *The First Universal Nation*, New York, Free Press.

Yearley, S. (1996) *Sociology, Environmentalism, Globalization*, London, Sage.

THE NATION-STATE, EMANCIPATORY SPACES AND DEVELOPMENT STUDIES IN THE GLOBAL ERA

Frans J. Schuurman

Introduction

There is no denying that development and development studies are closely tied to modernity. When modernity moved into crisis and postmodernity threatened to replace it, development studies also moved into what was called 'the impasse' and the notion of development received some serious attacks, various kinds of alternative 'development' notions were presented. We are talking here of the period from the beginning of the 1980s onwards, with an acceleration in the ideological crises after 1985. Careful attempts were made either to reconstruct an explanans and possibly a new explanandum for development studies or to deny that there was a crisis (a denial by the real die-hard Marxists). All this has been documented in various publications (e.g. Booth 1994, Crush 1995, Leys 1996, Escobar 1995, Koehler and Gore 1996, Schuurman 1993).

Since then development studies has been facing another challenge: globalization. The specific reason why development studies feels challenged by the concept of globalization is not only because globalization (even more than postmodernity) is heralding the end of the modern age, it is also because there is a changing view on the role of the nation-state. It is the nation-state that, within the modern age, has played a vital role in development studies. Even when world-system theories were dominant within development studies it was always, in the end, nation-states (as centres, semi-peripheries, and peripheries within a world-system) that constituted the essential spatial contexts for analysis, theory construction, and policy guidelines. Globalization discourses announce the end of the nation-state; in fact it is this decline of the nation-state that is at the core of many globalization theories. If this has any bearing at all, where does it leave development studies? It is not only that globalization is calling into doubt the modernity project and with that the object of development studies (development) but it is (at least rhetorically) also attacking the explanatory and methodological core, the subject, as well: the nation-state.

Some would say that there are also some positive aspects to all this. Development studies, as part of the modernity project, has always awarded itself a heroic aura. For others, however, (notably the post-developmentalists) development studies and its twin, anthropology, formed part of a project of imperialism. Anthropology puts peoples in the South on the map as 'others' and development studies finishes the job by declaring them ready to be developed and then goes on to indicate the way to do it. If the concept of globalization is a metaphor for the end of the modern age and an end to these imperialist practices, and in the process eliminates anthropology and development studies as well, then so be it, and good riddance. Kearney (1996:15) puts it as follows: "Developmentalism was a reflex of modernism. The death of modernism spelled the death of developmentalism". I will not give an immediate answer to this line of reasoning. I prefer to do that indirectly in the ensuing analysis.

Let me explain my angle of approach. The object of development studies has a strong normative basis: development as an emancipatory project. The target groups (varying with the ideological tides) were labelled the poor, the marginalized, the excluded, or the subaltern classes. (The postmodern critique on this was that labels changed without the persons in question having had any say in the matter, a just critique on the misplaced essentialism within anthropology and development studies). This emancipatory project had, as mentioned, the nation-state as the most important spatial and ideological referent. What about the emancipatory spaces in the global era? Are there any left and, if so, do they have spatial dimensions, and what are they? Are collective identities in the global age still forged through a specified space (=place)? Do emancipatory strategies have an explicit spatial dimension? Does, perhaps, globalization characterize itself not so much by a fragmentation of spaces but by a deterritorialization? Where do emancipatory struggles take place if globalization is supposed to be place-less, distance-less and time-less?

Before I can address these questions I will have to start with a rather elaborate prelude, which cannot be more than the rough outline of a critical assessment of globalization. From an 'objective' point of view looking at the globalization debate there are at least three types of problems that catch the eye. Firstly, there are many different definitions of globalization. Everyone seems to use or interpret globalization differently, emphasizing this or that global characteristic. This creates great confusion. Secondly, there are the so-called globalization myths, i.e. faulty manipulation or interpretation of data to sustain or infer that there is something like globalization. Thirdly, there is a noticeable degree of teleological, tautological, and reificatory elements in many globalization discourses (sometimes in this text referred to as 'glob-talk'), usually in a highly interrelated manner. In this contribution I address these problems as follows.

First I will present a rough taxonomy of glob-talk, followed by some short remarks on the issues of teleology, tautology, and reification which seem to be present in nearly all the globalization discourses. Then I will present my own definition/approach to globalization. The chapter will then proceed to discuss some critical issues in globalization literature (which, in fact, is a further elaboration of some of the positions in the taxonomy). That section will concentrate on the status of the nation-state. In the concluding section I will discuss what this means for emancipatory spaces in the global age.

A taxonomy of glob-talk

A cursory view of the globalization literature produces at least nine different types of glob-talk. The following taxonomy is really a sliding scale with no clearly defined boundaries. Also, most of the globalization authors tend to combine various positions. As such, this taxonomy is based on my (subjective) reading of their publications.

1 *The true globalists* (Martin Albrow, Partha Chatterjee, Manuel Castells). Their position is that there are major transformations going on in society, politics, and economy and that these transformations are taking place on a global scale. These transformations do not form part of modernity, late-modernity, or postmodernity; they indicate the coming of a new era: globality. Some of these authors stress that we still lack an adequate discourse to describe and analyse the global age. We still have to make use of concepts that come to us from the modern age and are not really adequate to describe the true nature of globalization.

2 *The cyberspace globalists* (Mike Featherstone). The microchip revolution ushered in the 21st century before the end of the 20th century. The computer age has had such a profound effect on production, consumption, and interpersonal relations that, like the true globalists, the cyberspace globalists believe that major transformations are taking place. The difference between the true globalists and the cyberspace globalists is constituted in the belief that it is cyberspace that is going to be the major political, economic, and cultural arena for the 21st century.

3 *The neo-liberal globalists* (Kenichi Ohmae, Francis Fukuyama, John Naisbitt). For this group of authors globalization is also a process with an ontology of its own. It is the global spread of market logic, liberalism, and democracy. This is a rather heterogeneous group. In general, the position is rather structuralist in the sense that globalization has an inner logic which cannot be stopped. 'Go with the flow' seems to be the message and 'all will benefit in the end'.

4 *The cosmopolitanist/new-age/postmodernist/culturalist globalists* (Rajni Kothari, David Korten, David Held). Here globalization is also a fact but it is primarily cultural in nature. Space and culture are delinked, non-traditional identities are strengthened in the face of a threatening homogenization because of the onslaught of globally diffused information. Traditional identities are under threat, indigenous people are alienated from their cultural heritage through the global movement of consumer capitalism. The globe is the political arena for the conglomerate of new social movements, indigenous move-

ments, environmentalist movements in increasingly global (transnational) coalitions.

5 *The hybridization globalists* (Ulf Hannerz, Arjun Appadurai). These authors interpret globalization as a dialectical process where 'the global' meets 'the local'. This results in an increasingly hybrid praxis. Authenticity of culture (an anchor point in the previous position) is rejected. Culture is becoming increasingly hybrid, and probably always was.

6 *The neo-Marxist globalists* (Ellen Meiksins Wood, William Tabb). Their position is that globalization is a fact and it is capitalism gone global. It is time to get the classical Marxist analytical framework out of the cupboard because if there ever was a time for using scientific Marxism, it is now. These are the times of the purest form of capitalist logic no longer contaminated by the existence of non-capitalist modes of production or unequal exchange on the international market. Class struggle should be internationalized and, in fact, it is doing just that.

7 *The historical globalists* (Paul Hirst, Grahame Thompson, Deepak Nayyar). Their position is that there is globalization but it is nothing new. The claim that it is new is fashionable and exaggerated. We have seen earlier periods with a tremendous amount of internationalization of money and trade. The international economy between 1870 and 1914 was hardly less integrated than today.

8 *The non-globalists* (Michael Mann). They insist that there is no such thing as globalization. At most there is regionalization but even that is nothing new. The whole globalization discourse is one without any ontological foundation. These critics tend to concentrate on the nation-state, which they still consider as important as it ever was. In this they differ radically from the globalists who tend to concentrate in their discourse on the demise of the nation-state.

9 *The diehard modernists* (Ernesto Laclau). The thesis here is that, contrary to what the true globalists assert, globalization is nearing its end. Since the Enlightenment modernity spread itself to all corners of the earth, as a truly global process. Among other things, this has led, for example, to the Universal Declaration of Human Rights. The feeling among the diehard modernists is that an increasing cultural relativism leads to a noticeable decline in modern universal norms and values. They see this cultural relativism fed by postmodernism, post-colonialism, a reveille of fundamentalism and a growing balkanization at global level. This had led to a disturbing denial of international solidarity by the fragmentation of erstwhile universalized values and norms concerning human rights and emancipation. Increasingly unenlightened autocrats see their chance to safeguard their political power by using a cultural relativist discourse. If there ever was something like globalization, it is now fragmenting.

Teleology, tautology, and reification in glob-talk

On many occasions, irrespective of the position taken up in the above taxonomy there is teleology, tautology, and reification, which if combined can present a pretty convincing picture of globalization. Ferguson (1992:73), writing about the mythology around globalization, remarks that the concept of globalization carries

> "... overtones of historical inevitability embedded in inferences of globalization as a unidirectional process or a *fait accompli*. Such rhetoric, far from being value-free, implies reification and carries ideological baggage whereby globalization becomes the new dynamic, the motor of world change... this concept has taken on a life of its own: as a *sine qua non* for our age, its status may be moving from that of mythology to ideology."

This 'teleological doctrine', as Ferguson calls it, shares with other such doctrines interrelated sets of tautologies and reifications. The tautology in this case consists of explaining the core of globalization by referring to global processes in terms of other global processes.
Friedman (1994:200) is an example of this:

> "The collapse and transformation of great empires in both the Old World and the New World, the metamorphosis of 'tribal' social systems as a result of the reorientations of trade, the formation of colonial societies, the productions of hunters and gatherers and chiefdoms, as well as pluralism, lumpen proletariat and state-classes, are all part and parcel of the global system, engendered by global processes..."

This is the ultimate self-referential approach of globalization. The innocent reader is first presented the picture of some global processes that then appear to have been engendered by other global processes that remained unnamed. This kind of reasoning happens on many occasions: globalization appears defined in terms of its own consequences.

This approach is often combined with reification. Reification appears when globalization is awarded agency. Globalization can 'do' things like 'increasing human insecurity' which, incidentally, seems to be one of its favourite activities. A combination of tautology and reification leads to the following remarks: "[globalization led to] ... a reinvigoration of sub-national territorial identities, for example, amongst ethnic groups and indigenous people..." (Scholte 1995). This implies that globalization has some sort of agency which leads up to something, while in fact the reasoning can also be inverted, in this case that the rise of regional identities has global proportions and as such is a constitutive characteristic of something we can call globalization.

Now, I am well aware of the tradition within the social sciences to use phrases like "the system acts out in this or that way" as shorthand for saying "the accumulation of the intended and unintended consequences of the activities of individual and collective actors within a defined field of a social system". However, given the already very deterministic overtones within many globalization discourses (in the sense of "it is out there happening and there is nothing we can do to stop it"), I would prefer to avoid reification within the globalization discourse wherever possible. I am, by the way, not at all sure that I will not fall into this same trap in the remainder of this chapter.

Globalization as the global (uneven) spread of capitalism and modernity

Let me introduce the definition of globalization that I will use in this contribution. I define globalization simply, some would say simplistically, as *the global spread of capitalism and modernity*. It would take me outside the framework of this chapter to elaborate too much on why I prefer this definition, but the answer is concerned with the often seemingly paradoxical characteristics of globalization, like homogeneity and heterogeneity, globalization and localization, universalisms and particularisms, individualism and new localism. All these characteristics of globalization are only seemingly new paradoxes, they represent, however, globally projected contradictions that have always been present within capitalism and modernity, but increasingly so as a result of the disjunctive spatial developments of capitalism and modernity. In other words the global spread of capitalism and modernity is not a homologous process but disjunctive in terms of space and time. (This uneven spread of globalization seems to me a description of a somewhat higher level of abstraction than the much favoured description of space-time compression that has a more ontological content). Perhaps a combination of Giddens' four dimensions of modernity gone global with Appadurai's idea of disjunctive scapes would clarify my point of view.

In the modern age Giddens' four dimensions of modernity (militarism, industrialism, capitalism, and the nation-state) were spatially concentrated in the centre (first in the so-called empires, later on in the advanced capitalist countries). When these dimensions took on a transnational (global) character they did not do this in a nicely organized way, according to stipulated spatial and time coordinates. What resulted was an increasing spatial and chronological disjunction between the emergent scapes of the four dimensions of modernity, ushering in the typical characteristic of globality: the strange amalgams of homogenization and fragmentation. These contradictions are now globally projected, and, as such, also gain new dynamics, which, however, can still be understood to a large extent using what we know of the inner logics of capitalism and modernity and the interrelation between these two. This is not to say that we have to go back to Marx and Parsons to understand the global era. Much has been written since to clarify the dynamics of capitalism and modernity (and, in fact, much less marred by deterministic and structuralist overtones). What I meant to say was that we do not specifically need new concepts in a newly constructed global theory to understand our present condition.

Within the taxonomy of globalization which was presented earlier, my approach to globalization is a combination of the last three positions.

The role of the nation-state in glob-talk

In order to decide whether the role of the state and the status and position of the nation-state as such have definitely changed and moved into a different era called global let us first take a closer look at globalization from a historical perspective. When one looks at globalization from a historical perspective and one does not see it simply as a phenomenon that began in the 1970s and accelerated to its present speed at the end of the 1980s, then one sees that there have been previous periods that are sometimes referred to as globalization waves (Oman 1996). The importance of this point of view is that one is then able to ask whether these glob-waves are part of some systemic and/or agency-driven logic within capitalism and modernity to globalize. For someone like Ellen Meiksins Wood (1997a) it is clear that globalization is a result of the inner (above all systemic) logic of capitalism (exactly which logic that is, is subject to discussion: the law of the tendential decline of profit, the law of the rise in the organic composition of capital, the law of marginal costs and benefits, market-oriented laws etc.).

According to Charles Oman, the first globalization wave took place in the period 1870-1914. During that time many countries used the gold standard, the UK was the hegemonic economic power, there was a generalized powerful surge of colonialism (the whole world was practically or theoretically divided up between the imperialist powers), and there was a major technological advance in industry and transport which "shrunk" the world in terms of space and time. There was also an emergence of giant financial trusts (such as the Zaibatsu in Japan) and the separation of ownership and management hailed the advent of corporate capitalism. (According to Fukuyama, some societies missed the boat because of cultural constraints *vis-à-vis* this separation of ownership and management; so that part of the first globalization wave was not truly globalized.)

The second globalization wave took place some years after World War II (1950s-1960s), a period characterized by the US as a hegemonic economic and political power. During that time the dollar replaced the gold standard and there was a strong growth of international trade, multinationals and foreign direct investments, and the spread of Taylorism outside the US (Oman 1996:10).

Nayyar (1997:7) also points out that there is a common presumption that globalization is something new and a fundamental departure from the past but that it is seldom recognized that there was a similar phase of globalization between 1870 and 1914. He then goes on to prove that in relative as well as in absolute terms (i.e. in index-figures) there are many similarities between the present globalization wave and the first one in terms of international trade, international investment, and international finance. There is, for example, a similarity with respect to the share of export in the GDP of industrialized countries then and now (around 16%). Nayyar points out that on both occasions the US held an exceptional position, i.e. a share of exports in GDP of around 7% in 1992 and a similar percentage in 1913 (6%). Calculated in terms of 1980 prices, the total foreign investment in the world economy in 1914 was $347 billion compared with the actual stock of direct foreign investment in 1980 of $448 billion.

International finance grew very rapidly in relation to world trade from a ratio of 9:1 in 1973 to 90:1 in 1992 but, as Nayyar points out, at the end of the 19th century there was also a significant integration of international financial markets. Cross-national ownership of securities (including government bonds) reached very high levels at that time. Nayyar finds further similarities in a *laissez faire* attitude, a technological revolution in transport and communications, which brought about an enormous reduction in the time and costs of transport, and new forms of industrial organization, which played an important role in making globalization possible in both periods. In the first globalization period it was the advent of mass production/Fordism and Taylorism, which through huge cost reductions led to the accumulation and concentration of capital, reinforcing the process of globalization. In the second phase, as Oman pointed out, it was flexible production. In the first phase it was the economic hegemony of Great Britain and in the present phase it is the political hegemony of the US, while in both periods there was the national currency of a dominating economic power accepted as international exchange.

Nayyar then continues by stipulating the differences between the two globalization periods. In the first period, particularly, there was intersectoral trade (between agricultural and manufactured products), while in the second phase intra-industry trade and intra-firm trade became most important. While in the first phase 45% of the investment in the Third World and 55% of overall investment went to the primary sector, in the second phase these precentages were lowered to 20% and 10% respectively. Foreign investments in the first phase were realized in search of profit, in the present phase it was short-term capital movements in search of capital gains. To Nayyar the most fundamental difference, however, is that in the present globalization phase there are many restrictions on the flow of labour. It is capital which goes to labour, while in the past it was labour which went to capital, witness the large-scale migrations to the 'new' countries in North and South America and Australia.

Nayyar concludes that the game of globalization is still there but the players as well as the rules are new. Then, the game was dominated by imperial nation-states, now there are TNCs and international banks. Nation-states are no longer the main economic players but they remain important political players. In the context of this chapter it is important to stress that Nayyar finds it naïve to write off nation-states as important players in the globalization game. This is in spite of the historic fact that, in the imperial phase of globalization, nation-states played a more important (economic and political) role than they do currently. Nation-states still remain important in political and strategic terms. In his view it was the military strength of the imperial powers at the time which set the rules of the game, in contrast to the present day where it is the political clout of nation-states which backs up the rules imposed by the transnational corporations, the banks, etc. Here Nayyar stands in contrast to Martin Shaw, who thinks that military relations still define the relations between states and "... hence the parameters of the world system of power, and that the notion of undermining of (nation) states in an age of globalization has focussed too much on the economic/cultural definitions of nation-states" (Shaw 1996:15). I am not sure I would agree with Nayyar on this specific point. Looking at the military operations of the USA over the last 10 years it still seems that military power is important in bringing unruly nation-states back into line.

Nayyar concludes by remarking that there is currently an uneven spread of globalization: sub-Saharan Africa, west Asia, central Asia and south Asia are increasingly excluded (in 1992 66% of the total exports from the Third World came from only 11 countries). It is here that Nayyar pleads for the need for strategic forms of state intervention to counteract the negative effects of increasing exclusion.

Jan Nederveen Pieterse (1996) also remarks that although globalization refers to a worldwide process, "it is not an even global spread of gain and loss" (Nederveen 1996:1). Ghai and de Alcantara (1994), citing a UNDP report of 1992, point out that between 1960 and 1989, the share of global income held by the richest fifth of the world population increased from 70% to 83%. At the same time the share of the poorest fifth dropped from 2.3% to 1.4 %. Between 1970 and 1989 the participation of sub-Saharan Africa in global trade dropped from 3.8 to 1%.

There is a general agreement on a widening of the gap between the developed, advanced economies and many developing countries (let's say those countries which traditionally formed part of the Third World). There is, however, no unanimity about the role played by globalization. For example, UNCTAD blames the negative effects of globalization for the developing countries on their being especially vulnerable to the downswings in global trade and finances. On the other hand, the World Bank asserts that the only way forward for these countries is to increase their participation in the globalization process.

What do the statistics add to these positions? Citing Petrella, Nederveen Pieterse points out that

"... there has been a marked downturn in the participation in the world economy by developing countries since the beginning of the 1980s. In 1980 the share of world trade of manufactured goods of the 102 poorest countries of the world was 7.9 per cent of world exports and 9 per cent of imports; in 1990 these shares fell to 1.4 and 4.9 percent."

If, then, there has been an impoverishment these figures seem to indicate that globalization is not directly involved, but according to Nederveen there are many ways in which developing countries are included in global processes: through structural adjustment programmes, global communications, development cooperation, migrations etc. He prefers, therefore, the term 'asymmetrical inclusions'.

The first conclusion from the figures presented above is that, for example, foreign direct investments have always been and still are concentrated in advanced capitalist countries with capital moving from one such country to another. Meiksins Wood (1997b:5) points out that more than 70% of all employment in the USA is in the service sector, much of it in industries that cannot simply be shifted to other economies with a cheap and unorganized labour force. Meiksins Wood recognized that capitalism always had an expansionary drive but that for many of its consequences (such as cutbacks in social provision) governments and political parties can be held responsible. This is an important point because it presents the possibility of looking beyond the systemic logic of expansionary capitalism for identifiable actors within the system. Then, according to Meiksins Wood, the state is in the forefront of a whole row of corporate actors (like MNOs, international financial and political organizations, organized crime, international media etc.). According to Meiksins Wood, the nation-state may be losing functions in the process of globalization but it is gaining new ones as the main conduit between capital and the global market. In the global market, capital needs the state (Meiksins Wood 1997b:12) "Behind every transnational corporation is a national base, which depends on its local state to sustain its viability...". She puts it even more strongly:

> "... the nation-state is the main agent of globalization. U.S. capital, in its quest for "competitiveness", demands a state that will keep social costs to a minimum, while keeping in check the social conflict and disorder generated by the absence of social provision."

She does not deny that it is possible for the state to change its form and give way either to more local or to larger political authorities, but the idea of the state as such will continue to be crucial. The examples that she gives of international working-class solidarity as a unifying principle include protests,not just against exploitation by the same transnational corporation but also against the actions of particular nation-states in sustaining the conditions of capital accumulation (Meiksins Wood 1997b:14). Her analysis includes four conclusions that are important to us in the context of this chapter. Firstly, "capitalism, contrary to conventional Marxist wisdom, has always had tendencies to fragment class struggle and to domesticate it..., making it very local and particularistic"

(Meiksins Wood 1997b:10); this is a point that Stuart Hall also emphasizes in his writings about globalization and identity. Secondly, the nation-state may be losing functions in the process of globalization but it is gaining new ones as the "main conduit between capital and the global market" (Meiksins Wood 1997b:12). Thirdly, as capital is going global it creates its own counterpoints as it always has done, as in its national or earlier imperialist phase. Fourthly, globalization is not a natural, inevitable process, it has identifiable (corporate) actors which are answerable to normative issues.

In short the Left should not look for refuge in localized, fragmented political struggles or in a "completely abstract internationalism (Meiksins Wood 1997b:15). Talk of emancipatory struggles in the context of a global civil society is, according to Meiksins Wood, like "whistling in the dark".

In the discussion on the current importance of the nation-state Rajni Kothari takes up a middle position when he puts forward the idea that

"the new framework of capitalism is based on a transition from the politico-military model of international management and domination (the phase of "imperialism") to a technofinancial system of global (as distinct from international) integration into one overarching world market. [this leads to] the erosion of a state-based structure of national and international interactions" (Kothari 1997:234).

It does not seem logical to Kothari to see the shift of a power base from politico-military to techno-financial as an indication of the weakness of the state. On the contrary, he sees it as a more subtle form of control. In other words the definition of the state (where there is always an element of exercising a certain amount of legitimate violence) should be updated. Kothari's approach does not seem to be a bad idea but perhaps a slightly different interpretation should be added. During the period of the Cold War the advanced industrialized countries used the existence of the communist bloc (especially the Soviet Union) as a legitimation to uphold the military strength of individual countries (especially the USA) and of NATO (a military strength, by the way, which also played a significant role in the post World War II economic growth). The same reasoning was valid for the communist bloc. Military interventions from both sides in their own periphery were accepted strategies. With the end of the Cold War this legitimation of the armed forces ended. The search was then on for new legitimation, which was found in a number of opportunities: Saddam Hussein represented the 'increasing threat from the South', the drug-barons represented global moral decay, and there was 'ethnic cleansing' in Africa and the Balkans, etc. US military power is still being wielded as the hegemonic global military force. In contrast to the previous period the legitimating discourse is now the defence of human rights, a defence against drugs, and an urge to help countries on the road to democracy and the free market system.

The role of the state as a direct and autonomous economic entrepreneur came thus to an end but the same does not hold for the politico-military role of the state. In this sense, the state still constitutes an important point of reference for organizations within civil society.

The above-mentioned authors took a line of reasoning which positioned the (nation) state above everything as a result of the spatial spread or concentration of trade and investment. Jan-Aart Scholte takes a different point of view. He defines globalization as the supraterritorial dimension of social life and subsequently discusses globalization in terms of the nature of collective identity, because, for Scholte at least, identity is crucial in social relations. According to Scholte (1995),

> "before the onslaught of the nation-state in the 19th century the social rela-
> tions were heavily focussed on the immediate territorial place. However,
> after the mid-19th century the nationality principle became dominant in the
> identity construction. This, at the same time, meant the suppression of all
> those alternative forms of identities which were based on different dimen-
> sions (e.g. regional, religious etc.), suppressed dimensions which now in the
> global era start "blossoming" again with sometimes disastrous consequences
> (ethnic strife in Africa, nationalist secessions in the Balkans, religious funda-
> mentalism in northern Africa/Algeria): in fact "pre-modern" forms of iden-
> tity rising in a global era."

The important question that Scholte raises is whether these 'pre-modern' forms of identity are a temporary anachronism emerging in an era where global capitalism and modernity are reconstructing themselves and temporarily creating ideological vacuums (the end of the Cold War, the *fin-de-siècle* and new millennium-like attitudes, etc) or are they heralding a new type/form/strategy of emancipation in a global era?

According to Scholte, much of present-day capitalism is bound up with national firms, national currencies, and national markets. Ethnic struggles and indigenous movements also tend to reproduce nationhood on a smaller scale, so "globalization also goes hand in hand with renationalisation". Globalization is not eliminating nations, only complicating the construction of collective identities, leading to hybridization and, as such, Scholte proclaims globalization to be a core feature of late modernity.

Emancipatory spaces in the global era

Many of the foregoing writers appear to be critical of writing off the role of the nation-state as the core issue of the globalization concept. This suggests that the nation-state remains an important referent for emancipatory struggles in the so-called global era. As much as capitalism seems to have succeeded in liberating itself from the strait-jacket of national social contracts, it is still important for counterforces to consider the nation-state as an important frame of reference and not concentrate only on something like 'global civil society' or even local space. In spite of this general conclusion about emancipatory space in the global age, things are slightly more complicated than this. Firstly, we should show a difference between, on the one hand, the nation-state as a frame of reference for the emergence and mobilization of a collective identity and on the other hand, the nation-state as a political arena for an ensuing emancipatory struggle. As mentioned before, during the modern period these two aspects were closely connected but globalization has changed that. The nation-state is still important, as has been pointed out several times, but it is no longer the only referent for the construction of either collective identities, or is it the only arena for political struggle.

Let us take a brief look at other potential emancipatory spaces in the global age. Cyberspace seems to be one of the favourite global sites where emancipation could take place. In fact the Internet is considered as prototypical of an emancipatory site in the global age: it is accessible, horizontal (i.e. not hierarchical), timeless, and spaceless. It can be used for the mobilization of a collective identity, especially for oppressed minority groups which might otherwise be more difficult; external support can be mobilized and information disseminated, etc. The Zapatistas in Mexico launching an Internet campaign to muster international support and the Kurds in Iraq letting the outside world know of the atrocities committed against them, are well known examples of the use of Internet and GSM. Useful as this may be in the emancipatory struggle of oppressed groups we have to realize a number of things. Firstly, the Internet and GSM are not accessible to all marginalized peoples, in fact there is an increasing social polarization emerging in relation to knowledge about and access to cyberspace.

Secondly, people do not live in cyberspace, although it sometimes seems that way. Whatever the uses of cyberspace are in the fostering of collective identities, there comes a time when the struggle has to be taken from the virtual to the real world. Thirdly, the enthusiasm of those who see the Internet as a tool in a globalized emancipatory struggle seems to overlook the increasing tendency to turn away from international solidarity and to stress cultural relativism, particularism, etc. As such, virtual emancipation runs the risk of finding itself in a realist global social vacuum. Still, the important point to grasp here is that, in the global era, it is not necessarily only physical space that musters collective identity.

Another space that seems to be increasingly favoured by globalization is local space, sometimes called third space (as different from private and public space). There seems to have evolved a global euphoria concerning the economic, political, and cultural emancipatory potentials of local space. Elsewhere I have extensively criticized this globalized euphoria (Schuurman 1997) so I will limit myself here to quoting David Harvey who, in no uncertain terms, condemns the idea of emancipatory projects limited to local space as a reactionary project because it furthers local fragmentation. In reference to the 'place-specific myths of Nazism in opposition to the rational utilitarianism of Enlightenment', Harvey warns against

> "a whole set of political, cultural, and spatial practices that sought to rein-force local community solidarity and tradition in the face of the universalism and globalism of money power, commodification, and capital circulation" (Harvey 1989:277).

According to Harvey, this perspective is especially likely under conditions of time-space compression, i.e. globalization

> "We thus approach the central paradox: the less important the spatial barri-ers, the greater the sensitivity of capital to the variations of place within space, and the greater the incentive for places to be differentiated in ways attractive to capital. The result has been the production of fragmentation, insecurity, and ephemeral uneven development within a highly unified glo-bal space economy of capital flows. The historic tension within capitalism between centralization and decentralization is now being worked out in new ways" (Harvey 1989:296).

Harvey's remarks are in line with the idea that decentralization furthers an inter-national zero-sum game between localities of which the poor will be the victims. As long as the current instability of the international economic and financial sys-tem lasts, as long as the decentralization discourse, emphasizing local space, contributes to hollowing out the state, and as long as there is no institutionalized social contract at the global and/or local level, it is rather premature to parade decentralization as the Post-Fordist panacea. Concentrating on the emancipatory potential of local space could well turn out to be a neoliberal cul-de-sac for the poor in the Third World.

What about global space, as a framework for identity formation and an arena for emancipatory struggles? If it is of limited importance then, according to Chatterjee and Appadurai, that is due to the continued existence of the concept of the nation-state in globalization discourses, which obstructs the development of discourse alternatives. Chatterjee (1997) cites Appadurai:

> "... no idiom has yet emerged to capture the collective interests of many groups in translocal identities... they are still entrapped in the linguistic imag-inary of the territorial state... This vicious circle can only be escaped when a language is found to capture complex nonterritorial, postnational forms of allegiance."

I have to strongly disagree with this reasoning because it conveys a message of a false consciousness, a victimization of helpless and voiceless actors, who are robbed of speech by the existence of the concept of the nation-state.

In contrast, Timothy Luke (1996) sees great emancipatory potential in what he calls 'the pluralization of voices'. According to him cultures, economies, and societies are split between "the demands of nominal nationality and actual transnationality as both local and regional communities become integrated into truly transnational rather than essentially national modes of production". Luke agrees with Vattimo by emphasizing the emancipatory aspect of globalization because "everybody can speak, no longer cowed into silence by the idea of a single form of humanity" (Luke 1996:127). The problem which I mentioned earlier was that if subaltern groups manage to let their voice be heard globally then who is out there listening to them? They might be shouting in a vacuum because of a crumbling international solidarity.

In conclusion, then: the nation-state as the locus of an emancipatory struggle and as the frame of reference for the construction of a collective identity is still important (and will remain so for the time being). Other spaces, however, have partly invaded a primacy that was present in the modern age. As such, there has been a certain fragmentation into new emancipatory spaces due to processes of globalization. These newly emerged spaces (cyberspace, third space, and global space) are not necessarily interrelated like Russian dolls (one fitting within the other); they may be disjunctive in space and time.

Finally, I want to confront briefly the issue of how this all relates to development studies. In the introduction I tried to make it clear that development studies is closely tied to the modern age, has a normative component in the sense of development as its object of study (the explanandum), and considers the nation-state as the central referent for the subject (the explanans). The views reflected in this chapter have hopefully made it clear that, first of all, what we call now the global age is a label used to indicate the global spread of capitalism and modernity. Secondly, that the world has become more homogeneous but also more unequal, and, thirdly, that the nation-state, although changing in form and function, still figures as important politically, ideologically, economically, and culturally in the global age. As such, there are still many reasons to consider development studies as an important field of research, especially in the construction of critical theory. Globalization challenges development studies to overcome the pitfalls of reductionism, determinism, reification, tautology, teleology, upward/downward and central conflation in terms of agency and structure, implicit imperialism, etc. Ours is an increasingly complex world and development studies can contribute significantly to explain these 'global times'.

References

Albrow, Martin (1996) *The Global Age. State and Society Beyond Modernity.* Cambridge, Polity Press.
Booth, D. (1994) *Rethinking Social Development. Theory, Research & Practice.* Harlow, Longman.

Chatterjee, Partha (1997) "Beyond the Nation? Or Within?", *Economic and Political Weekly*, Jan. 4-11, pp. 30-34.

Crush, J. (1995) *Power of Development*. London, Routledge.

Escobar, Arturo (1995) *Encountering Development. The Making and the Unmaking of the Third World*, Princeton, Princeton University Press.

Ferguson, Marjorie (1992) "The Mythology about Globalization", *European Journal of Communicatons* 7, pp. 69-93.

Friedman, Jonathan (1994) *Cultural Identity and Global Process*, London, Sage.

Ghai, Dharam and Hewitt de Alcantara, Cynthia (1994) *"Globalization and Social Integration: Patterns and Processes"*, Occasions paper no. 2, World Summit for Social Development, Geneva, UNRISD.

Hirst, Paul, and Thompson, Grahame (1996) *Globalization in Question. The International Economy and the Possibilities of Governance*, Cambridge, Polity Press.

Kearney, Michael (1996*) Reconceptualizing the Peasantry. Anthropology in Global Perspective*, Boulder, Westview Press.

Koehler, Gabriele, and Gore, Charles (eds.) (1996*) Questioning Development. Essays in the Theory, Policies and Practice of Development Interventions*, Marburg, Metropolis.

Kothari, Rajni (1997) "Globalization: a World Adrift", *Alternatives* 22, pp. 227-267.

Leys, Colin (1996) *The Rise and Fall of Development Theory*, London, James Currey.

Luke, Timothy (1996) "Identity, Meaning and Globalization: Detraditionalization in Postmodern Space-Time Compression". In: Heelas, Paul, et al. (eds.) *Detraditionalization. Critical Reflections on Authority and Identity*, Oxford, Blackwell, pp. 109-134.

Mann, Michael (1996) *The Global Future of the Nation-State*. Paper for the Conference, Direction of Contemporary Capitalism, University of Sussex, 26-28 April.

Meiksins Wood, Ellen (1977a) "Back to Marx", *Monthly Review* 49 (2), pp. 1-10.

Meiksins Wood, Ellen (1997b) "Labor, the State, and Class Struggle", *Monthly Review* 49 (3), pp. 1-18.

Nayyar, Deepak (1997) "Globalization: the Past in Our Present" *Third World Economics* 168, pp. 7-15.

Nederveen Pieterse, Jan (1996) *Globalisation and Emancipation. From Local Empowerment to Global Reform*. Paper for the CERES-Workshop on Globalisation. Wageningen.

Oman, Charles (1996) *The Policy Challenges of Globalisation and Regionalisation* Policy brief no. 11, OECD Development Centre, Paris.

Scholte, Jan-Aart (1995) *Constructions of Collective Identity*. Paper for the Conference The Organization Dimensions of Global Change: No Limits to Cooperation. Ohio, University of Cleveland.

Schuurman, Frans J. (1993) *Beyond the Impasse. New Directions in Development Theory*, London, Zed Books.

Schuurman, Frans J. (1997) "The Decentralization Discourse: Post-Fordist Paradigm or Neo-Liberal Cul-de-Sac?" *The European Journal of Development Research* 9 (1), June, pp. 150-167.

Shaw, Martin (1996) *The Global Revolution in the Social Sciences: the Globalization of State Power as a Defining Issue*. Paper for the Conference on Direction of Contemporary Capitalism. University of Sussex, 26-28 April.

Tabb, William (1997) "Globalization is *an* Issue, the Power of Capital is *the* Issue", *Monthly Review* 49 (2), pp. 1-10.

PART II

GLOBALIZATION AND CENTRAL ISSUES IN DEVELOPMENT STUDIES

INTRODUCTION TO PART II

Detlev Haude and Frans J. Schuurman

In his chapter on globalization and human rights *Reinhart Kössler* again takes up two issues which figured in Part I, notably universalism versus relativism, and the declining role of nation-states. Globalization has definitely given a new twist to views about the universal validity of human rights. Contrary to a popular view Kössler emphasizes that human rights are not an intrinsic cultural trait of Western culture but are historical products of fierce struggles, which are upheld by people's vigilance and active efforts. In fact, human rights arguments put forward from Western sources decline dramatically next to the actual practices in and by these states. Nevertheless, ASEAN governments especially see the Universal Declaration of Human Rights as a cultural imperialist text. However, as Kössler points out, these culturalist claims are sometimes used to legitimize state-initiated human rights violations. At the same time, it is also possible to discover democratic and human rights strands within non-European systems of thought.

In Kössler's view, the Right to Development, championed by governments in the South, is in fact supremely Eurocentric as a consequence of its state-centredness and its emphasis on material prosperity. What is missing in a globalizing world is an approach to human rights which goes beyond a modernist, Eurocentric, and nation-state focus and addresses global problems and global solutions. The Declaration of Human Rights, however, still emphasizes the role of states as safeguards of these rights.

In his contribution *Kristoffel Lieten* seeks to re-establish the importance of the debates on the developmental impact of multinational corporations. He does so within the context of a discussion on the impulse which developing countries are supposed to receive from the globalizing economic system. Lieten attributes the weaning power of Western capitalism to the effects of lopsided development, the reinforcing momentum of asymmetry and the downsizing of the role of the state. Seemingly successful instances of transition (in South-East Asia) were associated with policies which were radically different from the presently fashionable structural adjustment policies and with no central role for multinational corporations (MNCs). Evidence emanating from a major study on MNCs in India in the 1980s suggests that in four crucial fields of development initiatives, MNCs turned out to be a part of the problem rather than a part of the solution.

The article asserts that the bankification of the world system inhibits the transformative power of the market system in developing countries. The argument is a theoretically informed attempt to return to the development debates of the 1970s. These debates may, fruitfully, be resurrected in the 21st century in order to more fully understand economic globalization.

Mohamed Salih starts his chapter on globalization and sustainable development with the thesis that the current debate on sustainable development has been complicated by globalization's ability to influence and hence redefine the conventional conceptions of environment and development. Two lines of argument are highlighted in the debate about linking these two powerful and equally overloaded concepts of globalization and sustainable development. The first explores whether globalization is conducive to global environmental protection and if so under which environmental management regime(s). The second questions whether the ethos of global environmental protection and that of free trade environmentalism, both embedded in the globalization discourse, are reconcilable. Salih goes on to argue that the social science engagement in this debate is still to a large extent inept in answering the question of whether globalization is detrimental or beneficial to global environmental protection. Hence, instead of narrowing the gulf between global environmental policy and developmental practice, the two are widening it. Concomitantly, treating each in isolation from the other also widens the gulf within the ranks of those concerned with the undesirable manifestations of globalization.

In view of this, the chapter argues that the social sciences are confronting the formidable challenge of unpacking concepts deeply entrenched in the confines of disciplinary research, yet are begging for an interdisciplinary understanding of issues that traverse, encompass and expand several social science disciplines. Globalization and sustainable development are aggregate manifestations of regimes of social, economic, and political expressions informed by the totality of the context(s) within which they interact. These manifestations are too wide in scope and content for any social science discipline to be able to handle. Another, perhaps somewhat less explicit, conclusion which can be drawn from this chapter concerns the recurrent issue of the role of the state. As in the case of the previous chapter on human rights, Salih emphasizes that the protection of the global environment will rely more on the capacity of strong states than on the goodwill of global institutions. One obvious reason for this could be that global institutions still lack the political power. It is also true that, as Salih stresses, legal instruments aimed at protecting the (global) environment will have to be combined with persuasive socio-economic incentives. It is not difficult to imagine that states will have to play an important role here.

The next two chapters discuss various aspects of globalization and gender. *Marianne Marchand* and *Anne Sisson Runyan* start with the observation that international political and economic studies have so far largely lacked feminist and/ or gender perspectives. Globalization presents a challenge insofar as it overthrows older dichotomies like male/female, state/civil society, etc. by the multiple contradictions it creates. The authors show that globalization is simultaneously reinforcing gender roles in certain arenas and opening up new spaces for resistance. Depending on specific historical circumstances and situations, OECD countries, as well as former socialist and developing countries create, for example, different 'sites' for feminist struggles and changing gender roles. One of the main tasks of gender analysis and feminist struggle is to expose the cases in which globalization is seen and promoted as a construction mainly shaped by and striving for masculine domination. Fulfilling this task could result in both a better understanding of the increasing burden on women through globalization as well as a first step on the way to overcoming gender-based inequality.

Tine Davids and *Francien van Driel* in their contribution also propose to go beyond the by now well-established dichotomies in globalization studies specifically where gender is concerned. The authors propose a different approach to globalization and, as such, draw attention to the usefulness of a multi-dimensional gender model as an analytical and methodological tool of deconstruction. In examining the interconnectedness of the global and the local, they expose a dichotomous way of thinking and the production of stereotypes and clichés in related scientific research. The debate on the feminization of poverty as an example of an effect of globalization is taken as an example of such a misleading and dichotomous approach. In contradistinction, using a multi-dimensional gender model, these authors analyze how women are part of and deal as active vocal subjects with local discourses in which global processes obtain their meaning. Both authors draw on their fieldwork in Mexico and Botswana to exemplify their approach. In their conclusion Davids and van Driel explicitly aim at stimulating the wider applicability of the multi-dimensional gender model as a pattern of thought and inspiration in the globalization debate.

While McLuhan's global village stood at the beginning of the globalization debate, today it is the global city with its manifold problems that catches our attention. *Ton van Naerssen*, while embracing the phenomenon of the global city, points at the same time to salient differences between the mega-cities of the North and the South. Both are undergoing quick and fundamental restructuring especially through migration and economic and cultural influences. The cities of the North (the 'world cities') retain, however, a dominant position, while their Southern counterparts suffer more of the problems arising from the unprecedented population growth and global reshuffling of economic activities. Nevertheless, many cities in the North and South share many problems which are connected to social polarization and ecological degradation, forcing them to look for policy solutions which increasingly have to take into account the dynamics of the global urban network. Reviewing two urban development programmes, van Naerssen draws the conclusion that existing and future problems can only be solved by a combination of action from above and from below (e.g. by community-based organizations), depending on the socio-political situation in particular cities. Again, cities of the South are falling behind in finding solutions, since often neither the political climate nor the financial means are appropriate for the necessary restructuring efforts.

GLOBALIZATION AND HUMAN RIGHTS: SOME DEVELOPMENTAL REFLECTIONS

Reinhart Kössler

The catch-phrase of globalization has given, among many other effects, a new twist to the debate about the universal validity of human rights, as well as the ways and means to assert such rights. This is a vital and intricate problem. The following contribution aims to take a closer look at the actual relationship between globalization and human rights and to draw conclusions in terms of a viable human rights strategy on a global scale. After considering some central traits of globalization, with particular accent upon global inequality, I want to address the issues of universalism vs. relativism of human rights, as well as that of the unity and internal tensions existing between particular human rights contained within the relevant instruments today. This is finally related back to underlying material problems in a more detailed discussion of the controversial right to development.

The tensions of globalization

Globalization may be considered a complex and multi-dimensional set of processes of rapid change, while at the same time delineating a programme of fundamental and multi-dimensional change and an ideology to legitimize such change. The most basic change on which current processes termed globalization rests is the significant technological advances achieved during the last quarter of the 20th century. The spread of micro-electronics has penetrated practically every field of production, and it has caused fundamental changes in the fields of communication and information processing. In all likelihood, it is this change that immediately springs to mind when most people think of globalization. Communication around the globe in real time has tremendous implications. It has revolutionized markets around the world, and money markets in particular. The contraction of time and space has created, among citizens of the Western world at any rate, the feeling of becoming direct witnesses to current events considered to be of major importance, be they exploits in outer space, sports events, natural catastrophes, or the 'video wars' in Iraq and Yugoslavia.

As has already been recognized by many observers, however, this is not where the story ends. Certainly, globalization can be considered as indicative of the current state of a world society nexus, and even traces of MacLuhan's 'global village' may be found, in particular in its cyberspace version. World society, however, in so far as we are justified in using such a term, is far more complex and problematic than even the most incisive consequences of the information revolution would suggest. The reason is precisely that the world is not just made up of information or even information possibilities and never will be. A thorough understanding of the current world society nexus will not be possible without reference to its material aspects and substrates, and thereby also, to the dimension of inequality on a world scale.

One centrally important feature of globalization is the risk of the common destruction of humankind by means of human agency, pending since the advent of nuclear weaponry in 1945. At a fairly early date, Karl Jaspers had seen the only possible 'sense' of this potential peril as the chance that 'actual danger' might constitute a consciousness for the challenge of creating a 'world order of right' in the face of fatal danger (Jaspers s.a.: 262). This is a far cry from the current globalization euphoria, but it should be kept in mind as a strong pointer to its inherent risks, as well as to historic chances that go well beyond economic change. Globalization as risk was taken up later, especially in the discussion of unintended side effects of modernity that have led to a proliferation of risks and now force society to deal with these effects in the form of 'reflexive modernization' (see esp. Beck 1986).

Discussions on the consequences of globalization, in particular those highlighting the virtualization of economics tend to leave out these interrelated aspects which cannot be broached here (cf. Altvater/Mahnkopf 1999). Similarly, fascination with the advancing communications technology, its potentials and consequences tends to obscure the fact that the processes termed globalization have involved different parts of the world in very uneven ways. Thus, it is well known that world trade has both intensified enormously *and* been concentrated amongst the capitalist industrial countries of the North, with the addition of the Newly Industrial Countries. This leaves out the greater part of humankind. The quotas of effective requirements for available raw materials and waste deposits per country and per capita are also heavily weighted towards the needs in the centres of industrial capitalism. This fact alone demonstrates that any idea of generalizing the form of life associated with industrial mass production and mass consumption is completely illusory on a world scale. These facts are cited here only as a reminder of the basic circumstance which frequently seems to be forgotten when talking about globalization or the coming about of world society. Regardless of their various denominations, these nexuses are very real and tangible in their results, and they are, at the same time, marked by gross inequalities and stark structural hierarchy among national economies as well as amongst the people living within them.

It is here that the notion of a 'world society' runs into serious problems. Differences and inequalities, both among and within various national states, can be smoothed away by conceptual arrangements, for example by defining society as nothing more than an all-encompassing system made up by communications. This cannot be other than world-wide today (cf. Luhmann 1997), but this is done whilst glossing over the salient features of 'world society' thus understood, namely differences. Mainstream sociology has, for a long time, tried to argue that difference in modern society stems mainly or even exclusively from functional differentiation. Time and again, it has been shown that differences of wealth and of ascriptive life chances, of class, gender, and race have nonetheless persisted.

Difference persists even in the age and in the face of globalization, and it may very well be said that globalization is, in very important ways, *about* the confrontation and (re-)organization, (re-)arrangement of difference. At a basic level, this is borne out by the finding that in spite of globalizing upheavals, the location of enterprises persist in being of pivotal importance (cf. Kappel 1995). Most importantly, while the increase in the mobility of various resources has been very uneven, this is particularly so in the case of the mobility of people. Globalization has further intensified world-wide social and above all, economic nexuses. This, however, has not been accompanied by a similar degree of mobility, even though mobility, and air travel in particular, have increased enormously. The persistence of separate labour markets, basically defined by national state boundaries, has occasioned the recent salience of 'the maintenance of extremely divergent conditions of income and living within the world market' as one main objective – and problem – of effective governance; this is co-extensive with a shift from the model image of the welfare state to that of the 'national competitive state' (Hirsch 1995:104).

Frequently, the effects of globalization are presented as eroding the functional powers of national states, in particular the capacity to effectively tax incomes generated within their realms, and thereby, to uphold vital functions in terms of infrastructure and public welfare. This, however, is not the end of the story. It would seem that not only are people much less mobile than information or even physical goods, but that their movements, in an age of deregulation in the circulation of goods, are severely regulated and restricted as soon as these movements can be considered as constituting movements of labour power. This is now a much debated, as well as deplored, fact in terms of the 'new lines' erected along the US-Mexican Border or at the eastern boundaries of Germany and the Mediterranean coasts of the European Union (cf. Rufin 1996). But the same strategic pattern is strikingly apparent in the behaviour of relatively privileged states in the South that attract migrants, albeit as refugees, in search of a better future. A particularly disconcerting example of this is South Africa. Here, starting immediately with the advent of majority rule in 1994, state controls and repression, aimed against the influx of unwanted and therefore 'illegal' immigrants, were stepped up decisively (cf. Goebel 1999). Almost inevitably, such measures are connected with serious infringements on the human rights of 'illegal' immigrants including losses of liberty, bodily harm, and even death at the hands of those effecting deportation or preventing access to the target country (cf. Dietrich 1999; Höfling-Semnar 1995). In a country such as Germany, this has been complemented throughout the 1990s by a set of "sovereign strategies of the national state" (Cyrus 1999:213ff) that lend the lie to the wholesale theses of the erosion of such states' powers. When it comes to sealing off their own territories, these states are capable of fielding a full array of means, including not only technical appliances but also selective treatment of international human rights instruments. Such sovereign strategies point to 'intended fracture points in the architecture of the international human rights constitution' (ib.: 220) which give leeway to the voluntaristic and interest-guided action of individual national state bodies.

The plight of international refugees, asylum seekers, and illegal immigrants forms an important dimension of the whole cluster of processes termed globalization. Within a human rights framework, it merits particular attention, since not only are human rights violations of various kinds involved in decisions for (forced) migration, but such violations are also perpetrated, on a more or less regular basis, in the course of state-sponsored efforts to fend off and forcibly reverse such migration. The latter fact is reminiscent of the situation created, after World War I, by the arrival in Western Europe of a mass of 'refugees' whom 'it was impossible to get rid of' and when 'the state, insisting on its sovereign right of expulsion, was forced by the illegal nature of statelessness into admittedly illegal acts' (Arendt 1986:281, 283f). As Hannah Arendt has pointed out, this also had grave repercussions for the internal civic rights situations in the target countries: 'This was the first time the police in Western Europe had received authority ... to rule directly over people' (ib.: 287), which in turn, in Arendt's view, marked an important step in the decline of the civic nation state as guardian of human rights.

Currently, the erosion of civic and, consequently, of human rights is apparent in the erection of ever-stricter border regimes. A corollary of this is a restrictive interpretation of human rights which are not treated as applicable to asylum seekers or, generally, illegal immigrants. This militates against any conception of the 'equality of all humans'. In turn, a conception of democracy as 'a privilege for specific groups, a select "garden of human beings" ... puts into balance nothing less that the relationship between democracy and human rights' (Höfling-Semnar 1999:247).

Therefore, the persuasive power of state-sponsored human rights arguments from Western sources obviously falls away dramatically when contrasted to actual practices in and by these states themselves. This consideration is important when turning to the issue of the 'universalization' of human rights. As long as this is propagated by particular state governments and called upon to justify external actions right up to military intervention, the actions of these states and governments themselves and their own human rights' records are of considerable importance.

Further, such a line of thought can remind us of a fundamentally important fact: nowhere in the world today are human rights anything like a solid reality or even an intrinsic cultural trait. They are the historical products of fierce struggles and they are upheld only by people's vigilance and active efforts. This goes a long way towards placing the inevitable issue of universalism vs. (cultural) relativism of human rights not in a static state, but rather, in a dynamic perspective of a vibrant civil society, which is seen here as a vital social field on which social tensions and countervailing interests, including advocacy of human rights, are played out.

Human rights and their contradictions

Human rights, as contained in the Universal Declaration of Human Rights (UDHR), fall into several groups or 'generations'. These are differentiated both by their content and by the time they have taken to be formulated. Basically, the provisions of the classical Bill of Rights, as contained in the first ten amendments to the U.S. constitution or in the first explicit declaration of human rights, adopted by the revolutionary French National Assembly in 1789, can be considered as the origins of the 'first generation' of civic and personal rights and liberties. Apart from rights concerning the protection of personal integrity, including freedom of belief and religion, these rights, now enshrined and elaborated in Articles 1-21 of UDHR, also encompass the right to participate in public affairs. A 'second generation' of rights is concerned with guaranteeing and safeguarding precisely the pre-conditions for exercising this and related rights effectively. Articles 22-28 of UDHR are concerned with social rights, including the individual's right to work, but they also contain provisions on the level both of the individual nation state and on that of the international order for state action to ensure a decent living for their citizens. Active citizenship would be a meaningless and empty shell without such provisions to ensure individuals a minimum measure of material conditions, free from the immediate concern of bare survival (cf. Pateman 1970). Article 28 of UDHR expands this principle, going beyond the confines of the national state and calling for an adequate social and international order. Along these lines, international human rights' instruments have been developed after the adoption of UDHR by the UN General Assembly in 1948. These include, besides the international pacts on civic and social rights, the declarations on the Right to Peace and the Right to Development, referred to as 'third generation' human rights.

All human rights are fraught with a number of problems, not least the fact that they are difficult to enforce. In only a few countries are human rights part of operative law. Their validity is hemmed in further by salvatory clauses subjecting constitutionally guaranteed rights and liberties to particulars to be provided in other legislation. Rights catalogues contained in individual constitutions are, as often as not, as extensive as that of UDHR, excluding, for instance, such vital social rights as the right to work. On the other hand, the enforcement of human rights on an international scale is hampered by the intricacies of an international law that can be enforced in most cases only if individual states are willing to co-operate. Experiences with international tribunals on human rights' violations testify to these difficulties.

The main international controversy over human rights, however, has centred on their supposedly 'Eurocentric' character. There can be little doubt that conceptually as well as in terms of original textual versions, human rights do indeed stem from a (Western) European context. At first sight, therefore, it makes some sense to consider the universalization of human rights, as has been postulated, in particular after World War II, as another form of Western ideological dominance or cultural imperialism. Thus, need-orientation, collectivity, and environmental integrity are claimed as mainstays of an autonomous reconstruction of non-Western cultures, and in clear confrontation to any modern concept of state (cf. Sardar 1999:57ff; 48). In a far cruder form, the charge of cultural imperialism is backed up by playing off individual rights against the right to development construed to reside in collectives and preferably in states. This will be dealt with in more detail in the following section. First, I should like to address the charge of cultural imperialism.

By construing human rights as a means and an expression of dominance or as an outgrowth of Western culture, and therefore as inappropriate or incongruent in other parts of the world, one central feature of this catalogue of rights is omitted: these rights are, in fact, far from being intrinsic to Western culture. One might even say, with greater justification, that human rights are a result of centuries of struggle against forms of government and indeed, against cultural and political traditions that were dominant in the West up to 200 or more years ago and cannot be considered as definitely overcome, even today. Such traits have included long-term imprisonment without sentence, a whole array of public corporal punishment, capital punishment executed in public by a wide range of brutal and ugly methods for minor offences or for religious heresy. They also included physical torture, witch-burning, etc. Capital punishment hit a long-term high in 18th century England, on the very eve of industrial revolution, when *habeas corpus* had already been on the statute books for several decades (cf. Hay et al. 1975). Occasional witch hunts taking place as late as the tension-ridden post-World War II period in Germany, targetted refugees from the former Eastern provinces (cf. Beer 198:163). Fundamental human rights, then, were secured against established state routine and in all probability, in many respects, also against deeply ingrained popular attitudes and ways of thinking. They have to be re-asserted constantly in the face of tendencies to fall back on seemingly effective short shrift repressive methods of dealing with difference and conflict.

The 'second generation' social rights were formed in a long and conflictive process of workers' and popular struggles during the 19th and the greater part of the 20th centuries. Women's civil rights were asserted strongly at the time of the French Revolution, but bitterly contested until well into the 20th century and still form a contested terrain in terms of their specific contents and regulatory powers in social relations (cf. Pateman 1988). The process of 'universalization' of human rights, then, is not restricted to geographical diffusion. The more important and indicative aspect of this process is its progressive inclusiveness (see also Holthaus 1996). Let us take political rights. From being restricted to a minority in society, these have been expanded to transcend the barriers first of economic wealth and power, and later, of gender discrimination.

Moreover, such achievements can by no means be considered as a 'western tradition', even in the sense of an irreversible cultural achievement. The experience of two world wars, above all the secular crimes of Nazism, bear ample testimony that any 'process of civilization' is nothing like an objective path, running in one direction only. 'Second generation citizens' and human rights are on the retreat in the present age of neoliberalism. Even in the West, then, human rights are by no means an intrinsic feature, but an achievement of long struggle, in need of constant protection. Consequently, at their inception during the French Revolution, the declaration of human rights was therefore seen, not in any sense as a continuation of the *ancien régime*, but as a totally new departure, in stark contrast to the absolutist state, nothing less than 'the founding of a new society' (Gauchet 1991:13).

Human rights, then, are not fixed cultural traits or traditions of a particular world region. Representing values, their formulation and enforcement are dependent on social processes and on the presence of agents willing and able to set into motion and to pursue such processes. This emphatically political view of human rights is corroborated by the mode of their propagation or universalization. The view that human rights are being grafted upon societies with traditions that find themselves in fundamental discord to these values is distorted, to say the least. Universalization of human rights, in terms of geographical diffusion and progressive inclusiveness, is foremost an outcome of the fact that increasing numbers of people have claimed these rights, that they have struggled and made sacrifices for them.

After all, global propagation of Western concepts and structures did not begin with human rights. It took the violent and exploitative forms of colonial conquest and domination, with the consequences of untrammelled greed to procure commodities for the emergent world market. The colonial state therefore did universalize Western features and patterns that are clearly at variance from human rights – valorization of natural resources and human labour power, and an administration geared towards most efficient use of the subject countries and their peoples. It is not hard to find corollaries to this 'rationalizing universalization' (Schiel 1999) within the West itself – above all the rationalizing, homogenizing national state itself.

In contradistinction to this, there is another universalizing tendency which Schiel has called 'civilising universalization', thus highlighting the expansion of *civil* rights, competencies, and structures implied by the process (ib.:12). Colonialism, then, can be seen as the world-wide expansion of rationalizing universalization, while the colonial subjects were denied the fruits of civilizing universalization that had been attained or were being achieved in the capitalist core countries of Western Europe and Northern America. Anti-colonial movements, once they advanced from the primary stage of mere resistance to conquest, were inevitably pushed towards laying claim to exactly those rights and liberties that seemed self-evident to colonial masters but were denied to colonial subjects. Obviously, this does not imply that after independence, human rights were generally respected, but this argument reminds us of the relational and contextual nature of any discourse on human rights. These rights are claimed, foremost, by those to whom they are denied. On the internal field of struggle for rights, human rights advocates therefore confront culturalist claims of state-powered human rights violators. As far as these form part and parcel of sustained efforts to take over, and develop further, the technological as well as the institutional aspects of *rationalizing* universalization, such claims disclose their ideological nature. It is quite possible to discover human rights and democratic strands within non-European systems of thought, such as Confucianism (cf. Lee 1997; 1999). Again, this can only underscore both the malleability and adaptability of cultures, and the possibilities and opportunities that lie in a creative assimilation of achievements, such as human rights, by those who have to face the challenges of globalized capitalism.

Lastly, the relativist argument itself rests on the decidedly modern, and 'Western' feature of differentiation and decentration of value spheres (cf. Habermas 1998:206f). This is the precondition that different cultures can be considered as potentially equivalent. The *principled* rejection of claims to cultural superiority is itself an outflow of the intellectual trajectory that has been at the origins of the present catalogue of human rights. This would not apply, of course, if *one* claim to cultural superiority were played off against *other*, similarly grounded claims. Then the relativist argument would, *a fortiori*, appear as a mere ideological cloak to strategies for legitimizing domination and the exertion of power and violence.

A right to development – for and by whom?[1]

In a time of enhanced globalization, inequality of life chances and life levels on a world scale has become an ever more acute problem. This has been sketched out by a brief look at the interconnected problems of (illegal) migration and human

---

1. The following is adapted from Kössler 1999:19-27; Kössler 1998:chpt. 5.

rights. The same point can be made by referring to the need for mutual recognition as humans, arising out of the world social nexus and urging a minimum of equity among the participants of that nexus. As has been indicated, this need is recognized already in UDHR Art. 28, but it has been restated in a separate declaration by the UN General Assembly which does not form part of UDHR proper. In 1986, the General Assembly declared development *'an inalienable human right'* (art. 1.1).[2]

While the Right to Development, like other so-called third generation human rights, notably the Right to Peace, is not contained in UDHR, it may be derived from UDHR Article 28, stating that *'Everyone is entitled to a social and international order in which the rights and freedoms set forth in this Declaration can be fully realized.'* Similarly, chapter IX, Article 55 of the UN Charter stipulates the obligation of member nations to work together, i.a. for *'economic and social progress and development'*, and also for *'universal respect for, and observance of human rights and fundamental freedoms.'*

Clearly, these authoritative formulations are aimed at an international obligation to safeguard human rights, not only in the sense of preventing flagrant violations of 'classical', personal human rights, but also in the sense of creating conditions for the effective enjoyment of human rights. These documents, therefore, point strongly to the intimate relationship that exists between personal human rights and civil freedoms – so-called first generation human rights – and the conditions for their material fulfilment, which have given rise to social and economic rights (second generation), as well as to rights concerning the international order (third generation). Thus, the right to development stipulates a number of material conditions that have to be fulfilled for a person effectively to enjoy his or her human rights, be they personal freedom, bodily integrity, freedom from discrimination, or the right to political participation etc. All such rights and freedoms will remain hollow if they are not bolstered up by minimum standards of living, enabling a person to claim and actively use them. In a celebrated example, the sanctity and privacy of a home is irrelevant to a person who does not have one, but it is of utmost importance as soon as people begin to enjoy their own homes.

This makes it important to uphold the entire catalogue of human rights. There may be tensions between the individual rights, but these are obviously grounded in the real world. If Western critics of 'collective rights' have advocated a tight restriction on the narrowly defined personal rights and civic liberties, they have ignored the fact that these can only be enjoyed and exercised if certain minimum material conditions are met, as defined in the second and third generations of human rights. Conversely, the critics that have specifically denounced personal rights and freedoms, rather than the entire UDHR, as uniquely western and therefore Eurocentric have for the most part disguised

---

2. In the following, quoted articles (art.) refer to: Declaration on the Right to Development, as documented in Nuscheler (ed.), 1998:78-81.

behind these seemingly noble words the unwillingness of state bodies to respect personal rights and liberties. As has been indicated little criticism is heard from the same quarters about the concept of national sovereignty, which is, of course, at least as 'Western' and 'Eurocentric' as personal human rights are.

From this angle, the Right to Development may be considered to emanate from the logic of the rights vested in the UDHR, but then the question appears all the more important; how is such a right defined and who is supposed to exercise it. The right to development as defined by the Declaration entitles *'every human person and all peoples ... to participate in, contribute to, and enjoy economic, social, cultural and political development, in which all human rights and fundamental freedoms can be fully realized'* (art. 1.1.) This *'implies the full realization of the right of peoples to self-determination'* which in turn is seen to stipulate, *'subject to the relevant provisions of both International Covenants on Human Rights, the exercise of their inalienable right to full sovereignty over all their natural resources'* (art. 1.2). In its articles 2, 6 and 9, the declaration underscores the indivisibility, interdependency, and mutual equivalence of all human rights and fundamental freedoms, which explicitly have to be taken into account also in fulfilling the responsibility of *'all human beings ... for development, individually and collectively'* (art. 2.2). At the same time, the aims of the declaration are conceived as an international responsibility of *'all states'* who *'should co-operate with a view to promoting, encouraging and strengthening universal respect for and observance of all human rights and fundamental freedoms for all without any distinction as to race, sex, language or religion'* (art. 6.1).

In all this, it is *'the human person'* who is pointedly identified as *'the central subject of development'*. Therefore the individual in this sense is also designated as the one who *'should be the active participant and beneficiary of the right to development'* (art. 2.1). In this way, conventional, above all first generation human rights were explicitly invoked and re-affirmed by the declaration. Later claims that the Declaration contained a 'justification for the primacy of development' over individual human rights, as advanced in particular by the 'Asian bloc', have no basis in the text and are even explicitly refuted in article 9.2, barring any justification of human rights violations on such grounds (Nuscheler 1998:61).

The re-assertion of individual human rights has been interpreted as a 'political deal', exchanging a 'recognition of the principle of universality' of human rights against consenting to a formal 'acknowledgement of the ... "Right to Development"' (ib.:60). Nevertheless , states figure very strongly in the declaration, and there is an unmistakable tension between assertions of the rights and duties of individual persons and of states. This is, of course, already obvious from the strong assertion of state sovereignty. And it is states who are accorded *'the right and the duty to formulate appropriate national development policies that aim at the constant improvement of the well-being of the entire population and of all individuals, on the basis of their active, free and meaningful participation in development and in the fair distribution of the benefits resulting therefrom'* (art. 2.3). Consequently, it is also *'states'* that *'have the primary responsibility for the creation of national and inter-*

national conditions favourable to the realization of the right to development' (art. 3.1), while they merely *'should encourage popular participation in all spheres as an important factor in development'* (art. 8.2). States are pledged to co-operate, especially in *'eliminating obstacles to development'* and in the promotion of *'a new international economic order based on sovereign equality, interdependence, mutual interest and co-operation among all States'* (art. 3.3), and further in *'sustained action'* for *'more rapid development of developing countries'* (art. 4.2). This was clearly aimed at the agenda of the Group of 77 and of the UNCTAD conferences, which still showed some momentum in the mid 1980s when the declaration was drafted. At the same time, any hints at operative ways of realizing the Right to Development, in the concept set forth in this declaration, clearly hinge on the central role of individual nation states. Of course, such formulations may have had their rationale in current attacks on national sovereignty at a time when Structural Adjustment Programmes were grafted onto one country after another in very stereotyped and destructive ways during the debt crisis that rocked the world economy and national development strategies at the time. Still, these signs and problems apparently were not taken as pointers to the fundamental difficulties that the implementation of a nationally defined economic or development strategy unmistakably faced, not even a decade later even in industrial core countries. For better or worse, globalization makes these formulations about the sovereign state implementing development strategies sound obsolete and unrealistic.

Again, just as human rights in general and second and third generation rights in particular, the right to development is not positive law, grounding concrete, legally enforceable claims. Doubtlessly, the Right to Development could not exert much influence 'on budget debates or in the negotiations of the Uruguay Round' (Nuscheler 1996:12). Moreover, more difficulties obviously exist here than in the case of personal rights and liberties, which could be given status as operative law in the bills of rights contained in some national constitutions. Development, however conceived, is a far too complex a process to be cast into legal instruments obliging governments to refrain from certain actions or even to execute others. Even greater difficulties would be incurred if such provisions were to be contained in international accords or regimes, although regimes, even on complex positive policy issues, are not entirely out of reach (cf. Zürn 1998:224-232). In many countries, however, the Bill of Rights is not directly operative law. In a country like Germany where it is, another fundamental right, once especially cherished for being a positive reflection of learning from the country's evil past, the right to asylum, has been amended to the point where it can only be claimed in legal courts with the greatest difficulty (cf. Höfling-Semnar 1995:220ff). Thus, the right to asylum, as a legally enforceable right, now falls pitifully short in Germany – and most probably in most other countries – of the standards proclaimed in UDHR, art. 14 or in the Geneva Convention. Surely, it would be too cynical to infer from this that the right to asylum, since hardly enforceable, was now devoid of meaning and value and could possibly be completely discarded on such grounds. Nobody would go along with such reasoning. By the same token, criticism of the Right to Development, simply because there are obvious difficulties with its implementation , misses the mark.

The Right to Development has been played off as a *collective* right against the *personal* human rights and liberties. Such arguments have been advanced, not only by Third World, but especially by (South) East Asian governments, claiming precedence of industrial development over individual freedoms, while at the same time asserting divergences in the cultural heritage of 'their' countries in the face of the Eurocentrism inherent in human rights; these arguments have also been championed, inversely as it were, by critics of later generation human rights, who claim that the notion of human rights should be restricted to the catalogue of 'classical' Bills of Rights, i.e., individual freedoms. These claims and criticisms are in glaring contradiction to the Declaration of 1986 (esp. art. 9.2).

The statements of ASEAN governments during the run-up to the UN Human Rights Conference in Vienna in 1993 and in particular, the 'Bangkok Declaration', have digressed from the wording of the Declaration in one important respect: they saw *states* as the subjects of the Right to Development. This would indeed mean that the status of individual human rights would no longer be 'undisposable, but dependent on the state' (Tetzlaff 1993:35). This was rejected by the Vienna Declaration which, at the same time, re-affirmed that denial of development must be considered as a human rights violation and that this means that peoples must be 'free to pursue their economic, social and cultural development' (§ 2, doc. in Tetzlaff 1993:306). In the same document the interdependence and mutual re-enforcement of democracy, respect for human rights, and development are stressed. This notwithstanding, lack of development is expressly not considered a justification for the denial of human rights by the Vienna Declaration (§§ 8, 9). These formulae are indicative of the tensions that exist in the real world between individual and collective rights, above all regarding development, in any case once this is interpreted to be vested in the state.

Further criticism directed against the Right to Development, in any case in the form it has been given in the Declaration and subsequent documents, castigates this right, besides being a 'soft law' at best, as a 'right to everything' and therefore basically devoid of content (Nuscheler 1998:68ff). Undoubtedly, this underscores once again the difficulties involved in giving practical meaning to this right. A different, more restrictive formula, however, would miss the fundamental fact that 'development' is indeed about 'everything'. What is at stake here is the entire range of living conditions. From the perspective of an interpretation of *habeas corpus,* which recognizes the material pre-conditions of effectiveness of this right, this would also encompass health and a sound environment. Again, the aims stipulated in the Declaration and subsequent documents also contain vital preconditions for the effective exercise of such rights as political participation, freedom of information and publicized opinion, or the right to an education. As one of the staunchest critics of the Right to Development also notes, moral obligations, such as those contained in the instruments stating and re-affirming the Right to Development, will hardly result in immediate practical steps taken by any government, but they can give added momentum to demands and initiatives from within civil society to remind governments of the obligations they have incurred. In this sense, the Right to Development may well serve as a 'benchmark' (Nuscheler 1998:71) for the evaluation and monitoring of the performance and policies of governments, particularly in the industrialized countries.

Again, this gives added weight to the concept of development articulated in the relevant documents. An examination yields two inter-related problems, which I consider much more serious than the objections discussed so far. While reference is made to individual persons, the Right to Development is seen effectively to reside above all in states or at best, in 'peoples', which are in turn described as sovereign and thus equated with states. Also conceptually, the Right to Development is situated squarely in the field of international, and above all UN, diplomacy and at the same time, indeed by this token, directed at the (development) policies of individual states. The meaning of development as it emerges from these documents is strictly centred on the state. Over and above this, development is not further explained , except for some reference to sustainability. It appears to be about an ever- increasing 'well-being', about the removal of development blockades, about the external economic situation of developing countries, and finally, about overcoming a 'lack of development', which is, of course, a tautology.

There is little to be found here of the shift of emphasis, generated since the 1980s, away from mere growth towards aims and concepts such as sustainability but, especially, empowerment. The texts also turn a blind eye to the rising role of non-state actors on all levels. On the other hand, the concept of development which is declared a human right in these documents, accords quite accurately to the different versions of the old, modernizing paradigm of late development, set within the boundaries of the nation state. This is not only a decidedly modernist, and in this sense Eurocentric, concept of development, it is an illusory perspective. As long as development is not seen as addressing global problems and calling for global solutions, it cannot consist in replicating experiences that were based, after all, on the exploitation of the many, colonized or not, by the privileged few.

In this way, the official formulations of the Right to Development ignore the demands raised by new social movements or the women's movement internationally for a 'different' or 'other' development, which to some limited extent have been reflected in official political discourse and practice. Thus, the Vienna Declaration simply mentions women's rights and the Right to Development side by side without suggesting any form in which these might be articulated. These documents are a far cry from a 'model of development which is tuned to the concrete interests of the peoples and persons concerned, to the realisation of their economic, social, cultural, civic and politic human rights'. Such a model could indeed convey the perspective of 'a radical new conceptualization of development', which then would not state a Right to Development as an overarching human right to remain strictly formal in the last analysis, but conversely, would 'equate the notion of development with all-round, universal fulfillment of human rights' (Nowak 1993:224f).

Obviously, this refers us to the principle of global equity and along with that, to a fundamental change in dominant cultural values and goals and lifestyles, along the lines of 'planetary ethics' (Nederveen Pieterse 1999:82). But the consideration of the Right to Development and its problems may give us one further clue. If it has been deemed to a large or even primary degree the responsibility of people in the West to review the privileges most of them enjoy today in comparison to the vast majority of humankind, we have to go further. The Right to Development has been championed primarily by governments of the South and brought forward, on important occasions, as a counterweight against the supposedly Eurocentric contents of personal human rights and fundamental freedoms. From the perspective outlined here, it would appear now that there can be found no document more Eurocentric in its fundamental thrust and statements than the Declaration of the Right to Development. Later documents, such as the Vienna Declaration on Human Rights (1993), have referred to cultural specificities, but the basic concept of development as contained in the Declaration of 1987 centres on modernity radiating from the West as the goal of development, i.e., economic growth. Surely, this is understandable from the perspective of poor countries, where redistribution would not overcome destitution, but where growth, in terms of the nationally bounded territory, is a necessity. At the same time, however, this goal definition is a clear expression of the conceptual and cultural hegemony of the metropolitan societies, and this in one of the central documents that was supposed to help overcome global inequality. Here development is seen as meaning the generalization of the Western, Fordist life model, in material terms at least, even though it may be shorn of its mass democratic dimension. This means that no escape route is mapped out here from the Western defined paradigm of development.

As indicated above, if this perspective, which is considered necessary and long overdue , is to get any further, concerted and global efforts are called for. Because of the present situation of dominance, sacrifices from the privileged of today will be called for. Survival on this planet, however , will hinge to no small degree on their willingness to overstep the boundaries that today still restrict solidarity to the members of a particular nation or to some form of charity. Recognizing the fact that world society is becoming a reality in a world still marked by many different inequalities , the demand for unrestricted civic solidarity remains apposite (cf. Kössler/Melber 1993:82-94). With this perspective, the Right to Development would no longer be aimed at the illusory concept of spreading and possibly, universalizing the Fordist model of development, which in reality only amounts to buttressing the principle of a hierarchically structured world society. Rather, this Right would then be directed towards indispensable re-orientation, towards a truly global perspective of equity among humans, as well as between humans and nature. Only such a development could make something good come from the richness of human endeavour and offer the perspective of sustainability not only for women and men living in the present, but also for posterity.

References

Altvater, Elmar/Birgit Mahnkopf (1999) *Grenzen der Globalisierung. Ökonomie, Ökologie und Politik in der Weltgesellschaft*. 4th, rev. ed. Münster, Westfälisches Dampfboot.

Arendt, Hannah (1986) *The Origins of Totalitarianism*. London, André Deutsch (1951).

Beck, Ulrich (1986) *Risikogesellschaft. Auf dem Weg in eine andere Moderne*. Frankfurt-on-Maine, Suhrkamp.

Beer, Matthias (1998) "Flüchtlinge – Ausgewiesene – Neubürger – Heimatvertriebene. Flüchtlingspolitik und Flüchtlingsintegration in Deutschland nach 1945, 'begriffsgeschichtlich betrachtet'". In: Matthias Beer/Martin Kintzinger/Marita Krauss (eds.): *Migration und Integration. Aufnahme und Eingliederung im historischen Wandel*. Stuttgart, Steiner, pp. 145-167.

Cyrus, Norbert (1999) "Im menschenrechtlichen Niemandsland: Illegalisierte Zuwanderung in der Bundesrepublik Deutschland". In: Dominik et al., pp. 205-231.

Dietrich, Helmut (1999) "Die 'unsichtbare Muer'. Eine Skizze zu Sozialtechnik und Grenzregime". In: Dominik et al., pp. 290-323.

Dominik, Katja/Marc Jünemann/Jan Motte/Astrid Reinecke (eds.) (1999) *Angeworben – eingewandert – abgeschoben. Ein anderer Blick auf die Einwanderergesellschaft Bundesrepublik Deutschland*. Münster, Westfälisches Dampfboot.

Elias, Norbert (1976) *Über den Prozeß der Zivilisation*. 2 vols. Frankfurt-on-Maine, Suhrkamp (1936).

Gauchet, Marcel (1991) *Die Erklärung der Menschenrechte. Die Debatte um die bürgerlichen Freiheiten 1789*. Reinbek, Rowohlt (La Révolution des droits de l'homme, Paris 1989).

Goebel, Christian (1999) *Am Ende des Regenbogens. Einwanderung, Fremdenfeindlichkeit und Nation-Building in Südafrika*. Frankfurt-on-Maine, IKO.

Habermas, Jürgen (1998) *Die postnationale Konstellation*. Politische Essays. Frankfurt-on-Maine, Suhrkamp.

Hay, Douglas et al. (1975) *Albion's Fatal Tree. Crime and Society in Eighteenth Century England*. London, Allen Lane.

Hirsch, Joachim (1995) *Der nationale Wettbewerbsstaat. Staat, Demokratie und Politik im globalen Kapitalismus*. Berlin/Amsterdam. Edition ID-Archiv.

Höfling-Semnar, Bettina (1995) *Flucht und deutsche Asylpolitik. Von der Krise des Asylrechts zur Perfektionierung der Zugangsverhinderung*. Münster, Westfälisches Dampfboot.

Höfling-Semnar, Bettina (1999) "Ignoranz, Realitätsferne und Zugangsverhinerung. Flucht und deutsche Asylpolitik". In: Dominik et al., pp. 232-249.

Holthaus, Ines (1996) "Frauenmenschenrechtsbewegungen und die Universalisierung der Menschenrechte", *Peripherie* 61, S. 6-23.

Jaspers, Karl s.a.: *Vom Ursprung und Ziel der Geschichte*. Stuttgart/Hamburg, Deutscher Bücherbund (1949).

Kappel, Robert (1995) "Kern und Rand in der globalen Ordnung. Globalisierung, Tripolarität, Territorium und Peripherisierung", *Peripherie* 59/60, pp. 79-117.

Kössler, Reinhart (1998) *Entwicklung*. Münster, Westfälisches Dampfboot.

Kössler, Reinhart (1999) *Meanings of Development*. Windhoek (NEPRU Occasional Paper No 14).

Kössler, Reinhart/Hennning Melber (1993) *Chancen internationaler Zivilgesellschaft*. Frankfurt-on-Maine.

Lee, Eun-Jeung (1997) *Konfuzianismus und Kapitalismus. Markt und Herrschaft in Ostasien*. Münster, Westfälisches Dampfboot.

Lee, Eun-Jeung (1999) "Konflikt und Wandel der konfuzianischen Tradition in Korea – Historischer Rückblick und Perspektiven", *Peripherie* 73/74, pp. 162-183.

Luhmann, Niklas (1997) *Die Gesellschaft der Gesellschaft*. 2 vols. Frankfurt-on-Maine, Suhrkamp.

Munck, Ronaldo/Denis O'Hearn (eds.) (1999) *Critical Development Theory. Contributions to a new paradigm*. London/New York, Zed Books.

Nederveen Pieterse, Jan (1999) "Critical Holism and the Tao of Development". In: Munck/O'Hearn 1999, pp. 63-88.

Nowak, Manfred (1993) "Menschenrecht auf Entwicklung versus menschenrechtliche Entwicklungs-zusammenarbeit". In: Tetzlaff (ed.) 1993, pp. 215-226.

Nuscheler, Franz (1996) Das "Recht auf Entwicklung". Fortschritt oder Danaergeschenk in der Entwicklung der Menschenrechte? Bonn, Dietz.

Nuscheler, Franz (1998) "The 'Right to Development': Advance or Greek Gift in the Development of Human Rights?" In: id. (ed.) 1998, pp. 54-73.

Nuscheler, Franz (ed.) (1998) *The International Debate on Human Rights and the Right to Development (=INEF Report 30)*. Duisburg.

Pateman, Carole (1970) *Participation and Democratic Theory*. Cambridge, Cambridge UP.

Pateman, Carole (1988) *The Sexual Contract*. Cambridge/Oxford, Polity.

Rufin, Jean-Christophe (1996) *Die neuen Barbaren. Der Nord-Süd-Konflikt nach dem Ende des Kalten Krieges*. München, DTV.

Sardar, Ziauddin (1999) "Development and the Location of Eurocentrism". In: Munck/O'Hearn 1999, pp. 44-62.

Schiel, Tilman (1999) "Moderner 'Gartenstaat' und Menschenrechte. Südostasien zwischen kulturellem Partikularismus und rationalisierendem Universalismus". *Peripherie*, 73/74, pp. 6-28.

Tetzlaff, Rainer (ed.) (1993) *Menschenrechte und Entwicklung. Deutsche und internationale Kommentare und Dokumente*. Bonn, Dietz.

Zürn, Michael (1998) *Regieren jenseits des Nationalstaates*. Frankfurt-on-Maine.

MULTINATIONALS AND DEVELOPMENT: REVISITING THE DEBATE

Kristoffel Lieten

Introduction

Throughout the 1970s, a number of critical studies on the impact of multinational corporations (MNCs) in the developing countries were published (for example Jalée 1968, Vernon 1973, 1977, Helleiner 1972, Barratt Brown 1974, 1974, Radice 1975, Hymer 1976). The studies were critical of the MNCs in more than one sense, and conjured a future in which (developing) countries would exercise more autonomy and more state-aided development. Many of the social scientists concerned with or residing in the Third World turned against the MNCs with their imposing commercial, technological and political power. The dismay at the dependency of formally independent states, summarized in the title of Vernon's book *(Sovereignty at Bay)*, appealed to many. In the 1980s and 1990s, with a few exceptions (Reiffers 1982, Michalet 1985, Dunning 1981,1992, Lieten 1987, Dixon et al 1986, Jenkins 1987), the focus had shifted, and it has continued to shift. It has shifted to such an extent that the TINA syndrome rules the roost.[1] Immanuel Wallerstein (1996:356) exclaims:

> By the 1990s, it became hard to remember that anyone was ever optimistic. No one today seems to think there will be significant change in a relatively short run, a prosperous world for everyone. And everyone, or almost everyone, it seems, has given up on state action as the remedy. 'We were all Keynesians once', I suppose is the new slogan. Now, bless our souls, even most of us who were most radical in our politics a short time ago, are 'free marketeers'.

The shift, apart from ideological, has also been a shift into different theoretical concerns. In the 1970s, the number of studies on MNCs was insignificant in view of the overriding significance that these companies have in industrial, commercial and even social life. Even then, in the high days of research on MNCs, the

---

quantity of research was inversely related to the social relevance. At the end of the millennium, the interest has dwindled even further into insignificance. Some research has dealt with foreign investment, mainly in terms of financial flows and in terms of the impact on employment (Buckley and Clegg 1991, Buckley and Mucchielli, 1997; Calvo et al., 1998, Slaughter and Swagel, 1997; Watkins, 1997), but by and large, MNCs have been glossed over in the debate on development. The present ideological attachment to the benefits of the capitalist market have constructed a scholarship in which TINA dominates. The problem of development and underdevelopment is approached as if MNCs do not exist. While the public realm has come in for scrutiny, the private realm, although it has a continuously expanding influence over society, remains largely protected from investigation.

The axiom behind the advocacy of liberalism is that MNCs will run the system efficiently, and will bring about development. What hinders the fruition of this process are the encumbrances which, as yet, have not been removed: worldwide trade restrictions, overgrown state institutions, rent-seeking and parasitic government bureaucracies, etc. A further drive towards liberalization, privatization and downsizing the state will provide the parameters for wholesome development.[2] What used to be the unproblematic sequence of stages in The Stages of Growth. A Non-Communist Manifesto (Rostow 1960) with *The End Of History* (Fukuyama 1992) has graduated into the closure of all alternative ideologies and paradigms. Development theory has become the prescription of one principle for the entire globe. That principle usually remains unnamed in its practical application: MNCs are to bring that principle to fruition.

On a broad canvas, I intend to outline a number of ideas and to question the accepted wisdom. In the first place I shall argue that the transformative power of capitalism as such has lost much of its drive. In the second place, among others drawing from an earlier study on MNCs in India, I shall look at the record in some of the fields where MNCs are supposed to help bring about development. In the third place, briefly, I shall argue that the overall failure of MNCs, as established in the first and second section, has to be located in the new dominant mode of capital investment which has moved away from industrial capital into financial capital, the bankification of the world system.[3]

Transformative power

The common factor, and the explanatory factor, underlying the genesis and the continued existence of the Third World, is the colonial past.[4] The appearance of

---

2. Wertheim (1997) has introduced the interesting analogy of a chess grandmaster who tells his pupils not really to do what he teaches them, but actually to observe what he himself does and operate accordingly. In other words, the policy prescriptions are adopted less in the western world than in the developing countries under the umbrella of the Structural Adjustment Policy.
3. For the terminology I am indebted to Fidel Castro who used it in his speech at the New Delhi session as the out-going chairman of the Movement of Non-Aligned Countries in 1981.

the colonial powers in quite a few countries which had reached a reasonable level of development – reasonable at least in comparison with the European countries of that epoch – had a devastating effect on the local industries and on the regional trading networks. Burgeoning local artisanal production became liquidated (for example the mousseline in Bengal), a balanced trading network was replaced by a Western surplus realization mechanism (for example textiles into India, opium into China and spices, tea and bullion into England), and agriculture was destabilized into a plantation and tax endeavour. Entire populations with an intricate social and economic network were decimated (as in Latin America), packed off into overseas slave trade (as in Africa) or internally shifted into plantation territory (see Wolf 1982:129-261; Hobsbawm 1969). The recollection of the genesis of colonialism helps us to remember that in this first phase of 'globalization' the asymmetrical world structure came into being. Aided by the resource inflow from the colonized world, England – and later other European countries – could start on its industrial revolution and could start structuring the world division of labour in the interests of its pattern and needs of industrialization. Colonial expansion and economic retardation in the conquered world went hand in hand (Bagchi 1982).

Industrialization which much later entered the colonialized countries (by and large not earlier than the beginning of the 20th century) was initiated by foreign companies, either alone or in association with local brokers as indigenous partners. By that time, industrialization had passed from its localized, competitive 'manufacturing' stage to the industrial stage, and from a broad-based competitive form of capitalism into a monopoly stage in which the scale of capital investment and technology and the external economies changed the parameters. Probably the most important consequence, more important than the foreign control, was the fact that the broad-based competitive and labour-intensive system had been bypassed. A lopsided development, rather than development of underdevelopment, was the outcome.

The optimal process of integration of the small-scale production (and consumption) market in a centralizing and concentrating industrial process presupposes a gradual evolution. Such a gradual evolution, as a consequence of the predatory usurpation of the indigenous economy, was pre-empted. The ensuing disconnection of the efficient, capital-intensive and high-income industries from the vast hinterland of poverty and inefficient, labour-intensive small-scale industries was reinforcing a dual structure. The typical South-American city with its sky-scrapers and urban highways and with its *favelas* and *barracos* is at the same time a metaphor and an illustration of lopsided development. Islands of modern-scale and big-scale investments thrived on and co-existed with tradi-

---

4. We are aware that formally colonialism in Latin America had ended by the end of the nineteenth century, and that some countries have never been colonized, but even if and when colonialism came to an end, neo-colonialism continued to keep the politically independent countries, economically and financially in a state of dependency and/or marginality.

tional ways of life and traditional modes of production. The process of globalization appears to have reinforced the marginalization and exclusion. "There is no doubt", as an IMF study (Slaughter and Swagel 1997: 1 and 4) has mentioned, "that globalization has *coincided* with higher unemployment among the less skilled and with widening income inequalities... We might have expected trade liberalization to boost the demand for unskilled labor and raise unskilled wages, but in fact the opposite has happened in some developing countries." The lagging demand for consumer goods on the internal market has been a direct consequence and the further cause of an anaesthetized capitalist structure.[5]

The theorizing on the mode of production discussion in agriculture, and on the articulation with the world economy which preoccupied many discussions in the 1970s has a strong empirical ally in history. Both long-term historical trends and the defining elements of the present epoch do suggest a weakening pull of transformative capitalism. Over the last 200 years, capitalism may have extended its influence over much of the world, and may have undermined the social and economic staying power of feudalism but, in terms of revolutionizing the productive activities, in the primary and especially in the secondary sector, it has failed in many respects.

Long-term development, in spite of positive departures in a number of developing countries, presents a conspicuous picture: the Third World is falling ever further behind. Whereas the per capita income in the OECD countries between 1960 and 1990 rose from $1,400 to $16,000, in the developing countries, it rose from $130 to $700 on an average. It has been calculated that the latter territory in 1850 accounted for 65% of the world income; the share had gone down to around 30% in 1950 and to around 20% in 1970. Even on the basis of the real GNP, the local purchasing power GNP, the share of developing countries has dropped from 17% to 15% between 1960 and 1990 (various issues of the World Bank Development Report and the UNDP Human Development Report).

The long-term trend conjures up the image of a contest between a racing car and a bicycle. The cycle track, unlike the racing circuit, although occasionally passing by modern building and factories, is uneven, full of potholes and unguarded crossings. The developing countries are expected, more or less on their own, to accomplish the transition to a 'developed' industrial society, to become competent and qualified competitors in the world arena.

If this is the state of affairs, what great message or theory is promised for the years to come? Development is occurring in an era that has substantially different features to the era of European industrial development, from the second half of the 18th century through the first half of the 20th century. Some of the messages have been summarized by Gunnar Myrdal in his authoritative work *Asian Drama*. The transition, moreover, in view of the features associated with globali-

---

5. See e.g. Prabhat Patnaik (1995:137) in a perceptive article elaborating on the essential role of the state in widening the market within the particular context of a constricted market, and also Laclau (1971) in his seminal contribution on the articulation of modes of production.

zation, has to be achieved in a much shorter period than it took for Europe to move from the industrial revolution to its present monopoly stage.

Only a few countries seem to have succeeded. Even those countries that moved onto a fast track – the reference here is mainly to the Tigers and Dragons in East Asia – have encountered serious problems in sustaining the transition. The less favourable conditions in comparison with the European transition, include the crystallized global power structure with a definite subordinate position for developing countries: financially, commercially, technologically, military, etc. Many countries are no match for the size and influence of MNCs.[6]

Changing context

In contrast with the parameters under which Europe affected its transition, the Third World is faced with restricted access. The access to natural resources is limited; even its own resources are often in foreign hands. Access to finances is limited and a source of further haemorrhage through severe debt. The international division of labour, despite laudable departures by a few industrial sectors in some countries, too often keeps developing countries tied to their traditional monocropping and specialized exports. Export markets are fairly protected, by policy measures or otherwise. Population surplus cannot be shipped to foreign countries to be colonized. Even in the field of human development, which is a necessary basis for industrial development, progress is slow. Many countries in Asia and Africa have not as yet reached the standards that South Korea had reached in the mid-1950s. Progress, particularly since the 1980s, has been hampered by the withdrawal of money from human development expenditure to cover debt repayment. For example, Pakistan, in every way low on the list of human development, in 1995-96 had a total debt servicing (internal and external) amounting to 68.0% of current expenditure and 12.6% of GDP.

For the European, the US, the Japanese, the Russian, the Chinese and also the South Korean development models the supremacy of the state over civil society was typical, and also, with the exception of Korea, the strong position of the state in the world arena.[7] The states had the power to regulate the internal economy and to have the trade following the flag onto foreign markets. The states in the OECD countries, despite all public commitments to privatization and deregulation, have remained a strong intervening power on behalf of national economic

6.   The overwhelming asymmetry is illustrated by the fact that the biggest MNCs have a turnover which is higher than many of the biggest developing countries. There actually are only seven developing countries (China, Brazil, Mexico, Argentina, Republic of Korea, India and Indonesia) which are bigger than the turnover of the biggest MNC (General Motors). GM is bigger than Thailand, Ford Motors is bigger than Saudi Arabia, Mitsubishi is bigger than South Africa, Shell, Exxon and Toyota are by far bigger than for example Malaysia, Egypt, Pakistan, Peru and Bangladesh, etc. (UNDP 1999:32 and 185-6).

7.   Noam Chomsky (1993) has aptly called one of his books Year 501. The Conquest Continues, suggesting that what started with the conquest of Latin America by Columbus in 1491 has never ceased over the ensuing five centuries.

interests, and of the MNCs originating from their territory. On the other side, in the southern hemisphere, under the impact of structural adjustment, state resources and powers have been depleted to the extent that in many African countries particularly, the state has virtually ceased to exist as an instrument of development policy planning and implementation.

The power of the state in many developing countries is further emasculated by the multistructurality of the economy, and therefore also of the political system. In contrast with the rise of modern state power in Europe, where the entrepreneurial class established its dominance over the state and its institutions, the dominance of the entrepreneurial class in many developing countries is contested by pre-capitalist forces in agriculture and by non-resident investment and trading companies, and their collaborators. Political instability in conjunction with a reduction in national income and a rolling back of state support for public goods has ultimately led to a growing disorder and destabilization in many areas of the Third World.

Globalization and destabilization are coinciding phenomena; a causal relationship is probable (cf. George 1993, Walton and Seddon 1994). Destabilization can even be the consequence of an intentional process, through direct military intervention or back-up to military coups, through low-intensity warfare (through the support to armed rebellions), and generally through the effects of what generally has been called cultural imperialism. The latter, in the age of burgeoning satellite communication, has widened its scope exponentially. A Third World government, which wished to work on a sovereign economic policy, and which (re-) introduced measures that severely restrained the free access of western goods and investments, would certainly attract punitive measures, measures usually defended by a stereotyping of the human rights situation in those countries (as in Iran, Cuba, Libya, North Korea, Iraq, and Yugoslavia, etc.).

The asymmetry and the structurally different bases between 'North' and 'South' help to explain why, despite almost two centuries of post-colonialism in Latin America, half a century in Asia and somewhat less in Africa, a structural breakthrough towards a diversified and balanced (industrial) society has not occurred. The transformative power of capitalism seems to have waned. This appreciation is very much at variance with the triumphalist agenda, as it has been drawn by the advocates of the present monetarist and free trade policies. Introduced basically as an answer to problems of state finances and economic integration in the OECD countries in the late 1970s, the policy has been made to apply with a vengeance to developing countries. Its acceptance by many Third World governments, who had previously sworn by a different policy, came with the imposition of the Structural Adjustment Policy package. Participation in the world economy, the so-called outward orientation, would lead, it was promised, to unprecedented economic development, unlike the long periods of stagnation under inward orientation, import substitution and state activity in industry. Privatization and liberalization have become the core elements in the new policy.

They should help to channel investments by indigenous entrepreneurs and, in the framework of the globalizing world, by MNCs. The export-led development would follow in the wake of FDI, and, on the other hand, would accelerate further FDI.

FDI flows

The eulogies and jubilation of the 1980s, confirmed by the downfall of socialism in Eastern Europe, had lost much of their arrogance by the mid-1990s and started to lead to a new introspection. In the period of unrestrained globalization have MNCs been able to deliver the goods? Have they brought about economic development in the Third World and have they brought the Third World any closer to the standard of living in the rest of the *global village*?

Not without substance – statistics can be read differently – has Ankie Hoogvelt (1997:75) alluded to "a modestly thickening network of economic exchanges within the core, a significant redistribution of trade participation within the core, the graduation of a small number of peripheral nations with a comparatively small population base to "core" status, but above all to a declining economic interaction between core and periphery."

In the colonial period, right up to 1960, the Third World had received half of total direct investment flows. Thereafter, the share declined, and in an activist language which leaves no room for doubt, she alleges that "an ambitious net of capitalist catchment may have been thrown during the colonial era, but having caught the fish, it has pulled back and settled comfortably on the shores of a relatively small part of the world." (Hoogvelt 1997:76-7).

In the 1990s, private capital inflows, however, did increase. Foreign investments have been growing faster than the expansion in international trade. FDI in 1996 was close to $340 billion. In 1998, it reached $660 billion, and for the following year, the increase was calculated at around 25%. Its increase in the first half of the 1990s was twice as much as the increase in worldwide exports. At the same time, foreign investments in developing countries have witnessed a spurt in the 1990s to the extent that, for example in 1996, they attracted as much as 37% of FDI (see the long-term trend in Table 1). By the end of the century, however, it appears to have come down again to around one quarter of total FDI ($198 billion in 1999 on a total of $827 billion).

One explanation for the increase is the sourcing of production in a cheap labour environment, and, depending on the optimal production environment, the production of goods in a number of stages, passing through different countries. FDI was partly connected with the privatization of public enterprises and with portfolio investment. The attraction of some of these countries to foreign capital was also related to the expectations of large gains in the domestic stock markets from price appreciation and the higher real domestic rates of interest as compared to OECD countries. Avramovic (1992; see also Bello 1998) suggests that part of the capital inflows represented repatriation of capital held abroad by local nationals. This was very much the case with China.

Table 1   FDI Flows, 1965-1996 (Billion US $)

	1965-69	1970-74	1975-79	1980-83	1983-87	1988-92	1993-96
Industrial Countries	5.2	11.0	18.4	31.3	59	139	152.2
Developing Countries	1.2	2.8	6.6	13.4	18	37	79.8
Developing Countries Share of World Total	18.7	20.3	26.4	30.0	23.4	21.0	34.4

Source: *World Bank Development Report 1985:126 for the period up to 1983, and Goldar and Ishigami 1999 for the period thereafter.*

A closer look at the spread of FDI over the developing countries reveals that the investment flows initially went into Latin America and later into East Asia, particularly into China. In the early 1990s, just ten countries received three quarters of all transfers, with China alone accounting for close to 40%. The countries favoured for FDI (the Chinese coastal provinces, Thailand, Colombia, Taiwan, Malaysia, Turkey, Brazil, Mexico, and Indonesia) happen to be countries with established achievements of foreign trade and with a developed internal market. The reasonably sharp increase in FDI flows to the Third World obfuscates the fact that many countries were bypassed. Kevin Watkins (1997:12) argues that two thirds of the world population, including virtually each country in Africa, is virtually written off the map as far as foreign investment is concerned:

> "As investment activity becomes increasingly concentrated in this core group of countries, the idea that benefits will eventually trickle down through the global economic system appears at best far-fetched – and at worst an exercise in delusion. This has important implications. (FDI) is an important conduit for the transfer of new technologies. As international trade becomes more and more knowledge-intensive, access to these technologies become increasingly important to future competitiveness -and the difficulties faced by LDCs in attracting foreign investment threaten to exclude them from the major source of technological innovation, exacerbating their technological weakness in the process."

Griffin and McKinley (1993) have calculated that the richer developing countries (with an real per capita GDP of between $4,000 and $10,000), in 1990 received close to 60% of FDI investment in the Third World. The 51 poorest countries (with a per capita GDP of less than $1,500) received less than 5%. Much of this FDI went into Nigeria. Ethiopia, Zaire (now Democratic Republic of Congo), Myanmar, Vietnam, while other major countries, such as Pakistan, Bangladesh, Sri Lanka, and Nepal in South Asia, received merely a trickle (see Table 2).

Table 2 FDI to Developing and Transition Countries, 1997

Country or Combination of Countries	FDI (Billion US $)
Russia	13.2
Poland and Hungary	7.0
China	45.3
Brazil	16,3
Mexico	12.1
Argentina	6.3
Chile, Venezuela, Colombia, and Peru	15.8
Singapore, Korea, Taiwan, and Hong Kong	17.2
Indonesia and Malaysia	8.9
India	3.2
Subtotal: 85% of all FDI transfers to the region	
Pakistan	0.80
Bangladesh	0.15
Sri Lanka	0.14
Nepal	0.02

Source: UNDP 1999:27 and 44-52.

Countries that attract FDI may expect an outflow of remittances on account of profit repatriation. It is not unusual for developing countries to have a negative flow of resources, except for the years in which FDI has increased substantially. Griffin and McKinley (1993) have calculated that it is precisely in the poorest group of countries, that the ratio of profit remittances to FDI has been higher than in the richer developing countries, and that foreign direct investment "evidently, is not a mechanism for equalising physical capital among all countries." Table 3 indicates that, as a consequence, net FDI to the poorest countries in 1990 amounted to a meagre 0.01% of real GDP. It requires more than a strong imagination to defend the position that MNCs act as harbingers of economic development. Even in the richer developing countries, where the net FDI transfer was ten times higher, it amounted to hardly 0.10% of real GDP.

Table 3 Spread of FDI over the Developing Countries (DCs), 1990

	Share of Population	Share of Total Real GDP	Share in FDI	FDI per capita (US $)	FDI % of Real GDP	Net FDI as % of real GDP
Richer DCs	14.8%	35.9%	59.2%	22.03	0.42%	0.10%
Middle DCs	46.6%	46.7%	35.9%	4.22	0.19%	0.09%
Poor DCs	38.6%	17.4%	4.9%	0.70	0.07%	0.01%
	100%	100%	100%			

Note: Net FDI is calculated as the FDI minus repatriated as well as reinvested profits.
Source: Calculated from Griffin and McKinley 1993, various tables.

The strong state

The cheap and abundant labour supply in the (poorest) developing countries, it appears, is not a factor that induces MNCs to invest in the countries most in need of external stimuli. The adherence to a structural adjustment policy and to an outward orientation of the economy do not seem to help either. The countries that were doing well, including the People's Republic of China, happen to be countries that combine a high degree of economic stability and financial stability and, as such, offer an attractive environment for private investment flows (Wegener 1998). It is important to understand how such relative stability has come about. The countries concerned had achieved stability on the basis of a continuing strong position of the state in the economic regulation of the economy and on the basis of the creation of an internal market.[8]

Alice Amsden (1989:130; see also Hamilton 1984 and Lingle 1998) writes "In Korea, it was the government and not the market mechanism which took the central decisions in the allocation of resources and the stimulation of private industry." The basis for the Korean transition was laid by the radical land reforms, in conjunction with a military dictatorship[9] and massive supplies of foreign aid in the 1950s and 1960s, for obvious geo-political reasons. The leading role of the state, institutionalized through its strategic position in the *chaebol*, the South Korean corporate houses, and the subordinate role of foreign enterprises have remained an essential feature of the South Korean economy, both in the initial stages and in the maturing period.

The Korean success story, it should be added, was very much stimulated by the export drive which started from the late 1960s onwards, i.e. after the period when the strategy of import substitution and the creation of an indigenous market had come to a close. The export drive materialized in no small measure because of the US policy of subcontracting in the production chain for which attractive tax rebates were available. Such sub-contracting on its own may not have generated industrial growth. The international subcontracting, also referred to as 'offshore assembly', according to a World Bank study (World Bank

8. It may be recalled that the World Bank (World Development Report 1987) had forcefully argued that outward orientation did pay off in terms of higher investment, higher output and higher exports. In its typology, strongly outward orientation was considered synonymous with the acceptance of the global liberal and privatized economy, and did make countries grow stronger than moderately outward oriented countries and then inward oriented countries. Its listing of the strongly outward oriented countries was statistically unreliable (it contained only four countries: South Korea, Taiwan, Singapore and Hong Kong) and could lead the argument the other way round. The countries which had done reasonably well, and which on that basis had achieved a fair amount of outward linkages, happen to be countries which erected a state-protected import-substitution industry.
9. Robert Wade (1990) reminds us that Syngman Rhee and Chiang Kai-shek had the necessary state power, supported by American military might, to implement harsh measures and eliminate the feudal and parasitic elements in the economy. Singapore and Hong Kong also had authoritarian regimes. This was also the case where countries had done fairly well in a later period (Indonesia, Thailand, Malaysia, and of course China and Vietnam).

Report 1987:47), 'is akin to the putting-out system' in pre-industrial England, linking at that time the capitalist with the pre-capitalist sector. It is an unreliable and unenviable position to be in, dependent on an oligopolist demand side. If thriving under amenable conditions, it could lead to full-fledged capitalism; if not, as it was argued in Sweezy et al. (1957), it could also lead to a solidification of the old society. If indeed offshore assembly, outsourcing, relocation, etc. by MNCs are merely putting-out exercises, then it could be explained why, despite decades of post-colonial opportunities, barely any development has occurred and the transition has been a painstakingly lopsided affair.[10]

Three caveats have to be added to the role of MNCs and the process of glo- balization in the ostensible success story of East Asia. In the first place, exports were not an MNC-driven affair, although MNCs did contribute to exports, and were expected to do so under the investment licence obligations. In the second place, the end of the containment policy for the time being has deprived many Third World countries of western aid and trade concessions. While in the 1960s and 1970s, the influence of the western countries, and of their MNCs, was con- tested by the actual (and potential) power of the Soviet Union and China on the one hand and the fairly influential Non-Aligned Movement on the other hand, the end of the millennium witnessed the imposition of NATO power. Naked political might may be in the process of being substituted for economic aid that was essential during the days of the domino theory.[11] In the third place, exports by the Four Tigers in East Asia, and later by the Dragons in South-East Asia, could thrive under optimal conditions in the world economy. Apart from the buoyancy of the western economies, which lowered the need for protecting their markets and its industries from untoward Third World competition, the manu- factured export potential of developing countries was limited. William Cline (1982) has calculated that if the East Asian model of the 'Gang of Four' were to be generalized among developing countries, there would be a seven-fold increase in imports originating from the Third World. This would amount to as much as 61% of OECD imports, and even to 74% in the case of the USA. Cline (1992:88-9) therefore concludes that the generalization of the model would result in untenable market penetration into industrial countries:

---

10. Paul Baran's diagnosis of the pathology seems to have come through with the passing of time. He isolated monopoly industry as an essential feature of the morphology of backwardness, extending the merchant phase of capitalism by obstructing the transition of capital and men from the sphere of circulation to the sphere of production. Capitalism in the developing countries henceforth had a twisted track: 'Having lived through all the pains and frustrations of childhood, it never experien- ced the vigor and exuberance of youth, and began displaying at an early age all the grievous featu- res of senility and decadence. To the deadweight of stagnation characteristic of pre-industrial society was added the restrictive impact of monopoly capitalism (Baran 1962:210).

11. Development aid, it should be remembered, has never been as low as in the 1990s. The pious com- mitment made at the beginning of the first development decade in 1970 to commit 1% of GNP, has never been fulfilled by the OECD cluster of countries. Effective allocation of the US, the UK and Germany in 1997, as per the OECD, DAC statistics, was as low as 0.10 %, 0.28 % and 0.31 % respec- tively. The OECD average amounted to 0.27 % only.

"These findings suggest it would be inadvisable for authorities in developing countries to rely in their long-term plans upon the same kind of export results that have been obtained by the four East Asian countries... without provoking protectionist response ruling out its implementation. Elevator salesmen attach a warning label that their product is safe only if not over-loaded by too many passengers at one time; advocates of the East Asian export model would do well to attach a similar caveat to their prescription."

OECD market penetration from developing economies could be somewhat more palatable if performed by Western MNCs and indirectly benefiting Western economies, but this does not seem to be on the agenda, except for agricultural and mining products. The widespread belief that product market integration will lead to more imports from developing countries has caused some concerns because of their expected impact on employment levels in the advanced econo-mies. The assumption that the corporate sector strives to relocate production to low-wage countries, however, does not reflect the real picture: "these beliefs appear to be at odds with the empirical evidence that globalization has only a modest effect on wages, employment, and income inequality in the advanced economies" (Slaughter and Swagel 1997:11). The modest effect follows from the limited market penetration in the OECD by Third World manufactured prod-ucts.

Indeed, the cheapness of labour in developing countries as such is not a major consideration for relocating production to developing countries. The poorest countries, with indeed by far the lowest wages levels, hardly attract any FDI. Why, then, did MNCs decide to invest in some developing countries and not in others? The conclusion in the World Development Report 1985 (*International Capital and Economic Development:* 129) states it clearly: "Countries with large internal markets and import-substituting strategies are among those that have received the largest amount of direct investment." In other words: "(MNCs) are usually attracted to invest abroad by a country's natural resources or its favourable economic environment.... One common motive for a company to undertake foreign investment is a threat to an existing export market" (ibid: 125).

The sequencing in the process suggests that MNCs enter when internal industrial development has progressed in such fields and to such a degree that the market, moreover an expanding market, was being secured by indigenous producers. The relocation of investments of the take-over of a local firm became the modus operandi through which the MNC could gain a guaranteed access to the local market.

Basic problems

Development, in its common meaning, involves a multistructural process with a solution to at least four basic problems: the generation of means of investment, the integration of diverse sections of the economy in a forward and backward functionality, the productive use of a growing magnitude of labour market entrants and the modernization of the production process. While this appears to have happened in East Asia, the replicability in other areas of the world seems questionable. Unfortunately, there is too little empirical backstopping available to consider the case. In a study on India in the 1980s, much in line with what Kidron (1965) had established earlier, we came to a fairly negative conclusion on the role of MNCs originating from one country (Shell, Unilever, Lipton, Philips, Akzo, etc., all having their headquarters in the Netherlands). Summarizing the main result of the study (see Lieten 1987), it can be stated that MNCs made hardly any contribution to solving the four basic problems mentioned above.

The import of capital was much less than the yearly exports of profits and royalties; further investment was financed through capital drawn from the local capital market and from re-invested profits; the taxes on profit were low. The operations of the MNCs, moreover, cost the country dearly in terms of a negative trading balance, a balance which grew more negative as the process of liberalization gathered pace after 1980. The MNC exports, it should be added, were to a significant extent traditional export products, such as carpets, shirts, and shrimps. The MNCs were weak in developing backward linkages, except for the period up to 1980 when the Government of India implemented an import substitution regime that compelled the companies to look for alternative supplies on the national market. No impulse was given to the solution of the unemployment. Actually, the opposite happened: the work force over the years, despite a solid increase in production, stagnated and in some cases even dwindled. Jobless growth turned out to be the key element in the behaviour of the MNCs, and, it should be added, in the pattern of industrialization that was associated with India's shift from a relative sovereign economic system to involvement in globalization. As a consequence of structural adjustment policies from 1990 onwards, government corporations started to size down the number of labourers. As such, job growth in the state-led manufacturing sector was 53% from 1977 up to 1990, to be diminished with 12% up to 1996. Employment in the private corporate sector on the other hand grew with only 33% over the entire two decades.

Indian industry presents a classic example of jobless growth. The insistence by the IMF on the implementation of the what is known as the exit-policy (the licence to fire workers) will find more industrial workers unemployed. The insistence on privatization, carried out with a vehemence by the 'Hindu nationalist' government, will have a similar effect.

MNCs are expected to bring in new technologies and new production lines that are to form the basis for the ensuing growth in the consumer sector. Investment in the basic goods industries in India has, by and large, been the work of the government and of indigenous private initiatives. In one field, the MNCs have made a contribution. MNCs turn out to be mainly active in the consumer goods industry, frequently in competition with local industries and acquiring them in the process, as happened for example in the soft drinks, the bulb, and cosmetics industries, and increasingly also with the software industry. The MNCs that had been studied were active in those product lines catering to the taste and the purse of the modernizing middle classes. Most MNCs in LDCs operate in these product lines. Cosmetics, television, music systems, tea, jam, and ice-cream, etc. may have gratified many Indians with bulging purses, and some who did not have the money to spare. However, neither the product range nor the technology embodied in them can be considered as contributing to 'development' and to a transitional breakthrough of a 'developing country' (see Lieten 1987 for a more comprehensive treatment).

It has been argued that India had a restrictive, inward-looking regime, and that, therefore, the economic breakthrough could not come about. Beginning around 1980 with the first IMF, and speeded up with the radical changes in economic policy around 1990, India opted for an export-led and foreign-capital-driven development. The fruits of such development should have become visible, but they have not. The Indian upper middle classes have gained access to such luxury gadgets associated with a western life style as cars, air-conditioning, cable television, cellular phones, computers, and king-size cigarettes. The goods remain by and large restricted to a one-digit percentage of the population. The vast majority of the population has hardly seen progress. GNP growth patterns have remained at the levels of the 1960s and 1970s, occasionally going up, as they did over the last two decades, attracting eulogies for the policy of liberalization, and then falling again, as they had done in the past. While on the one hand growth has not picked up, on the other hand, the government has lost much of its power to direct investments into development-promoting and socially-necessary product lines. It has also lost much of the power to check regional imbalances and to fight poverty. The skyscraper economy was established by the end of the millennium.

Concluding remarks

The free access of MNCs to developing countries is a direct consequence of the participation in the globalizing economy that again, more often than not, has been linked to the negotiated agreement on a structural adjustment policy. MNCs could now, more than ever before in the post-colonial period, be expected to start operating on a level field, and to impart development, unfettered by restraining and distorting government policies. It has also been noted, however, that globalization has not led to an increasing share of investments and trade going to the Third World.

Various reasons can be suggested for why this has not happened. The important point in the mean time is that is has not happened, and that MNCs, despite the gigantic resources at their disposal, have not been a major player in the development of Third World countries, at least not in a positive sense. Where a development transition has taken place, the policy has been based on the generation of internal resources and on a strategic role for the state. Such a transition has been facilitated by the conducive geo-political context of containment. The MNCs have not been the battering ram with which an inhospitable environment, much more inhospitable in comparison with the onset of industrialism in the western countries, could have been moulded. As an additional disconcerting variable, moderate to severe debt has touched virtually all developing countries. The unprecedented flow of resources from the developing countries into the core areas of the world economy in the wake of these debts has made development around the turn of the century into an even more painful, slower, lopsided and chaotic process than it otherwise already would have been. MNCs are waiting in the wings, themselves hampered by the debt crisis. They are unable to effect the transition in scores of countries where the economic, financial, and political conditions are not amenable to the strategies of the corporate sector.

The picture which has emerged from this chapter, and which purposely has skipped over the positive impact which multinationals may have in specific countries and in specific fields, brings into focus the long-term dynamics. The long-term constraints and disabilities by multinational corporations to cause a structural break in the asymmetric world structure, which has emerged with the onset of colonialism, have been addressed. The evidence suggests clearly that the constraints and disabilities have continued to impede the process of transition from underdevelopment to development in a sizeable area of the Third World.

References

Amin, Samir (1996) "On the Origins of the Economic Catastrophe in Africa". In: Sing Chew and Robert Denmark, Robert *The Underdevelopment of Development*, Thousand Oaks, Sage, pp. 200-218.

Amsden, Alice (1989) *Asia's Next Giant: South Korea and Late Industrialisation*, New York, Oxford University Press.

Avramovic, Dragoslaw (1992) *Developing Countries in the International Economic System*, UNDP, Occasional Paper No. 3.

Bagchi, Amiya Kumar (1982) *The Political Economy of Underdevelopment*, Cambridge, Cambridge University Press.

Baran, Paul (1962) *Political Economy of Growth*, New York, Monthly Review Press.

Barratt Brown, Michael (1974) *The Economics of Imperialism*, Harmondsworth, Penguin.

Bello, Walden (1998) "The End of a Miracle", *Multinational Monitor*, Volume XIX, Nos 1 & 2.

Buckley, Peter and Clegg, J. (1991) *Multinational Enterprises in Less Developed Countries*, London, Macmillan.

Buckley, Peter and Mucchielli, J. (1997) *Multinational Firms and International Relocation*, Cheltenham, Elgar.

Calvo, G.A. et al. (1998) "Inflow of Capital to Developing Countries in the 1990s". In: Milner, Chris, *Developing and Industrializing Countries*, Cheltenham, Elgar.

Claesens, S. (1998) "The Emergence of Equity Investment in Developing Countries: Overview". In: Milner, Chris, *Developing and Industrializing Countries* Cheltenham, Elgar.

Chomsky, Noam (1993) *Year 501. The Conquest Continues*, London, Verso.

Cline, William R. (1982) "Can the East Asian Model of Development be Generalized?", *World Development* X, No 2, pp. 81-90.

Dasgupta, Biplab (1998) *Structural Adjustment, Global Trade and New Political Economy of Development*, New Delhi, Vistaar.

Dixon, Chris, et al. (1986) *Multinational Corporations and the Third World*, London, Croom Helm.

Dunning, John (1981) *International Production and the Multinational Enterprise*, London, Allen and Unwin.

Dunning, John (1992) *Multinational Enterprises and the Global Economy*, Wokingham, Addison-Wesley.

Fukuyama, Francis (1992) *The End of History and of Last Man*, London, Verso.

Griffin, Keith and McKinley, Terry (1993) *A New Framework for Development Cooperation*, UNDP, Occasional paper No. 11.

Goldar, Bishwanath and Ishigami, Etsuro (1999) "Foreign Direct Investment in Asia", *Economic and Political Weekly*, Vol XXXIV, No 22, M50.

Hamilton, Clive (1984) "Industrialisatie in de Vier Kleine Tijgers van Oost-Azie", *Derde Wereld*, December 1984, pp. 68-94.

Helleiner, G.K. (1972) *International Trade and Economic Development*, Harmondsworth, Penguin.

Hobsbawm, Eric (1969) *Industry and Empire*, Harmondsworth, Penguin.

Hoogvelt, Ankie (1997) *Globalization and the Postcolonial World. The New Political Economy of Development*, Houndmills, MacMillan.

Hymer, Stephen (1976) *The International Operations of National Firms*, Cambridge, Massachusetts, MIT Press.

Jalée, Pierre (1968) *Le Tiers Monde dans l'economie mondiale. L'Exploitation imperialiste*, Paris, Francois Maspero.

Jenkins, R. (1987) *Transnational Corporations and Uneven Development*,London, Methuen.

Kidron, Michael (1965) *Foreign Investments in India*, London, Oxford University Press.

Kitching, Gavin (1989) *Development and Underdevelopment in Historical Perspective. Populism, Nationalism and Industrialization*, London, Routledge.

Krugman, P. and Benables, A.J. (1998) "Globalization and the Inequality of Nations". In: Oxley, Joanna and Yeung, Bernard, *Structural Change, Industrial Location and Competitiveness*, Cheltenham, Elgar.

Laclau, Ernesto (1971) "Feudalism and Capitalism in Latin America", *New Left Review*, No. 66, pp. 19-40.

Lal, Sanjay (1995) *Changing Perceptions of Direct Foreign Investment in Development*. Antwerp, Institute of Policy Management, University of Antwerp, Paper 1995, E.19.

Levy-Livermore, Amnon, (ed.) (1998) *Handbook on the Globalization of the World Economy*, Cheltenham, Elgar.

Lieten, G.K. (1987) *The Dutch Multinational Corporations in India*, New Delhi, Manohar.

Lingle, Christopher (1998) *The Rise and Decline of the Asian Century. False Starts on the Path to the Global Millennium*, Tauris.

Michalet, Charles-Albert (1985) *Les Multinationals face à la crise*, Geneva.

Myrdal, Gunnar (1972) *Asian Drama. An Enquiry into the Poverty of Nations*, Harmondsworth, Penguin.

Owen, Roger and Sutcliffe, Ben (1972) *Studies in the Theory of Imperialism*, London, Longman.

Patnaik, Prabhat (1995) *Whatever Happened to Imperialism and Other Essays*, New Delhi, Tulika.

Radice, Hugo (1975) *International Firms and Modern Imperialism*, Harmondsworth, Penguin.

Reiffers, Jean-Louis, et al. (1982) *Transnational Corporations and Endogenous Development. Effects on Culture, Communication, Education, and Science and Technology*, Paris, Unesco.

Rostow, Walt Whitman (1960) *The Stages of Growth. A Non-Communist Manifesto*, Cambridge, Cambridge University Press.

Slaughter, Mathew J. and Swagel, Phillip (1997) *Does Globalization Lower Wages and Export Jobs?* Washington, IMF, Economic Issues No. 11.

Sweezy, Paul, et al. (1957) *The Transition from Feudalism to Capitalism. A Symposium*, Patna, Sanskriti Publications (a reprint of *Science and Society*, New York).

UNDP (1999) *Human Development Report*, New York.

United Nations (1988) *Transnational Corporations in World Development: Trends and Prospects*, New York.

Vernon, Raymond (1973) *Sovereignty at Bay. The Multinational Spread of US Enterprises*, Harmondsworth, Penguin.

Vernon, Raymond (1977) *Storm over Multinationals: the Real Issues*, London, Macmillan.

Vernon, R. (1998) *Transnational Corporations: Where Are They Coming From, Where Are They Headed?* In: Egelhoff, William (ed.), *Transforming International Organizations*, Cheltenham, Elgar.

Wade, Robert (1990) *Governing the Market: Economic Theory and the Role of Government in East Asian Industrialisation*, Princeton, Princeton University Press..

Wallerstein, Immanuel (1996) "Underdevelopment and its Remedies". In: Sing Chew and Denmark, Robert, *The Underdevelopment of Development*, Thousand Oaks, Sage, pp. 355-365.

Walton, John and Seddon, David (1994) *Free Markets and Food Riots. The Politics of Global Adjustment*, Oxford, Blackwell.

Watkins, Kevin (1997) *Globalization and Liberalisation: Implications for Poverty Distribution and Inequality*, UNDP, Occasional Paper 32.

Wegener, R. (1998*) Private Kapitalzuflüsse in die dynamischen Länder Asiens*, Berlin, Deutsches Institut für Entwicklungspolitik.

Wertheim, Wim (1997) *Third World Whence and Whither*, Amsterdam, Spinhuis.

Wolf, Eric (1982) *Europe and the People Without History*, Berkeley, University of California Press.

Globalization, Sustainable Development and Environment: A Balancing Act

M. A. Mohamed Salih

Introduction

The current debate on globalization and the environment has revolved around four major themes, all informed by the multitude and complexity of a set of environmental concerns dubbed, even by the most conservative commentators, as symptoms of a global environmental crisis.[1] From climate change to biodiversity loss and from air pollution to fresh water contamination, the symptoms of a global environmental crisis have often been treated from an essentialist position. This theme acknowledges the significance of the natural interdependence of the environmental life support system (air, water, and soil) on a global scale. To that extent, the most common theme in the debate on globalization and the environment is that, if it is environmental then it must imply global consequences on the human and non-human world. This assumption implies that the impact of any large-scale development interventions (industrialization, raw material extraction and processing, mega-irrigation projects, timber logging, mining, fossil energy exploration, production and processing, and consumption, etc.) in the environment would influence the quality of the environmental life support system. Such large-scale environmental interventions are part of an ecological modernization process that has contributed to an unprecedented modification of the global environment. In essence ecological modernization carries the insignia of globalization and its capacity to produce momentous transformation in the way human lives are ordered and reordered, which in turn results in further modifications of the global environment.[2] Ecological modernization can therefore be

---

1. Tolba M. and El Kholy (1992) *The World Environment 1972 – 1992*: Two Decades for Challenge, provide a comprehensive review of the environmental problems considered global by the United Nations Environmental Programme (UNEP). These include climate change, biodiversity loss, population growth, fresh water pollution/contamination, air pollution, greenhouse effect, deforestation, land degradation/desertification.
2. Optimists such as Hannigan (1995:184) argue that ecological modernization and technological advancement will contribute to the annexation of time and space on a global scale through the dematerialization of production (virtual work-place etc), reduce transport and allow people the opportunity to work at home.

defined as a manifestation of a complex and far-reaching development or process or modernization in one of its most common interactions with the natural environment.

If the use and abuse of technology is an inseparable part of development and environmental modification then it is only logical that technology has also been conceived as the saviour from global environmental destruction. In the process, the quest for ecological modernization becomes a global imperative resulting in ecological damage as well as ecological repair.[3] Second, ecological modernization is associated with high per capita energy consumption and, also as a result of industrialization, the penetration of technology into almost every aspect of life, from household appliances to transport and the manufacturing of goods and services or development redefined as ecological modernization.

Paradoxically, under the ecological modernization project, a major reduction in energy consumption (the main contributor to air pollution, climate change, ozone layer depletion, and greenhouse effect, etc) may not be possible without major alterations to today's lifestyles. The view that technological advancement and raw material fabrication are our potential saviours from an impending global environmental crisis is not supported by the current expansion of new environmentally harmful products.[4] The implications of such developments for ecological modernization are immense, particularly in the event of further compression of the environmental space and the increase of ecological debt incurred by the industrially advanced world.

The second theme in the debate is more concerned with the environmental consequences of the production of the goods and services required for the satisfaction of an increasing world population. The views expressed by social scientists attached to the Club of Rome are commonly known. For instance, Meadows et al. (1972) argue that if the current trends of industrialization, population growth, and depletion of non-renewable natural resources continue unchecked, the earth would reach *The Limits to Growth* within a hundred years. What is needed to reverse these trends; not only to curb population growth, but also to work towards a sustainability revolution (Meadows et al. 1995)? Global economic growth would then set the limits to the capacity of the environment to provide the raw materials and energy resources needed to maintain economic growth. Generally, this theme is common in multilateral environmental initiatives and the manner in which they have responded to what has been dubbed the global environmental crisis. These initiatives are exemplified by a long sequence of global environmental conferences considered by the development lobby as an anti-

3. Beck (1993) in *Risk Society* and Giddens (1996) in "Urbanism, Globalization and Environmental Politics".
4. For more on this refer to Tylor (1970) *The Doomsday Book* and Ehrlich and Ehrlich (1996) *Betrayal of Science and Reason: How Anti-environmental Rhetoric Threatens Our Future.*

climax to civilizational progression.[5] Within this theme, the Group of Lisbon (1995:xvii), takes the view that the key to responding to global environmental change is not one of merely getting 'carrying capacity' right, but that "the response to present and immediate future needs and opportunities demands a system of co-operative governance. Only by linking the multitude of socio-economic networks at various territorial levels around visible targets and common objectives can one realistically hope to achieve social justice, economic efficiency, environmental sustainability, and political democracy, as well as avoid the many possible sources (economic, political, ethnic) of global implosion".

The most doomsday-like scenario treats exponential development as a threat to long-term human survival in a healthy environment and transforms the daily struggles for survival to struggles over progress. This possible scenario would result in a global implosion summed up by Beck's (1995) risk society, characterized by uncertainty and lack of control over its future destiny. In the risk society: 1) Environmental hazards are global and cannot be delimited spatially, temporally, or socially; they encompass nation-states, military alliances, and all social classes, and, by their very nature, present wholly new kinds of challenge to the institutions designed for their control and the legitimatization of their anonymity. 2) The established rules of attribution and liability – casualty and guilt – break down. 3) The hazards can only be minimized by technological means, never entirely eliminated. The technocracy of hazard squirms in the thumbscrews of the safety guarantees which it is forced to impose on itself. 4) The lack of provision for catastrophe prevention or prediction plainly exposes the paradigm error; the bewitchment of reason caused by the false belief that the 20th century was only a continuation of the 19th. The security system, which anticipates social provisions for the worst conceivable case, brokedown with the advent of large-scale (nuclear, chemical, ecological, genetic) hazards. Although Beck has moderated his position vis-à-vis the risk society thesis, it still poses some serious questions concerning what type of development developing countries should pursue.

The third theme is advocated by a large number of multilateral institutions and social scientists, mostly pro-South in their views on the relationship between the developing countries and the dominant global economic forces.[6] Their basic argument is that the development of globalization and the liberalization of trade and finance are not environmentally neutral, and often do not oper-

---

5. For example, the Stockholm Conference on the Human Environment was the first global conference of the environment followed by the United Nations Conference on Environment and Development (UNCED). These conferences eventually resulted in the global proclamation of the Bruntland Report entitled Our Common Future (1987) and Agenda 21 (1992). The Earth Summit (1992) was followed by several global initiatives, all directly or indirectly related to Agenda 21. These include the Population Summit (Cairo 1994), the Social Development Summit (Copenhagen, 1995), the Women's Summit (Beijing (1996), and the Climate Change Summit (Tokyo, 1997).

6. Of particular relevance here is, among others, the work of Shiva (1993), Sachs (1993), Adams (1990), North (1995), Taylor and Thomas (1999).

ate in a world free of national and regional interests. The implication here is that the rich North is responsible for the bulk of global pollution. If that is the case, what is needed then is a differentiated rather than uniform approach to whether curbing economic growth should be adopted equally by poor and richer countries. Pro-South social scientists also place a larger proportion of the blame for the global environmental crisis on the countries of the North. For example, the South Commission (1990:218) argues that,

> The countries of the South are today victims of the delirious environmental effects of policies and patterns of development in the North. These include, such global phenomena as the thinning of the ozone layer, nuclear radiation, and the green house effect, as well as such direct acts as the dumping of hazardous wastes and the location of polluting industries in the South. Attempts by the developing countries to bring the global commons – in particular the oceans and outer-space – under effective international jurisdiction have been defeated in practice by the lack of co-operation of the developed countries.

On the other hand, social scientists of various radical environmental persuasions argue that, the global sustainable development movement usurps a neo-colonial ideology aim to frustrate the development of the South.[7] This view, however, is not new; it originated in historical materialism and Engels' (1940) thesis on the *Dialectics of Nature* and Marx's contribution to the relationship between the expansion of capitalism and the destruction of the natural environment.[8]

The fourth theme found expression in Agenda 21, as well as a variety of United Nations conventions, treaties, and declarations espouse, and a number of 'establishment' scholars who work within this dominant paradigm. The common view here is that global environmental protection could be realized by adopting sustainable development as a global ideal. As a global imperative, sustainable development is built around six axes: (i) reviving growth; (ii) changing the quality of growth; (iii) meeting essential needs for jobs, energy, water, and sanitation; (iv) conserving and enhancing the resource base; (v) reorienting technology and managing risk and (vi) merging environment and economics in decision-making.

The main thrust of sustainable development, therefore, is that global environmental protection and economic growth should proceed hand in hand. More importantly, sustainable development hinges on the premise that global environmental institutions and governance should manage global environmental problems. The creation of the Sustainable Development Commission and Global Environmental Facility (GEF), the Global Governance initiatives after the Earth

---

7. Among the authors who espouse this view are Rich (1994), Sachs (1994), Merchant (1994), Shiva, (1993), Agarwal and Narian (1991) and Redclift (1984).
8. The contemporary relevance of Marx and Engels to the political economy of natural resource is quite apparent, particularly in the work of Redclift (1984), Brookfield and Blaikie (1989), Merchant (1994).

Summit of 1992, are but a few pointers in the direction of creating a multi-layered integration of management of global environmental change and the economic, political and technological developments responsible of this change.[9]

Although some social scientists and activists were quick to dub sustainable development's emphasis on reviving growth as a contradiction in terms, others began the search for methods and theories that could reconcile economic growth and global environmental protection.[10] Some of the most stimulating research in this area is what Eckersley (1995:15) refers to as free market environmentalism, which conceives of sustainable development within the dominant free market paradigm. In this paradigm, nature itself is, to some extent, treated as a commodity subject to market principles linked to its ability to supply environmental goods and services.

However, for other social scientists such as Wilson and Bryant (1997:107-8), (i) the market attaches a commonly recognized economic value to environmental resources. This value is dependent on the importance of the resource in question to environmental managers. (ii) The market provides the means by which environmental resources can be exchanged. (iii) As a direct response to valuation and exchange, the market has a direct bearing on the operation of multi-layered environmental management. (iv) The market serves as an important means by which resource scarcity is regulated. (v) Externalities highlight what can be termed market failure; that is, that the market does not capture the full environmental implications of human-environmental interactions. Free market environmentalism has to deal with this not at a resource, sector or national level, but all of these levels as well as integrating them at global level.

Ironically, while the debate on the global nature of the environmental crisis continues, the constellation of the world political and economic order began to shift away from global hegemony of two superpowers to unipolarity. In Axford's (1995) words, "global hegemony has slipped beyond the capacity of any single state, thus ushering in the emergence of a truly global managerial entrepreneurial class whose transnational economic transactions are efficiently enhanced by global private banks, financial markets and corporations". The advocacy of a rather muted free market principles and trade in production, services, and finance, has also worked its way to replace the primes of exchange relations informed by the sovereignty of national economies controlled by the state. The global scale operations that have doubled the World trade in new pro-

---

9. Global Environmental Facility (GEF) and other financing arms of the World Bank were established as a result of the Earth Summit with the aim of disbursing funds for the protection of the global environment. According to *Our Global Neighbourhood* (1995:216) global environmental governance emphasises the need to put into action a global legal, intellectual and institutional groundwork for a concerted effort to achieve sustainable development.

10. For more on the views of social scientists who doubted the possibility of reconciling economic growth and global environmental protection see Adams (1990) *Greening Development: Sustainable Development in the South*, Redclift (1987) *Sustainable Development Exploring the Contradictions* and Rich (1995) *Mortgaging the Earth*.

duction materials in less than two decades could not have been possible without the formidable technological and organizational development. [11]

New trends in globalization, including robotization, the dematerialization of production (media and communication), and post-Fordism (franchising the great corporate conglomerations) are not environmentally neutral. The political economy of these new trends is exemplified by the structural power of mobile capital and private investment, which has contributed to the decline of the state and its ability to control economic activities and the factors of production, including environment and natural resources. Two observations merit some attention here: first, while the protection of the global environment requires a globally concerted action, the prevailing economic globalization and its manifestation in trade, the information revolution and the accompanying technological advancements are growth driven. Second, globalization is born in the womb of a neo-liberal ideology hostile to attempts aiming at market regulation or control over the new entrepreneurial class's capacity to expand production, extract materials and exploit the riches of nature wherever they prove profitable. The question that begs a serious answer is whether it is possible to reconcile the ethos of neo-liberal globalization and the imperative of global environmental protection.

While the introductory section of this chapter has been devoted to the environment-development nexus seen as a process of ecological modernization, the following section takes issue with the debate on globalization and the environment, with specific reference to the debate on free market environmentalism and its potential contribution to global environmental protection. The section argues that development research has, to some extent, not been able to cope with the enormity of the configuration of the intricate relationship between globalization, sustainable development, and the quest for economic growth.

Globalization and the environment

One of the questions we face is whether global resource competition for high and sustained growth would foster or hinder the realization of global projects such as free trade and global environmental protection. Is it practically possible to reconcile globalization, free trade, and global environmental protection? Even if it is possible to reconcile free trade and the environment protection on a global scale, what institutional mechanisms are needed to address these issues? In this respect, globalization and the environment can be explored by examining one of the most influential trends, which (if a perfect market ever existed) should ideally transform global trade and conversely the relationship between trade and environment in a globally open trade regime.

---

11. For more details and critical insights on this formulation of globalization see Hirst and Thompson (1996) *Globalization in Question: The International Economy and the Possibility of Governance.*

In essence, I argue that free market environmentalism is an extension of the ethos of neo-liberal globalization and therefore both treat global environmental protection as subservient to global capital flows and the expansion of trade and economic growth. However, paradoxically, the globalization of the environmental issues and the quest for free trade constitutes the foundation stone of open globalization, which, if properly implemented, would allow for greater solidarity of a disenfranchised and diverse environmental movement (Martinez and Guha 1997). This explains why all regional trading blocs have signed protocols and conventions, which have committed them to regional and global environmental protection laws.

However, there is no agreement as to the exact impact of the liberalization of trade and free market globalization on the environment. The anti free market lobby, including environmentalists, argue that trade liberalization is harmful to the environment because it puts more emphasis on growth and development at the expense of global environmental protection. They also argue for greater decentralization of economic and political activities to empower people and enable them to care for their local environments. Trade liberalization without proper environmental protection policies, legal instruments and economic incentives (or liabilities) often results in land degradation and environmental disasters in the marginal and fragile global commons. This will hold globalization responsible for the dangers that threaten our global future.[12]

In a globally free trade regime, one of the institutions that will have a direct effect on the environment is the World Trade Organization (WTO), which represents the triumph of the trade liberalization lobby in conceiving the General Agreement on Tariff and Trade (GATT). The WTO is hailed as the epitome of how trade liberalization should lead to growth and therefore generates financial resources, which could be utilized to protect the environment. The WTO aims to liberalize four areas of economic activity previously considered to be the exclusive domain of the national legislation. These are: (a) trade in services, (b) intellectual property rights, (c) international investment flows, and d) agriculture.[13]

The WTO presumes that, by concentrating resources within each country into the most productive and competitive sectors, (i) free trade will enable countries to maximize their competitive advantage; (ii) a globally increased trade is essentially good for development, and the more people trade, the better off they will be. Brack (1998:1) supports this view by arguing that,

---

12. For more details on this subject refer to Ekins (1995) Harnessing Trade to Sustainable Development, WWF (1996) *Trade Measures and Multilateral Environmental Agreements: Backwards or Forwards in the WTO?* and Daly (1996) *Free Trade, Capital Mobility and Growth versus Environment and Community*, Institute of Social Studies, The Hague.
13. For more on the debate on trade and the environment refer to Clark (1995) "Global Competition and Environmental Regulation: Is the Race to the Bottom Inevitable?", Kinerade (1995) "Towards Ecologically Sustainable Development: The Role and Shortcomings of the Market", Charnovitz (1994) *Free Trade, Fair Trade, Green Trade: Defogging the Debate*, and Brack (1998) *Trade and the Environment: Conflict or Compatibility.*

In principle, the pursuit of both (free trade and global environmental protection), are compatible. According to the theory of comparative advantage, trade allows countries to maximise output from a given input of resources – which is a movement in the direction of environmental sustainability. Furthermore, trade liberalisation can help to remove distortionary subsidies and pricing policies, improving efficiency of resource allocation, and can encourage the spread of environmentally friendly technology.

Other aspects of global trade and the environment are articulated by Junior and Welford (1997:138), who argue that trade and economic globalization have greatly expanded the opportunities for the rich to pass on their environmental burdens to the poor by exporting both waste and polluting factories. Trade has a secondary impact on issues of equity as it results in impacts (positive or negative) on poverty, health, employment, human rights, democracy, labour laws, and self-determination. I add to these two points, one aspect of globalization that may have some positive result on the environment.

The pro-free trade lobby's assumptions have been contested by environmentalists who argue defiantly that the nature of comparative advantage in a globalized world has more to do with absolute price advantage than differences in comparative advantage. For instance, although many developing countries have comparative advantage in the production of tropical crops such as bananas, tea, and coffee, they continue to decrease in the international market due to their weak bargaining position in the world economy. In Eckersley's (1995) words,

> One obvious objection to free market environmentalism is that full-scale privatisation of the commons is not possible. After all, many environmental assets (e.g. clean air) are public goods, which, by definition are not amenable to being captured, commodified and bought and sold (i.e. they are non-excludable and able to withstand non-rival consumption).

The difficulty of integrating all environmental goods and services into the market economy raises issues of internalizing externalities that are not amenable to economic valuation, as the case of clean air cited earlier.[14]

The meagre attention given to the environment in the GATT process would suggest that no or little value would be attached to the potential environmental destruction caused by excessive use of natural resources in response to such policies. This is particularly true for developing countries, which depend on primary commodity production which, in 1992, insisted on the inclusion of the environmental issues in the GATT process and negotiations. From an environmental point of view free trade and the race for comparative advantage will

---

14. The intricacy of the linkages between trade and environment have persuaded economists such as Bartelmus (1994) and Pearce et al. (1993) not to be immune from engagement in the debate on ethics, affection, recreation and human freedom

lower environmental standards for the sake of free trade rather than raise them. Article I of GATT rules out discrimination between trading partners. Articles III and XVI, by forbidding the use of trade subsidies or restrictions for environmental purposes, mean that GATT already has difficulty in acknowledging the legitimacy of trade restrictions (for instance, on polluting substances) in the pursuit of global environmental protection.

However, it is difficult to analyze the development of world trade and its consequences on the environment in isolation from its differential effects on local communities, states, and regional entities. Wilson and Bryan (1996) explored the interdependence of local, national, regional, and global trade transactions and illustrated that multi-layered trade operations would result in the shrinking of environmental space. Earlier Opschoor et al. (1994) concluded that the expansion of global trade operations has resulted in an increased ecological debt and the shrinking of the environmental space available for the maintenance of the global environmental life support system. This process contributes, according to Opschoor et al. (1994), to the shrinking of the environmental space and the increase of the ecological debt, i.e. an increased 'environmental reach' through far-reaching 'environmental foot steps'. A global condition in which the environmental space is shrinking at an accelerating rate is detrimental to the well-being of the industrial world as well as the developing world, where polluting industries have often been relocated in places of lax legal systems. The interdependence of the environmental life support system and its response to large-scale environmental damage or degradation, emanating from an increasing trade in primary products and goods and services, cannot be more revealing.

Is there a way out?

The picture that I have painted so far is a gloomy one in which global environmental actors as well as the development lobby seem to have been locked into a losing battle against the powerful tides of globalization and an impending environmental crisis. The question that follows is whether the social sciences have managed, somehow, to leave their imprints on the debate by explaining the 'social' and its relationship to 'nature' and how they influence each other on a global-scale and what policy issues have likewise preoccupied them. Social sciences have contributed to the debate in the field of environmental policies and respective institutional mechanisms responsible for the mitigation of global environmental problems. What can environmental policies and institutions deliver in such a situation that requires more than a balancing act, and what are their limitations? These are difficult questions to answer and are certainly beyond the scope of this chapter. However, I will attempt to delineate some of the main factors that influence global environmental policies and institutions and their response to the processes that simultaneously influence globalization and sustainable development.

Environmental policies are part of international policies. This was first defined by Vig (1999:17) as joint responses to common problems that two or more national governments work out with one another, often with the active participation of inter-governmental organizations and non-governmental organizations. In the field of international environmental policy, Vig defines them as ranging from broad policy declarations and informal agreements to highly articulated conventions and treaties. According to Vig (1999: Ibid),

> The range of international environmental policies currently in force is vast, covering protection of endangered plants and animals; protection against transboundary pollution of air, water, and soil; protection of the atmosphere against acidification, ozone depletion, and climate change; protection of the oceans against oils spills and the dumping of radioactive and other hazardous chemicals, pesticides, and hazardous wastes, measures to combat desertification; and protection of Antarctica.

There is no gainsaying that international environmental policies represent a direct response to the consequences of ecological modernization. On a global scale this can be seen in the expansion of Western consumption patterns and lifestyles that have subsequently strained the functioning of the fragile environmental life support system on which the production of globally consumed goods and services depend. However, international environmental policies require global environmental institutions with transnational mandates to safeguard the protection of the global commons.

The major institutions entrusted with the implementation of international environmental polices are the United Nations General Assembly (UNGA), the United Nations Environmental Programme (UNEP), the Commission on Sustainable Development (CSD), the Global Environmental Facility (GEF). The three Bretton Wood Institutions (the International Bank for Reconstruction and Development, the IMF, and the World Trade Organization) have adopted reforms in the face of strong criticism for pursuing economic missions in ways that have further aggravated environmental problems (Soroos 1999:47).
Soroos (1999:48) laments by conceding that

> It is difficult to conceive of circumstances in which states would be willing to relinquish or pool their sovereignty to substantially strengthen global institutions charged with mounting a more effective response to the deepening environmental crisis confronting humanity. If anything, there is growing public disillusionment with global institutions and policies in both industrial and developing countries because of their perceived failure to be responsive to local needs and preferences.

The international environmental policies and institutions together constitute a diverse body of global environmental governance. The strong and active presence of Bretton Wood institutions and their quest for the liberalization of the world economy elucidates that global environmental governance is part of the globalization process. If traced from an evolutionary perspective of sustainable development, the Earth Summit and Agenda 21 have laid the foundations for the advocacy of global environmental governance within the wider concept of global governance. According to these foundations, there is no single model, form, or institution of global governance, nor is there a single structure or set of structures. However, recognizing the systemic nature of the issues with which it deals, it promotes systemic approaches to dealing with major global concerns. The aims of global governance include reforming and strengthening the existing system of intergovernmental institutions, and improving its means of collaboration with private and independent groups. Among other things, global governance will strive to subject the rule of arbitrary power – economic, political, or military – to the rule of law within global society.

I argue elsewhere (Mohamed Salih 1997a) that global environmental governance operates within the confines of, and consistent with, the principles laid down in global governance legal instruments, conventions and international environmental policy proclamations. *Our Global Neighbourhood* (1995:216) indicates that global environmental governance emphasises the need: 1) to put into action global legal, intellectual, and institutional groundwork for a concerted effort to achieve sustainable development; 2) to establish a Trusteeship of the Global Commons (TGC) and to be made responsible for acting on behalf of all nations, including the administration of environmental treaties; to enact an Earth Charter for world endorsement, pending the outcome of the global efforts exerted by the Earth Council and Green Cross to achieve this endeavour.

Considering the ultimate association between environment and development, it has become obvious that one of the most conspicuous outcomes of the Earth Summit is that the stage has been set for global governance aided by diverse trends of globalization to become the dominant paradigm and the most influential actor on the global scale. Global environmental policies, according to Rich (1994:273), have evolved around the premise that

> Global environmental management can work. The project as it emerged out of Rio has two principal approaches – a growing body of international environmental treaties among nation-states and increased foreign aid for environmental protection and management as well as poverty alleviation, channelled and managed mainly through the Global Environmental Facility (GEF) and other financing arms of the World Bank.

Notions such as global environmental policies imply not only that the natural economy has already been rendered subject to global capital operations, but also that sustainable development has been defined according to the logic of global capital operations and that of the dominant global governance institutions that support it. Seven years after the Rio Conference proclaimed Agenda 21 (1992) as the guiding principle for global sustainable development, the question remains as to why contradictory Northern political discourses have converged to agree on the assumption that what is ecological is by necessity global. Erroneously, however, that which is ecological is global, but that which is global concerns a socially, economically, and politically differentiated humanity. Global environmental governance has therefore been an integral part of the economic, social, and political processes responsive to Agenda 21 and other international environmental policy proclamations, conventions, and treaties.

The question that continues to beg for an answer is whether such grand global projects as environment and sustainable development, free trade, and even globalization are reconcilable within the new global context of development.[15] The global environmental movement is explicit about the need to establish a global resource management regime responsible for protecting the global commons from abuse by irresponsible nation-states or greedy corporate interests. Managing the global commons therefore requires global environmental policies, respected and implemented by all nation-states. Neo-liberal globalization, on the other hand, is premised on the need for trade liberalisation and opening up new markets and reaching out for new consumers.

The global environmental conventions, treaties, and laws, which resulted from the deliberations of multilateral environmental forums and negotiations, have contributed to the consummation of sustainable development as a global ideal.[16] As I have mentioned earlier, sustainable development advocates the need to integrate environment and development in decision- making. In my view, sustainable development meets free market environmentalism half way in defending decentralized private choice of the market as a superior economic management system to the command and control approach. According to Eckersley (1995:15-16), free market environmentalism asserts that bureaucratic regulations are inefficient and open to corruption in many environmental regulatory regimes concerned with the management of forests, water rights, and public lands. It also argues for the removal of government subsidies and intervention in the form of externality taxes to correct market failures.[17]

---

15. For full details of the debate on this matter refer to Stallings (1996) "Introduction" in *Global Change and Regional Response: The New International Context of Development* and Bierstreker (1996) "The Triumph of Liberal Economic Ideas in the Developing World".

16. For more details see Thomas (1992) *The Environment in International Relations*, Brenton (1994) *The Greening of Machiavelli: The Evolution of International Environmental Politics* and Vig and Axelrod (1999) *The Global Environment: Institutions, Law and Policy.*

17. For instance, *The World Bank and the Environment* briefs (1993:2-3) developed a fourfold environmental agenda that calls for: 1) Assisting member countries in setting priorities, building institutions, and implementing programs for sound environmental stewardship; 2) Ensuring that potential adverse environmental impacts from bank financed projects are addressed; 3) Assisting member countries in building on the synergies among poverty reduction, economic efficiency, and environmental protection; 4) Addressing global environmental challenges through participation in the Global Environmental Facility (GEF).

Because free market environmentalism has much in common with the current drive towards economic policy reforms (deregulation, free trade, and the market liberalization and open door economic policy), not surprisingly it argues for rolling back the state and assigning it a minimal role in environmental protection. Hence, as part of the core values of the global environmental agendas agreed upon by states (Agenda 21, 1992) and other international conventions, it advocates growth as an engine of sustainable development and hence environmental protection.

More than the good-will of global finance institutions that try to integrate the environment into their investment operations, the protection of the global[18] environment will depend on the capacity of strong states to implement economic policy instruments capable of harnessing/mitigating or abating the consequences of economic growth on the environment. Legal instruments or command and control policies, although important, will not be in a position to deliver results without persuasive socio-economic incentives.

The current environmental policy principles developed for OECD countries and applied in the developing countries have been summarized by Opschoor and Turner (1994:4) as follows:

(i)   The 'polluter pays' principle: i.e. the polluters pay the cost of meeting socially acceptable environmental quality standards.

(ii)   The prevention or precautionary principle: this explicitly recognizes the existence of uncertainty (environmental and social) and seeks to avoid irreversible damages in relation to the imposition of a safety margin into policy; it also seeks to prevent waste generation at source, as well as retaining some end-of-pipe measures.

(iii)   The economic efficiency/cost effectiveness principle: this applies both to the setting of standards and the design of the policy instruments for attaining them.

(iv)   The decentralization principle: to assign environmental decisions and enforcement to the lowest level of government capable of handling it, without significant residual externalities.

(v)   The legal efficiency principle: this seeks to preclude the passage of regulations that cannot be realistically enforced.

Reflections on these environmental policy principles and their practice in various parts of the world have produced mixed results, even in their proponents' view.[19] Business and international trade operators often misuse economic policy instruments, including market-based instruments such as a) taxes on emissions and tradable emissions permits and b) resource use-permits. However, I equally

---

18. For a concise summary with reference to the limitations of environmental policy principles in the countries of the south refer to Mohamed Salih (1997b).

19. Refer to Mohamed Salih (1999) Introduction in *Environmental Planning, Policies and Politics in Eastern and Southern Africa*.

doubt whether the economic policy instruments without legal instruments to enforce them could provide sufficient safeguards for effective environmental quality control. My reasons are as follows:[20]

(i)   Environmental taxes keep down the cost of compliance since the market determines that those who can most afford to act do so, and they deal with the total amount and distribution of the problem.

(ii)   Environmental taxes act as a continuous irritant to the polluters, who therefore have a continuing incentive to avoid the financial cost and taxes by introducing cleaner technology.

(iii)   The price of polluting products will tend to be higher than the price of clean products, and thereby the consumer will encourage producers to choose the latter.

(iv)   Environmental taxes can be used in a fiscally neutral manner to reduce other distorting taxes in the economy.

(v)   Reinforcement of environmental standards and the 'polluter pays' principle. If the influential regional trading blocs (EU, ASEAN, and NAFTA) adopt reasonable environmental standards and adhere to the 'polluter pays' principle, they may be able to ensure that pollution control and environmental costs are internalized into enterprise costs and product prices.

However, it is doubtful given the current variations in levels of economic development within and between states that the affluent ones would agree to sacrifice affluence for the sake of global environmental gains. In this respect, developing and small industrial countries seem fearful of the implications of implementing global environmental protection policies. On the other hand, enforcing compliance with global environmental legal instruments such as trade restriction may encourage non-co-operation in global environmental protection. However, without global environmental co-operation, international environmental laws are ineffective regulatory instruments.

Obviously, this discussion illustrates that social scientists are at the forefront of attempts to understand the forces behind globalization and environmental destruction, as well as attempts to contribute to the policy debate. In the process, social scientists have become more aware of the intricacies that may hinder the advancement of firm conclusions, such as those of the natural sciences. Essentially, the globalization-environment debate has questioned the ability of disciplinary boundaries to withstand the complex nature of environment and development and their multi-layered consequences on the totality of the human condition. The richness of the debate and its capacity to traverse several social and even natural science disciplines is in my view, to a large extent forced into the social sciences by the paradigmatic shift from development to sustainable

20. For more details on points i-iv refer to Weizsacker and Jestinghaus (1992) *Ecological Tax Reform: A Policy Proposal for Sustainable Development.*

development. This shift however speaks more for the ability of the social sciences to respond to new challenges than it does for whether the social scientists agree or disagree with the ethos of sustainable development as a global ideal.

The debate also integrates theoretical-philosophical policy and activists' research. As lamented by Redclift and Benton (1994:7-8), the relationship between structure and agency became more focused and there is hardly any contribution that can be described as purely theoretical or philosophical in nature. This is particularly true even for contributions from environmental ethics and environmental philosophy, which are defined as practical philosophies that engage the environmental consciousness of individuals and groups to restructure their relationship with the environment.

The social sciences have more than ever before been confronted with a myriad of data collected on a global level and that has little to say about the socio-economic and environmental conditions of the societies from which it has been collected. While some social sciences (e.g. economics) can generate data on a global scale, others are more concerned with the local consequences of globalization, better known as the global-local nexus.

Although globalization, environment, and development are not entirely new subjects, the intensity and complexity of their interaction pose new and complex questions that have structurally forced disciplinary social scientists to abandon their earlier hard-nosed attitudes towards interdisciplinary research.

Conclusion

The questions posed by globalization in its various manifestations, including sustainable development, are difficult to answer within the confines of any single social science discipline. Disciplinary approaches unconscious of their own limitations (and those of the social sciences as a whole to integrate development and the environment outside the policy realms) have not succeeded in hindering our understanding of the complex relationships linking powerful and over-loaded concepts, such as globalization and the environment. As the current debate illustrates, the uncertainty that has evolved around the future of development has also manifested itself in the uncertainty about our environmental future. Unfortunately, post development is also not an answer as globalization eats its way, sometimes violently, through the globe creating new dynamisms that traverse environment in its physical sense and development in its most celebrated economic sense. A new creative and all-encompassing understanding of the complex relationship between the global and the environmental of necessity requires a better understanding of the dynamic forces that steer the future of human destiny. The social sciences will betray their historical responsibility, if (and here I am ameliorating Beck 1995) they continue to treat the social and environmental problems of the 21st century as if they are a continuation of the 20th century. Global environmental consciousness has become a dominant factor influencing the definitions not only of what is local and what is global, but also the linkages between the local, the global mediated by the local-global nature of the environment. It has in a sense become increasingly difficult to manage the balancing act that satisfies the requirements of a liveable world within the core values linking globalization perceived by some as an economic ideal and a sustainable development ethos perceived by others as a global ideal.

References

Adams, W. (1990) *Greening Development: Sustainable Development in the South*, London and New York, Routledge.

Agarwal, A. and Narian, S. (1991) *Global Warming in an Unequal World: A Case Study of Environmental Colonialism*, Dehli, Centre for Science and Environment.

Axford, B. (1995) *The Global System: Economics, Politics and Culture*, Cambridge, Polity Press.

Brack, Duncan (ed.) (1998) *Trade and Environment: Conflict or Compatibility*, London, The Royal Institute of International Affairs.

Beck, U. (1995) *Ecological Politics in an Age of Risk*, Cambridge, Polity Press.

Bierstreker, T. J. (1996) "The Triumph of Liberal Economic Ideas in the Developing World". In Stallings, B. (ed.) *Global Change and Regional Response: The New International Context of Development*, Cambridge, Cambridge University Press.

Blaikie, P. M. and Brookfield (1989) *Land Degradation and Society*, London, Methuen.

Brenton, T. (1994) *The Greening of Machiavelli, The Evolution of International Environmental Policies*, London, The Royal Institute of International Affairs.

Brundtland Report (1987) *Our Common Future*, Oxford, Oxford University Press. World Commission on Environment and Development.

Charonvitz, S. (1994) "Free Trade, Fair Trade, Green Trade: Defogging", *Cornell International Law*, 27:3, pp. 498-505.

Clark, L Gordon (1995) "Global Competition and Environmental Regulation: Is the Race to the Bottom Inevitable?" In Eckersley, R. (ed.) *Markets, the State and the Environment*, Basingstoke, Macmillan.

Commission on Global Governance (1995) *Our Global Neighbourhood, Report of the Commission on Global Governance*, Oxford, Oxford University Press.

Daly, H. (1996) *Free Trade, Capital Mobility and Growth versus Environment and Community*, The Hague, Institute of Social Studies.

Dieren, Wouter v. (ed.) (1995) *Taking Nature into Account: A Report to the Club of Rome*, New York, Copernicus.

Eckersley, R. (1995) "Markets, the State and the Environment". In Eckersley, R. (ed.) *Markets, the State and the Environment*, Basingstoke, Macmillan.

Ehrlich, P. and Ehrlich A. (1996) *Betrayal of Science and Reason: How Anti-Environmental Rhetoric Threatens Our Future*, Washington DC, Island Press.

Ekins, Paul (1995) *Harnessing Trade to Sustainable Development*, Oxford, Green College.

Engels, Frederick (1940) *The Dialectics of Nature*, New York, International Publishers.

Giddens, A. (1996) "Urbanism, Globalization and Environmental Politics". In Goldblatt, D. (ed.) *Social Theory and the Environment*, Cambridge, Polity Press.

The Group of Lisbon (1995) *Limits to Competition*, Cambridge, Mass. and London, The MIT Press.

Hannigan, J. A. (1995) *Environmental Sociology: A Social Constructionist Perspective*, London and New York, Routledge.

Hirst, P. and Thompson, G. (1996) *Globalization in Question: The International Economy and the Possibility of Governance*, Cambridge, Polity Press.

Kinerade, P. (1995) "Towards Ecologically Sustainable Development: The Role and Shortcomings of the Market". In Eckersley, R. (ed.) *Markets, the State and the Environment*, Basingstoke, Macmillan.

Meadows, D. (1972) *The Limits to Growth: A Global Challenge; a Report to the Club of Rome*, New York, University Books.

Meadows, D.H., Meadows, D.L., and Randers, J. (1992) *Beyond the Limits: Global Collapse or a Sustainable Future*, London, Earthscan.

Guha, R. and Martinez-Alier, J. (1997) *Varieties of Environmentalism: Essays North and South*, London, Earthscan.

Merchant, C. (1992) *Radical Ecology: The Search for a Liveable World*, London and New York, Routledge.

Mohamed Salih, M. A. (1999) "Introduction", Mohamed Salih, M.A., and Tedla, S. (eds.) *Environmental Planning, Polices and Politics in Eastern and Southern Africa*, Basingstoke, Macmillan.

Mohamed Salih, M. A. (1997a) "Global Ecologism and Its Critics". In Thomas, C., and Wilkin, Peter (eds.) *Globalization and the South*, Basingstoke, Macmillan.

Mohamed Salih, M. A. (1997b) "Natural Capital". In O'Hara, P. (ed.) *Encyclopaedia of Political Economy*, London and New York, Routledge.

North, R. D. (1995) *Life on a Modern Planet: A Manifesto for Progress*, Manchester and New York, Manchester University Press.

Opschoor, J. B. (1999) "Foreword", Mohamed Salih, M.A., and Tedla, S. (eds.) *Environmental Planning, Polices and Politics in Eastern and Southern Africa*, Basingstoke, Macmillan.

Opschoor, J. B. and Turner, R. K. (1994) "Environmental Economics and Environmental Policy Incentives: Introduction and Overview". In Opschoor, J.B., and Turner, R.K. (eds.), *Economic Incentives and Environmental Policies: Principles and Practice*, Kluwer Academic Publishers.

Redclift, M. (1987) *Sustainable Development: Exploring the Contradictions*, London, Methuen.

Redclift, M. (1984) *Development and the Environment; Red or Green Alternatives*, London, Methuen.

Redclift, M. and T. Benton (eds.) (1994) *Social Theory and the Global Environment*, London and New York, Routledge.

Rich, Bruce (1994) *Mortgaging the Earth: The World Bank, Environmental Impoverishment and the Crisis of Development*, London, Earthscan.

Sachs, W. (1994) "The Blue Planet: An Ambiguous Modern Icon", *The Ecologist*, Vol. 24, No. 5. September.

Sachs, W. (ed.) (1993) "Introduction", *Global Ecology: A New Arena of Political Conflict*, London and New Jersey, Zed Books.

Shiva, V. (1993) "The Greening of the Global Reach; Global Environment or Green Imperialism?" In Sachs, W., (ed.) *Global Ecology: A New Arena of Political Conflict*, London and New Jersey, Zed Books.

Soroos, M. S. (1999) "Global Institutions and the Environment". In Vig, Norman J., and Axelrod, R.S. (eds.) *The Global Environment: Institutions, Law and Policy*, London, Earthscan.

Stallings, B. (ed.) (1996) *Global Change and Regional Response: The New International Context of Development*, Cambridge, Cambridge University Press.

South Commission (1990) *Challenge to the South*, The Report of the South Commission, Oxford, Oxford University Press.

Taylor, Annie and Thomas, C. (1999) *Global Trade and Social Issues*, London and New York, Routledge.

Thomas, C. (1992) *Environment in International Relations*, London, Royal Institute of International Relations.

Tolba, M. K. and El Kholy, O. (1992) *The World Environment 1972 – 1992: Two Decades for Challenge*, London, Chapman and Hall (United Nations Environmental Programme).

Tylor, G. R (1970) *The Doomsday Book: Can the World Survive?*, London, Thames and Hudson.

Vig, Norman J. and Axelrod, R.S. (1999) *The Global Environment: Institutions, Law and Policy*, London, Earthscan.

Welford, R. (1997) *Hijacking Environmentalism: Corporate Responses to Sustainable Development*, London, Earthscan.

Wilson, G. A. and Bryant, R. (1997) *Environmental Management: New Directions for the Twenty-First Century*, London, University College London.

Weizsacker, E. U. von and Jestinghaus, J. (1992) *Ecological Tax Reform: A Policy Proposal for Sustainable Development*, London and New Jersey, Zed Books.

World Bank (1993) *Environmental Briefs*, Washington DC, World Bank.

WWF (1996) *Trade Measures and Multilateral Environmental Agreements: Backwards or Forwards in the WTO?*, Gland, World Wide Fund for Nature (WWF).

Yearley, S. (1996) *Sociology, Environmentalism, Globalization: Reinventing the Globe*, London, Sage.

FEMINIST SIGHTINGS OF GLOBAL RESTRUCTURING: CONCEPTUALIZATIONS AND RECONCEPTUALIZATIONS[1]

Marianne H. Marchand & Anne Sisson Runyan

> 'Young ladies don't understand political economy, you know,' said Mr Brooke, smiling towards Mr Casaubon.
> 'I remember when we were all reading Adam Smith. *There* is a book now.' – George Eliot, *Middlemarch*[2]

Introduction

In this citation from Eliot's influential work, the underlying assumption is that "young ladies" don't understand political economy because they don't have anything to do with it: the world of political economy is far removed from the experiential world and daily lives of young, middle class women in 19th century Britain. Moreover, as Eliot's character reveals, the dominant view in 19th century Britain was that "young ladies" were too emotionally inclined to be able to discuss matters of political economy rationally.

Times have certainly changed since George Eliot wrote these lines. It is nowadays increasingly recognized that the "world of political economy" and the daily lives of women are no longer (and never have been) two separate worlds. Moreover, about a century after her book was first published, (young) women not only understand, discuss and analyze political economy, but feminist and gender analyses of international political and economic issues are becoming increasingly prominent as well. The objective of this chapter is to continue this tradition by analyzing how globalization, one of the central themes of contemporary international political economy, and gender, as a relation of inequality based on social constructions of masculinity and femininity, are intricately connected.[3]

---

1. This chapter is reprinted, with permission from Routledge, as an abridged and slightly modified version of Marianne H. Marchand and Anne Sisson Runyan, 2000, "Introduction. Feminist Sightings of Global Restructuring: Conceptualizations and Reconceptualizations" in Marianne H. Marchand and Anne Sisson Runyan (eds.), *Gender and Global Restructuring: Sightings, Sites and Resistances*, London: Routledge, pp. 1-22.
2. G.Eliot, *Middlemarch*, London,Wordsworth Classics,1994 edition, p. 14 (emphasis in the original).

More specifically, this chapter sets out to go beyond conventional representations and interpretations of globalization. Such interpretations tend to be either
too narrowly economistic or to focus primarily on changes in the nature of and
relationships between the market and the state. In so doing, they pay little attention to attendant global/local restructurings of social, cultural, racial, ethnic,
gender, national, familial identities, roles and relations. However, gender analysis (in its several variations) is particularly well-equipped for developing a better
understanding of globalization's multi-dimensionality.

In its endeavour to reveal the comprehensive and complex nature of globalization through a series of gender analyses, the present chapter will focus in particular on three inter-related issues and concerns. First, it intends to develop
conceptualizations of globalization or global restructuring (the latter being our
preferred term) through applying a gender lens. This includes raising such questions as: What are the gendered constructions of the new global political economy? How can we reconceptualize global space from a gender perspective?
These questions imply that global restructuring represents nothing less than the
construction, reconstruction, and transformation of categories of knowing which
tend to produce new gender biases as well as reifying others.

The focus of our second concern is on the concrete sites or spaces of global
restructuring, such as the state, global city, economy, household and civil society,
in which actors operate and various transformative processes are being articulated. One of the important themes here is that various processes of global
restructuring are not occurring in isolation but are connected. Moreover, the
articulation of global restructuring processes leads to new forms of inclusion
and exclusion, while often exacerbating existing inequalities.

The third concern guiding this research deals specifically with the responses
and forms of resistance which global restructuring has evoked. These responses
and resistances include a range of activities, strategies as well as oppositional
voices, from women's groups, labour and environmental movements. In contrast to the more inclusive transformative agendas of these groups, there is also a
more exclusionary, sometimes even violent, resistance mounted against global
restructuring. This resistance is most often articulated through ethnic conflict,
emerging nationalisms, and religious fundamentalisms. Similar to the questions
raised with respect to the other two concerns, the underlying question is what
insights does gender analysis provide to make sense of a wide variety of dis-
persed, isolated responses and resistance practices? Additionally, does gender
analysis enable us to formulate, and even advocate, varying kinds of resistance
strategies which make sense from a feminist perspective?

In the remainder of this chapter we will further explore these issues and concerns. As there is still no comprehensive gender analysis of global restructuring
or globalization available, we will try to partially fill this gap in the literature by

---

3.   For a definition of gender, gender analysis, and feminist theory, see below.

outlining the major elements that such an analysis should include. To do so we will first embark upon a gender analysis of global restructuring. The subsequent section on sightings, sites, and resistances will provide more concrete discussions on the connections among these three instances of global restructuring.

Gender and global restructuring

By challenging dominant treatments of globalization and raising the issue of human agency, critical approaches (see Introduction) provide an opening for developing critical feminist or gender analyses of globalization, according to Sandra Whitworth (1994) and Jill Steans (1998). However, the problem that Whitworth and Steans signal is that most critical international political economy (IPE) authors tend to ignore these openings and thereby forego the opportunity to enrich and improve their analyses by engaging in a serious dialogue with critical feminist and gender analyses of international political economy. This analysis is part of the effort to foster such a dialogue by specifically showing the multiple ways in which gender plays a role in global restructuring.

Feminist scholars have repeatedly shown that gender operates at various levels at which it intersects with class, ethnicity, race, nationality, and sexuality to produce and reproduce an intricate web of inequalities between and among men and women. In other words, gender can be defined as "socially learned behaviour and expectations that distinguish between masculinity and femininity" (Peterson and Runyan 1999:5). Gender operates in at least three distinct, yet interconnected ways: 1) ideologically, especially in terms of gendered representations and valorizations of social processes and practices; 2) at the level of social relations; and 3) physically through the social construction of male and female bodies. In other words, developing a gender analysis of global restructuring requires more than inserting "women" into already existing IPE analyses. It involves going beyond a narrow materialist understanding of global restructuring. As various authors (Whitworth 1994; Steans 1998) have revealed, one of the problems with critical IPE is precisely its materialist underpinnings. Despite, for instance, neo-Gramscian attempts to recognize the role of ideas in their formulation of hegemony, they still privilege its materialist foundations by asserting the centrality of production (Cox 1987:2-9; Cox 1993: *passim*; Whitworth 1994). Moreover, neo-Gramscian IPE has been challenged because of its strong preoccupation with the activities of elites, which tends to marginalize the potential for counter-hegemonic forces at the grassroots (Drainville 1995).

In order to move beyond a narrow materialist analysis of global restructuring it is important to address its ideational dimensions as well. Such an analysis is in step with the recent turn in IPE/IR theory toward developing a better understanding of the roles played by ideas, identities, and culture in international affairs (see Lapid and Kratochwil 1997). Feminist IPE/IR is in a very good position to bridge the divide between a predominantly materialist IPE analysis and a critical analysis of the ideational/cultural underpinnings of global restructuring. First, within feminist theory there exists a strong research tradition concerning questions of identity construction and issues of representation. Second, there is a well-developed feminist literature on issues such as development, labour market structures, export processing zones, structural adjustment programmes, and free trade issues which are pertinent to the field of IPE. Together these two strong traditions within feminist scholarship provide an excellent starting point for developing a more inclusive interpretation of global restructuring.

According to Spike Peterson, understanding and interpreting global restructuring, and indeed social reality more generally, involves relational thinking which brings together three distinct dimensions: "[t]his involves understanding the world 'out there' (practices, institutions, structures of social re/production), how we think (meaning systems, ideologies, paradigms), and who we are (subjectivity, agency, self and collective identities) as interacting dimensions of social reality" (1997:185). In other words, relational thinking allows us to introduce subjects and subjectivity into an otherwise rather abstract discussion about processes, structures, markets, and states. Second, it sensitizes us to the specifically gendered representations and valorizations of global restructuring. For instance, are certain sectors of the market becoming increasingly masculinized, that is, spaces where "masculine" behaviour is being rewarded and which will consequently attract more men than women? Alternatively, are parts of (civil) society and the state becoming feminized? If so, what are the consequences of this? Third, relational thinking reveals the gendered power dimensions of global restructuring. How and to what extent is global restructuring embedded in and exacerbating unequal power relations? How are processes of inclusion and exclusion being mediated through gender, race, ethnicity and class?

In the next section we will touch upon these three interrelated aspects of global restructuring's material, ideological and discursive dimensions. The underlying thought is that a gender analysis of global restructuring involves more than a discussion about the latter's differential impact on women and men.

Sightings, sites, and resistances

In this section we will further develop a gender analysis of global restructuring which is informed by relational thinking. The question of how feminists[4] think about global restructuring is specifically captured by the part entitled "sightings," while the discussion on "sites" is concerned with the material structures and practices of global restructuring in specific places. Finally, "resistances" not only deal with concrete strategies and instances of opposition but also with the identities and subjectivities of those involved. Bringing these three elements –

---

4. The term feminism is being used here to denote a broad view or orientation which sees gender as an important ordering device in today's world. As such feminism embraces many perspectives. Thus, feminists are those who hold such a broad orientation (see Peterson and Runyan 1999: 256).

sightings, sites and resistances – together will show how (gendered) changes in production, labour organization, and household structures are intricately connected to transformations in the role (and policies) of the state and the rearticulation of society. There are, for instance, clear signs of multiple globalizations (or global restructurings), reformulations of gender relations, and the emergence of new forms of organizing to counteract the negative impact of political/economic/cultural restructuring worldwide. In the remainder of this section we will take a closer look at some of these gendered "unsettlings."

Feminist sightings: critiques of the gendered discourses of restructuring
As we have indicated, gender operates at the level of ideology by valourizing certain social institutions, actors, practices, and processes that are associated with men and masculinity at the expense of others that are associated with women and femininity. Feminist theorizing is centrally concerned with breaking down or deconstructing this hierarchical dualism of masculinity/femininity which constitutes an ordering system that determines what is deemed of value and what is not. Moreover, Western feminist theorizing, in particular, is concerned with the distinction between public and private spheres and the relegation of the latter to the former (see Peterson and Runyan 1999).

Feminist observers of global restructuring have pointed out that discourses of globalization[5] are highly gendered and that the relations of domination entailed in global restructuring could not be sustained without gendered symbolism and metaphors which serve to "naturalize" hierarchies. Such symbolism and metaphors act to ward off resistance by variously valourizing globalization, making it appear natural and inevitable, and dampening debate about its effects and alternative social, political, and economic arrangements. For example, as Julie Graham and Katharine Gibson (1996: Chapter 6) have argued, globalization narratives of neoliberals and even some critical theorists read like "rape scripts," which are based on the assumption that men and women play out fixed gender roles of aggressors (whose behaviour cannot be controlled) and victims (who are too weak to actually stop the violence). The invocation of (masculine) "capitalist penetration" into presumably weaker non-capitalist economic systems has also been noted by Charlotte Hooper (2000). She finds that *The Economist* sometimes actually uses the metaphor of rape in article headings to promote the entry of transnational capital into "underdeveloped" economies.

Thus, part of critiquing global restructuring requires countering such narratives, whether from the right or left, which project globalization as an "irresistible" (masculine) force. This countering can be assisted by deconstructing dominant constructions of, in particular, emerging Anglo-American hegemonic

---

5. In the remainder of this chapter, the term globalization script or discourse is being used critically to reflect a) the views of those who advocate globalization or b) its ideological connotation and dimension. Global restructuring will be used consistently to indicate material and ideational processes of transformation.

masculinity, associated with global "jetsetting," under global restructuring and revealing how many men (e.g. as workers) are also being subordinated by these constructions (see Hooper 2000). Interestingly, this newly emergent Anglo-American hegemonic masculinity reveals certain dualistic tendencies. On the one hand, it maintains the image of aggressive frontier masculinity. On the other, there are also seemingly more benign images of the same captains of global capital, which herald feminized skills of non-hierarchical management associated with networking, teamwork, and flexibility. This multi-tasked feminized management style is juxtaposed in globalization scripts with labour, which is portrayed as anachronistically needful of hierarchical rules and structures, and, thus, poorly suited for the brave new world of flexibility that global capital demands.

It is the use of above-described gendered constructs and symbolisms which provide the legitimation and rationalization for neoliberal economic policies. This is particularly evident with respect to development and structural adjustment policies promoted by economists from international financial institutions, donor countries and international donor agencies. The irony behind these narratives is that while these technical experts are prescribing export-oriented (agricultural and industrial) development policies to Southern states, the Organization for Economic Cooperation and Development (OECD) countries are phasing out much of their own manufacturing sector and moving toward a high-tech information and finance-based service economy (see for example Sassen 1991; Runyan 1996). This is the new "taut and terrific body economic" (Gibson-Graham 1996:107) of the "new man." The "old man" of industrial production is increasingly beleaguered and marginalized as indicated by a *Financial-Times* article entitled "Ivan the Terribly Lost" (Thornhill 1997). In this piece, the once proud symbol of Soviet manhood, the industrial worker or "Homo Sovieticus," has fallen prey to high "mortality, unemployment, alcohol abuse, and suicide" as the liberalization of the Russian economy passes him by (Thornhill 1997).

Feminists have also noted how gendered metaphors and symbolism in globalization discourses act to privilege particular agents and sectors over others, such as finance capital over manufacturing, finance ministries over social welfare ministries, the market over the state, the global over the local, and consumers over citizens. In each of these cases, the latter is constructed as "feminized" in relation to the former which is often depicted as masculine space (see for example Marchand 2000a). Although other critical theorists have observed these hierarchizations in the context of global restructuring, they have failed to connect them to gendering processes, including shifting meanings of public and private (Brodie 1994).

A well-established tradition of Western feminist scholarship has revealed that women's subordination stems from men's assignment to and control over the public realm of the state and the market and women's consignment to the private realm of the home and family (see, for example, Okin 1979; Elshtain 1981; Hartsock 1985; Tong 1989; Coole 1993). Neoliberal discourse, however, constructs the market as the private sector in contradistinction to the state as the public sector and either totally disregards the private realm of the household/family or lumps it into a very broad conception of (private) civil society that includes market actors and which is also counter-posed to the (public) state.

In neoliberal discourse on globalization, the state is typically "feminized" in relation to the more robust market by being represented as a drag on the global economy that must be subordinated and minimized. As critics have noted, however, the state also paradoxically takes on a new role by becoming more akin to the private sector (and thus remasculinized) as it is internationalized to assist global capital and as its coercive and surveillance capacities are being enhanced.

To make feminist sense of these conflicting engenderings of the state, it is first necessary to note that not all states have similar capacities to participate in the global economy. While OECD states are in a position to "male bond" with global capital and thus partially retain or recapture their masculine status, Southern (and other subordinated) states are forced to accept a more feminized status. Second, it is important to recognize that the state is not a homogenous entity. Within states (Central and East European, OECD as well as Southern), there are sectors that remain "domesticated" even as other sectors are internationalized. For example, ministries that focus on domestic health, education, and social welfare are becoming increasingly disadvantaged or "feminized" in relation to ministries of finance and economic affairs that are directly related to the global economy and, thus, invested with masculine authority. Such ministries are also displacing the power of elected officials as democratic processes are increasingly viewed as too cumbersome for the fast-track world of global economics. The restructuring which has so privileged these (masculinized) sectors, coupled with the still considerable coercive apparatuses of states, makes (parts of) the state complicit in restructuring processes rather than obsolete.

In this context it is important to note that Western feminist theorizing about the public and private in relation to the state has been challenged by non-Western feminists. For instance, in the case of the modernizing state the private becomes a space of contestation and redefinition as modernizing elites seek to "suppress" the private as a source of social and economic traditional values and "colonize" it with public statist values in order to undermine inward-looking, patriarchal family values (Kandiyoti 1991:435). Fundamentalist revolutions and resistances to this represent a masculinist reclaiming of private patriarchal space. Writing from the perspective of migrant women, Annanya Bhattacharjee challenges Western feminist assumptions about the home as an essentially private space by arguing that "home" for these women has far more "public" dimensions. For them, not only does home refer to "the (conventional) domestic sphere of the heterosexual and patriarchal family," but it also entails "an extended ethnic community" and "nations of origin" which shape their identities and roles (Bhattacharjee 1997:313-14).

Finally, Western feminist theorizing about public and private is also being challenged by women in the "transitional" or post-Communist states of Eastern Europe and the former Soviet Union. Historically, the Communist state sought also to obliterate private space in terms of capitalism, autonomous civil society organizations, and household privacy. Communist ideology purported to solve "the woman question" by enjoining unprecedented numbers of women to enter the formal workforce, and to some degree governance, by providing free access to childcare, healthcare, and abortion as well as paid maternity leave. Women living through post-Communist transitions in this period of global restructuring are turning Western feminist theorizing on its head as they question any value in seeking traditionally public roles in government given their deep suspicion of the state as a site of liberation (Funk and Mueller 1993; Beck 2000). Instead, those who are positioned to afford it are experiencing more senses of freedom through the private market, which is giving them their first taste of entrepreneurial careers, consumerism, and individual expression. Accompanying this is a sense of the private realm of home and family as a larger space for agency than the public realm of the state since under Communist regimes this area was the least likely to be effectively kept under surveillance.

Even as the private sector is valourized over the public sector more generally, the private realm is hyperfeminized in relation to not only the state and the market, but also civil society in which it is rendered either invisible or highly subordinated. Ironically, however, the private realm has become highly politicized as a site of and for restructuring processes. As feminists have observed, the global economy demands that women simultaneously step up both their productive and reproductive labour are met by contradictory rhetoric and public policies. For instance, in the US women are caught between neoliberal rhetoric which casts women as the "new entrepreneurs" by devaluing women's traditional family roles and neoconservative views which emphasize "family values" and cast women as selfish and irresponsible if they do not fulfill their mothering roles. The contradictory nature of both processes and rhetoric, requiring women to be simultaneously in the workforce, sustain family income and take on additional caring responsibilities, is leading to "a crisis in social reproduction" (Brodie 1994:58).

These and other shifts in the meanings and designations of public and private as both a form and result of global restructuring are also challenging and prompting reworkings of feminist theory. As the public arena itself is being redefined and subordinated to private capital, women are even further distanced from power even as they become workers and elected officials because the nature of work is being degraded and the powers of legislatures are being diminished. The locus of power is shifting from the public world of politics to the privatizing, and, thus, depoliticizing world of economics. However the latter is, in turn, repoliticized by labour, environmental and women's activists (among others) who are increasingly demanding more accountability and transparency from firms and international financial institutions.

Feminist sites: critiques of the market, the state, and civil society

There is a wealth of feminist research on the gendered impacts of economic development and global restructuring processes. These investigations of the relationship between gender and global restructuring tend to focus largely on the materialist or economic dimensions of restructuring and tend to reduce gender analysis of restructuring to the differential effects it has on women and men in the workplace and the home. Nevertheless, they have been instrumental in exposing the vast underside of restructuring and thus have acted to significantly counter neoliberal advocacy of globalization.

Feminist critiques of the global capitalist market have primarily focused on gendered divisions of labour in which men's work is privileged over women's work in terms of status, pay, and working conditions. Feminists have long pointed to the gender inequalities arising from the split between productive labour associated with men's paid work outside the home and reproductive labour associated with women's unpaid labour inside the home which was solidified by the rise of industrial capitalism in the West (see, for example, Rowbotham 1974; Eisenstein 1979). Such inequalities were (re)produced through early colonization practices and later post-World War II economic development strategies imposed on the South by the North (see, for example, Boserup 1970; Charlton 1984; Mies 1986; Sen and Grown 1986). More recently, feminists have observed that these inequalities are being both exacerbated and complicated with the advent of post-industrial capitalism (see, for example, Mitter, 1986; Joekes 1987; Ward 1990; Vickers 1991; Bakker 1994; Joekes and Weston 1994; Marchand and Parpart 1995; Kofman and Youngs 1996; Moghadam 1998).

Women have become preferred candidates for certain kinds of jobs needed in a global economy organized around services and just-in-time production processes. The main reasons for this are that women remain associated with unremunerated and service-oriented reproductive labour and are often seen as physically better suited to perform tedious repetitive tasks as well as being more docile and, therefore, less likely to organize than men (see, for example, Fernandez-Kelly 1983). The jobs women now perform, range from light assembly work in export processing or free trade zones and subcontracted sweatshop/homework labour to clerical and domestic work and sex tourism (see, for example, Enloe 1989; Peterson and Runyan 1993, 1999; Boris and Prugl 1996; Pettman 1996). Poor, working class, Third World, minority, immigrant, and migrant women, as the cheapest and most vulnerable sources of labour, are most sought for such jobs which are characterized by low wages, few benefits, little union representation, and minimal regulation and tend to be part-time, temporary, and highly insecure in nature (see, for example, Aslanbeigui, Pressman, and Summerfield 1994; Bullock 1994; Rowbotham and Mitter 1994; Alexander and

Mohanty 1997). Thus, what feminists call the "feminization of labour" in the context of global restructuring refers not only to the unprecedented increase in the numbers of women workers in the formal (and informal) labour force to service the global economy, but also to the "flexibilization" and "casualization" of (especially women's) labour to keep labour costs down and productivity up in the name of free trade, global competitiveness, and economic efficiency.

Another feature of the economic impact of global restructuring on women is the unprecedented rise in the migration of women (especially, but not solely, poor and working-class ones from Third World states) across borders to earn incomes and provide foreign exchange for their governments. Numerous feminist scholars have documented the rise in the international "maid trade," international sex trafficking and tourism, and other service labour that women migrants provide to elites in "global cities" (or world financial centres) (see, for example, Enloe 1989; Pettman 1996; Peterson and Runyan 1999; and Kofman 2000).

As we have noted, feminists have also called attention to cutbacks in social services provided by the state – a process which particularly disadvantages women as the major recipients and providers of such services (see for example, Harrington 1992; Dahlerup 1994; WIDE et al. 1994; Sen 1997). Such cutbacks were initially instituted during the 1980s through structural adjustment programs (SAPs) imposed on debt-ridden nations in the South by the International Monetary Fund (IMF) and World Bank. In addition to stepping up export production (for which women's labour is needed), SAPs require developing countries to reduce state expenditures particularly in the area of social welfare. As structural adjustment has become more globalized, welfare states in the North have subjected themselves to similar austerity measures involving significant reductions in public funding and the increasing privatization of social welfare programmes. Post-communist states (and most recently the so-called Asian Tigers), too, have fallen under the rigours of SAPs, drastically cutting and/or privatizing formerly free state services upon which women had depended for health, child, and elder care. Thus, privatization processes are essentially reprivatizing reproductive labour – that is, shifting public responsibility for social welfare back to the private realm of the home where women must pick up the slack. As we noted earlier, many women must now simultaneously be in the workforce and at home to serve the global economy, make up for shortfalls in working- class men's declining wages and jobs in industrial sectors, earn money to pay for privatized social services, and provide the reproductive services for which the state is abandoning responsibility. This is prompting various kinds of renegotiations of gender relations in households (see, for example Kromhout 2000; Moghadam 2000).

Feminist analyses of the economic effects of restructuring on women have been increasingly accompanied by analyses of the consequences for women of the political effects of restructuring on the state and civil society. Economic privatization is producing political privatization which takes several forms (see Eisenstein 1996). As Anne Sisson Runyan has described this elsewhere:

> One form is the oft-cited erosion of the state as it is internationalized or made more beholden and accountable to global capital than to citizens. In this process, the state is depoliticized through the reduction of all political issues to matters of economic efficiency. This, in turn, leads to another form of political privatization – the reduction of "public citizens" to "private consumers." (Runyan 1997:26).

This process derails traditional feminist demands on the state to provide full citizenship, human, equality, and social welfare rights for women (see Mikanagi 2000). Further undercutting the basis for state-centred feminist organizing is the rise of neoconservative political forces which blame "both the welfare state and feminism for the breakdown in the social and moral fabric" and see "the family as the fundamental building block in the new order, asserting that families should look after their own, and that state policies should act to make sure they do" (Brodie 1994:57). Fundamentalist religious and nationalist forces in civil society that are fostered by and provide support for neoconservative policies which focus on controlling women's lives and bodies represent the most reactionary responses to global restructuring (see Grewal and Kaplan 1994). As we have argued, these ideological shifts have led feminists to probe beyond the material economic and political effects of global restructuring on women and focus on how gender operates at the symbolic, ideational, and cultural level to produce and direct global restructuring in particular ways and to reduce resistance to it. These processes have also led them to search for alternative conceptions of resistance which highlight women's agency not just in large- scale economic (labour) movements, but also in cultural and political struggles at all levels from the household to the transnational arena.

Feminist resistances: local/national/global struggles, hybrid spaces, and multiple strategies[6]

The previous discussions on sightings and sites reveal global restructuring as a process that constitutes and is constituted by a myriad of unsettlings and renegotiations of boundaries and identities. Moreover, gender, as a significant boundary ma(r)ker and identity producer, is a focal point both of and for restructuring. On the one hand, restructuring depends heavily on gendered discourse and gender ideology for its own construction because they make it appear natural and inevitable. On the other hand, restructuring entails re-workings of the boundaries between and meanings of femininity and masculinity, which are intimately related to the shifting boundaries and meanings of private and public, domestic and international, and local and global. In this last section, we will

---

6. Parts of this section draw upon the discussion in Marchand 1997.

explore how global restructuring is constructing hybrid spaces and identities and thus new spaces for (feminist) resistance, even as it is reproducing and intensifying relations of domination.

The question of resistance has always received scant attention from International Relations (IR) and IPE scholars, especially those working within the (neo)realist tradition. And when attention has been paid, it has tended to concentrate mostly on forms of resistance that involve large-scale, organized, mass mobilizations, such as international labour, guerrilla, and independence movements. Following this same pattern, it is only recently that IR/IPE scholars have started to look at globalization and the politics of resistance (see the special issue of *New Political Economy* on "Globalisation and the Politics of Resistance" 1997). One explanation for this relative lack of attention toward resistance in the context of globalization has been discussed earlier: the dominant portrayal of globalization as inevitable and a 'bigger-than-thou' phenomenon has led to feelings of disempowerment (and thus eroding the basis for resistance). However, breaking through the various globalization myths, critical IPE scholars have started to explore and analyze possible counter-hegemonic forces and attempts to resist, reduce and channel the negative implications of globalization. Yet, the issue of resistance still remains under-theorized. Moreover, existing analyses are not only gender-blind (Marchand 2000b), but also employ rather narrow interpretive frames which tend to prioritize large-scale (sometimes violent) countermovements and overlook, for instance, more localized practices of resistance.

Developing a feminist analysis of and perspective on resistance involves, first of all, a recognition of the contextual nature of resistance. Resistance, in other words, is embedded in, structured by, as well as structuring global restructuring. As global restructuring involves not only transformations of the state, market and civil society, but also the reworkings of masculinity and femininity as well as gender relations, it tends to problematize such oppositional categories as private/public, home/work, domestic/international, and local/global by placing women (and men) simultaneously in these various realms. This recognition of the complexities surrounding the politics of resistance in an era of globalization, in turn, opens up the possibility to identify multiple forms of resistance and sites of intervention. In other words, resistance needs to be reconceptualized in order to go beyond a narrow interpretation of resistance, which would only consider a contemporary variation of the international working class struggle worthy of attention. As Chin and Mittelman (1997) suggest, such a (more inclusive) reconceptualization of resistance would involve the charting of various dimensions of resistance, including its various sites, strategies, forms and objectives. In addition, it is important to consider the (re-)articulation of collective identities as an integral part of the politics of resistance (see Castells 1997). Resistance can take on diverse forms and strategies, ranging from survival or coping strategies to (more or less) organized resistance and transnational organizing, all of which entail cultural as well as economic) struggles and the development of new identities and subjectivities. These various strategies bring not only the local/global nexus into play, but are also located at the interstices of private/public, home/ work, masculine/feminine and involve a renegotiation of the boundaries of the market/state/civil society.

A second area for feminist theorizing (and activism) is the shift in the balance of power within states, which tilts power in favour of ministries of finance and economic affairs. Traditionally, such ministries have been relatively insulated from direct political accountability toward the public (except for business lobby groups) and have had few, if any, interactions with representatives of women's groups. For NGOs involved in lobbying activities the major challenge of the 1990s was to raise the level of gender awareness and sensitivity at these ministries. The feeling that still pervades many of these bureaucracies is that gender issues, finance, and the (global) economy are totally unrelated.

Finally, processes of global restructuring have also had their impact on civil society and brought about increased social activism beyond national borders (see Keck and Sikkink 1998; Stienstra 2000). This phenomenon is often referred to as the emergence of a so-called global civil society. Here it is important to stress that this would not have happened without, on the one hand, the emergence of new communication technologies, such as the fax and computer, and, on the other, the United Nations, which has played an important enabling role by providing a meeting place for NGOs. Clearly, civil society is one of the most familiar grounds for feminist activists and women NGOs. Strengthening civil society is often seen as an important tool and objective in the struggle for democracy and in the fight to improve women's/human rights. It is also seen, from critical perspectives, as the place to start counteracting the negative impact of SAPs and trade liberalization. However, as noted earlier, civil society is also the terrain on which religious and nationalist fundamentalist groups, business networks, and other groups with "less-than-progressive" agendas are active. Moreover, it is important to keep in mind that a strengthened civil society is also on the neoliberal agenda. However, the elements of civil society neoliberals wish to privilege over the state are precisely those which will broaden and deepen relations of domination in the absence of any recourse to democratic governance at local, national, or global levels.[7]

These developments require feminist scholars to revisit their implicit and explicit assumptions about civil society and the formulation of more nuanced ideas about and understandings of civil society's power dimensions. For instance, one issue that deserves attention is how women's networks and NGOs can or are trying to take advantage of the more diffuse power structures within civil society to keep gender on the political agenda. Early indications are that the use of new technologies will become very important in this struggle as they may well structure the ways in which women's groups and other alternative net-

---

7. We wish to thank Valentine Moghadam for pointing this out to us.

works relate to each other, to the state, and to the market (see Castells 1997). From a feminist activist point of view, women's networks and NGOs should not only insist on making new technologies easily accessible, but they should also explore them to their fullest potential in terms of information-sharing and net-working-supporting capacities.

Concluding comments

In this chapter we have shown how processes of global restructuring involve simultaneous transformations of the state, civil society, and the market. We have also given some examples of how women (and men) in various parts of the world are involved in and affected by these processes. An important starting point for feminist academics, women's networks, and NGOs to counteract this (neoliberal and patriarchal) global restructuring is to reveal how all these processes are gendered. This can be done by employing relational thinking through "bringing people" (as highly diverse "women" and "men") into the analysis of global restructuring and by focusing on its gendered representations. In trying to counteract the negative impact of global restructuring, NGOs and grassroots organizations need to be aware of how their local concerns are related to larger processes of global restructuring and reflect upon how their activities may affect or influence these processes (and vice versa).

Feminist debates about and approaches to global restructuring further extend and complicate how we think (sightings), what we look for (sites), and what we do (resistances) in relation to global restructuring. Dominant constructions of globalization are being challenged by highlighting its cosmopolitan, masculinized character and its silencing of public-private renegotiations, as well as the underlying restructuring of gender relations. The material structures and practices of global restructuring are highlighted by focusing on specific places, spaces, and processes such as states, global cities, the labour force, migrations, and households. From a feminist perspective it is important not only to pay attention to economic forces but also to draw attention to cultural, political, and familial dimensions. Finally, the ongoing processes of global restructuring require the further development of feminist understandings of resistance. Relying on relational thinking (joining practices, thought, and subjectivity) a feminist approach increases our understanding of global restructuring and resistances to it and will highlight the complexities, multi-dimensionality and contradictions.

References

Alexander, M.J. and Mohanty, C.T. (eds) (1997) *Feminist Genealogies, Colonial Legacies, Democratic Futures*, New York, Routledge.

Aslanbeigui, N., Pressman, S. and Summerfield, G. (eds) (1994) *Women in the Age of Economic Transformation: Gender Impact of Reforms in Post Socialist and Developing Countries*, London, Routledge.

Bakker, I. (ed) (1994) *The Strategic Silence: Gender and Economic Policy*, London, Zed Books.

— (1997) *Identity, Interests, and Ideology: The Gendered Terrain of Global Restructuring*. In Gill, Stephen (ed.), *Globalisation and Democratisation: Structural Change and the New Multilateralism*, New York, United Nations University Press.

Beck, J.A. (2000) "(Re)Negotiating Selfhood and Citizenship in the Post-Communist Czech Republic: Five Women Activists Speak about Transition and Feminism". In Marchand, M.H., and Sisson Runyan, Anne (eds.) *Gender and Global Restructuring: Sightings, Sites and Resistances*, London, Routledge, pp. 176-193.

Bhattacharjee, A. (1997) "The Public/Private Mirage: Mapping Homes and Undomesticating Violence Work in the South Asian Immigrant Community". In Alexander, M.J., and Mohanty, C.T. (eds.) *Feminist Genealogies, Colonial Legacies, Democratic Futures*, New York, Routledge.

Boris, E. and Prugl, E. (eds) (1996) *Homeworkers in Global Perspective: Invisible No More*, New York, Routledge.

Boserup, E. (1970) *Women's Role in Economic Development*, New York, St. Martin's Press.

Brodie, J. (1994) "Shifting the Boundaries: Gender and the Politics of Restructuring". In Bakker, I. (ed.) *The Strategic Silence: Gender and Economic Policy*, London, Zed Books.

Bullock, S. (1994) *Women and Work*, London, Zed Books.

Charlton, S.E.M. (1984) *Women in Third World Development*, Boulder, Colorado, Westview Press.

Chin, C.B.N. and Mittelman, J.H. (1997) "Conceptualising Resistance to Globalisation," *New Political Economy* 2, 1, pp. 25-38.

Coole, D. (1993) *Women in Political Theory*, 2nd ed., New York, Harvester Wheatsheaf.

Cox, R. (1987) *Production, Power, and World Order*, New York, Columbia University Press.
    (1993) *Structural Issues of Global Governance: Implications for Europe*. In S. Gill (ed.) *Gramsci, Historical Materialism and International Relations*, Cambridge, UK, Cambridge University Press.

Dahlerup, D. (1994) "Learning to Live With the State – State, Market, and Civil Society: Women's Need for State Intervention in East and West", *Women's Studies International Forum* 17, pp. 117-27.

Drainville, A.C. (1994) "International Political Economy in the Age of Open Marxism", *Review of International Political Economy*, 1, 1, pp. 105-132.

Eisenstein, Z. (1979) *Capitalist Patriarchy and the Case for Socialist Feminism*, New York, Monthly Review Press.
    (1996) "Stop Stomping on the Rest of Us: Retrieving Publicness from the Privatization of the Globe", *Journal of Global Legal Studies* 4, pp. 59-95.

Elshtain, J.B. (1981) *Public Man, Private Woman: Women in Social and Political Thought*, Princeton, NJ, Princeton University Press.

Enloe, C. (1989) *Bananas, Beaches, and Bases: Making Feminist Sense of International Relations*, Berkeley, University of California Press.
    (1993) *The Morning After: Sexual Politics at the End of the Cold War*, Berkeley, University of California Press.

Fernandez-Kelly, M.P. (1983) *For We are Sold, I and My People: Women and Industry in Mexico's Frontier*, Albany, NY, State University of New York Press.

Funk, N. and Mueller, M. (eds) (1993) *Gender Politics and Post-Communism*, New York, Routledge.

Gibson-Graham, J.K. (1996) *The End of Capitalism (as we knew it): A Feminist Critique of Political Economy*, Cambridge, Oxford , Blackwell.

Grewal, I. and Kaplan, C. (1994) *Scattered Hegemonies: Postmodernity and Transnational Feminist Practices*, Minneapolis, University of Minnesota Press.

Harrington, M. (1992) "What is Exactly Wrong with the Liberal State as an Agent of Change". In V.S. Peterson (ed.) *Gendered States: Feminist (Re)Visions of International Relations Theory*, Boulder, Lynne Rienner.

Hartsock, N. (1985) *Money, Sex, and Power*, Boston, Northeastern University Press.

Hooper, C. (2000*)* "Masculinities in Transition: the Case of Globalization". In Marchand, M.H., and Sisson Runyan, Anne (eds.) *Gender and Global Restructuring: Sightings, Sites and Resistances*, London, Routledge, pp. 59-73.

Joekes, S. (1987) *Women in the World Economy*, New York, Oxford University Press.

Joekes, S. and Weston, A. (1994) *Women and the New Trade Agenda*, New York, UNIFEM.
    (1991) "Identity and its Discontents: Women and the Nation", *Millenium: Journal of International Studies* 20,3, pp. 429-43.

Keck, M.E. and Sikkink, K. (1998) *Activists Beyond Borders*, Ithaca, NY, Cornell University Press.

Kofman, E. (2000) "Beyond a Reductionist Analysis of Female Migrants in Global European Cities: the Unskilled, Deskilled, and Professional". In Marchand, M.H., and Sisson Runyan, Anne (eds.) *Gender and Global Restructuring: Sightings, Sites and Resistances,* London, Routledge, pp. 129-139.

Kofman, E. and Youngs, G. (eds) (1996) *Globalization: Theory and Practice,* London, Pinter.

Kromhout, M. (2000) "Women and Livelihood Strategies: a Casestudy of Coping with Economic Crisis through Household Management in Paramaribo, Surinam". In Marchand, M.H., and Sisson Runyan, Anne (eds.) *Gender and Global Restructuring: Sightings, Sites and Resistances,* London, Routledge, pp. 140-156.

Lapid, Y. and Kratochwil, F. (eds) (1997) *The Return of Culture and Identity in IR Theory,* Boulder, Lynne Rienner

Marchand, M.H. (2000a) "Gendered Representations of the 'Global': Reading/Writing Globalization". In R. Stubbs and G. Underhill (eds.) *Political Economy and the International System: Global Issues, Regional Dynamics and Political Conflict* (second ed.), Toronto, Oxford University Press, pp. 225-235.

(2000b) *Some Theoretical 'Musing' about Gender and Resistance.* In Téreault, Mary Ann, and Teske, Robin L. (eds.) *Feminist Approaches to Social Movements, Community and Power.* Vol. 1, *Conscious Acts and the Politics of Social Change.* Columbus, S.C., University of South Carolina Press (Forthcoming).

Marchand, M.H.and Parpart, J.L. (eds) (1995) *Feminism/Postmodernism/Development,* London, Routledge.

Mies, M. (1986) *Patriarchy and Accumulation on a World Scale: Women in the International Division of Labour,* London, Zed Books.

Mikanagi, Y. (2000) "A Political Explanation of the Gendered Division of Labor in Japan". In Marchand, M.H., and Sisson Runyan, Anne (eds.) *Gender and Global Restructuring: Sightings, Sites and Resistances,* London, Routledge, pp. 116-128.

Mitter, S. (1986) *Common Fate, Common Bond: Women in the Global Economy,* London, Pluto Press.

Mogdaham, V.M. (1998) *Women, work, and economic reform in the Middle East and North Africa,* Boulder, Lynne Rienner.

(2000) "Economic Restructuring and the Gender Contracts: a Casestudy of Jordan". In Marchand, M.H., and Sisson Runyan, Anne (eds.) *Gender and Global Restructuring: Sightings, Sites and Resistances,* London, Routledge, pp. 99-115.

Okin, S.M. (1979) *Women in Western Political Thought,* Princeton, NJ, Princeton University Press.

Peterson, V.S.(1997) "Whose Crisis? Early and Post-Modern Masculinism". In Gill, S. and Mittelman, J.H. (eds.) *Innovation and Transformation in International Studies*, Cambridge, Cambridge University Press.

Peterson, V.S. and Runyan, A.S. (1993 and 1999) *Global Gender Issues,* 1st and 2nd eds., Boulder, Colorado, Westview.

Rowbotham, S. and Mitter, S. (1994) *Dignity and Daily Bread,* London, Routledge.

Runyan, A.S. (1996) "The Places of Women in Trading Places: Gendered Global/Regional Regimes and Internationalized Feminist Resistance". In Kofman, E. and Youngs, G. (eds.) *Globalization: Theory and Practice,* London, Pinter.

(1997) "Gender and Gendered Regimes: Systems to Revise". In Haxton, E., and Olsson, C. (eds.) *Women and Sustainability in International Trade,* Uppsala, Sweden, Global Publications Foundation.

Sassen, S. (1991) *The Global City: New York, London, Tokyo.* Princeton, NJ, Princeton University Press.

Sen, G. (1996) "Gender, Markets and States: A Selective Review and Research Agenda", *World Development* 24, 5, pp. 821-29.

Sen, G. and Grown, C. (1987) *Development, Crises and Alternative Visions: Third World Women's Perspectives,* New York, Monthly Review Press.

Steans, J. (1998) *Gender and International Relations,* Cambridge, UK, Polity Press.

Stienstra, D. (2000) "Dancing Resistance from Rio to Beijing: Transnational Women's Organizing and United Nations Conferences, 1992-6". In Marchand, M.H., and Sisson Runyan, Anne (eds.) *Gender and Global Restructuring: Sightings, Sites and Resistances,* London, Routledge, pp. 209-224.

Thornhill, J. (1997) "Ivan the Terribly Lost", *The Financial Times,* London.

Tong, R. (1989) *Feminist Thought,* Boulder, Colorado, Westview Press.

Vickers, J. (1991) *Women and the World Economic Crisis,* London, Zed Books.

Ward, K. (ed) (1990) *Women Workers and Global Restructuring*, Ithaca, Cornell University ILR Press.

Whitworth, S. (1994a) *Feminism and International Relations: Towards a Political Economy of Gender in Interstate and Non-Governmental Institutions*, London, Macmillan

(1994b)"Theory as Exclusion: Gender and International Political Economy". In Stubbs, R. and Underhill, G.R.D. (eds.), *Political Economy and the Changing Global Order*, London, Macmillan.

Women and Development Europe [WIDE], National Action Committee [NAC]-Canada, Alternatives for Women in Development [Alt-WID], Canadian Reseach Institute for the Advancement of Women [CRIAW] (1994) *Wealth of Nations – Poverty of Women*, framework paper prepared for Globalization of the Economy and Economic Justice for Women workshop, NGO Forum of the ECE Regional Preparatory Meeting for the Fourth World Conference for Women, Vienna, Austria, 13-15 October 1994. Institute for Comparative Economic Studies.

GLOBALIZATION AND GENDER: BEYOND DICHOTOMIES

Tine Davids & Francien van Driel

Introduction

> Changes in the global political economy since the 1980's have had a dramatic effect on the lives of women, who have become increasingly integrated as players in the world's production and consumption processes. Women have been affected by globalization in the most diverse aspects of their lives and in the furthest reaches of the world. The effects have been multiple and contradictory, inclusionary and exclusionary. (Afshar and Barrientos 1999:1)

This is the opening paragraph to Afshar and Barrientos's anthology *Women, Globalization and Fragmentation in the Developing World.* The tone in the first line – *a dramatic effect* – indicates that something radical has been happening in the lives of women since the early 1980s. These radical changes in the lives of women can be traced back to changes in the global political economy; they are comprehensive and contradictory and either exclude or include women. But women have also become players in global production and consumption processes; players in a game that is played on a global level, according to the authors. The question that immediately surfaces is what the influence of globalization processes for women is. In this chapter the relationship between globalization and gender is studied more closely. There will be an analysis on the basis of the multidimensionality of gender concerned with how this relationship takes shape in the current debates on globalization. This is followed by a discussion on how to avoid the pitfalls that have been noticed in the debates on globalization using this analytical gender model. Furthermore, we will explore the application of this analytical model on the debate on gender and globalization. In doing so we hope to initiate a discussion on the applicability of this model to the debate on globalization in general.

This will be done according to the following steps. First, there will be a brief exploration into the way in which globalization is given meaning in the literature. The heterogeneity of standpoints within globalization literature is the starting point for shaping our thoughts on globalization and gender. The question as to whether it concerns homogenization, heterogenization, or creolization cannot be answered unequivocally and demands a method of analysis different from that usually used to analyze globalization processes. We must therefore consult women's studies and the way thinking about gender and difference has been shaped there. This discussion exposes not only the dichotomous way of thinking, but also the power of attributing meaning. Here ingredients are supplied for a different approach to the category of women. It is discussed how theories on 'the layeredness of gender' are an integral part of an analytical and methodological approach that can be helpful in analyzing the relationship between globalization and gender in a less common way. This perspective will then be used to study the way in which globalization and gender has been shaped within development issues. The question is whether or not this new discourse on globalization and gender will reproduce the same dichotomies and stereotypes. It will be answered through an analysis of the discourse on the feminization of poverty and personal research into female-headed households in Botswana. In the last part of this article the consequences of the alternative approach for future research will be discussed. Personal research into women and political representation in Mexico will be used to this end.[1] The effects of inclusion and exclusion are again discussed with the difference that women have now become players in a more complicated game in which they not only produce and consume, but in which they also give and appropriate meaning.

Globalization and localization: a tension between homogeneity and heterogeneity

Before it is possible to state ideas on the relationship between globalization and gender it might be pertinent to address briefly what characterizes globalization. We are mainly concerned with how globalization as a phenomenon is given meaning in the scientific discourse. This has made us think and has made us challenge it. There are different thoughts on globalization, which is demonstrated by Schuurman's taxonomy elsewhere in this book. In this taxonomy there are nine possible movements or positions that can be identified with regard to globalization. These positions are so varied that they move from a Utopian to a nihilistic vision. As a common denominator of the different positions one could say that globalization is, at the very least, about an increasing interconnectedness of the world through technology and flows of capital, commodities, people, and culture. Exceptions to these views are of course those in which there is no such thing as globalization in the first place and where it is assumed that there is at best a degree of regionalization.

---

1. The research into women and politics in Mexico was made possible in part by financing from WOTRO (Netherlands Foundation for Advancement of Tropical Research).

Disregarding this latter view and not wishing to enter into a discussion on whether globalization does or does not exist, we will take as our starting point the view outlined above as shared by multiple globalists. Then the confusion only really takes shape when we try to pin down and interpret that interconnectedness.[2] The question into the meaning of globalization, how linear the process is, and if it causes actual changes on a global scale has to do with the way in which different authors give meaning to these changes. Where one author is clearly within the bounds of modernistic thinking when it comes to an analysis of globalization, another is trying to break that very pattern of thinking (Albrow, 1997). This is best expressed in the way in which one author sees globalization as no more than a continuing homogenization of the world according to the Western model (Fukuyama, Kothari, Held, Naisbitt, Meiksins Wood & Tabb, see Schuurman in this anthology), while another would sooner describe globalization as a 'globalized production of difference' (Appadurai 1996:199).

Whether globalization is seen as a process of homogenization, heterogenization, or creolization depends largely on the perspective of analysis. It has been noticed that many analyses, including analyses that move within the field of development studies, adapt a macro-economical perspective. The dominant way of thinking about globalization within development studies is characterized by this macro-economical vision in which globalization is mainly seen as a process that, though complex and set in many fields, is still unilinear. The unilinearity of that complex process is then largely determined by a neo-liberal logic based on a modernistic way of thinking. Even when authors are critical of this neo-liberalization the pattern of thought is always within the bounds of a linear process.

Globalization hereby comes first as a process that is set in a global context, without problematizing that context. It occurs as an 'out there' process, but what does that context envelop and who does it concern? Global from whose perspective and according to which process? Only in a neo-liberal and then in an anti-liberal range of thought does globalization get its meaning. This means that globalization acquires a very specific meaning, with an emphasis on macro-political and macro-economical interconnectedness. Within gender and development literature a comparable development seems to be taking place. Recent gender and development literature is mostly *reactive* when it concerns macro-political and economical questions (cf. Pearson & Jackson 1998:9-10).

Literature that refers to topics such as the influence of structural adjustment programmes, internationalization of the job market, and the position of women within the global economy largely reflects a pessimistic vision (Sen 1997; Wichterich 1998). They are approaches in which changing macro-economical relations and their alleged negative effect on local circumstances are central. The image that is put forward by these analyses is that women are victims of neo-liberal processes. The problem with this angle is that something seems to be happening

---

2. Disregarding entirely whether or not globalization can be explained through its own effects. For a discussion thereof see Schuurman's chapter in this anthology.

beyond the power and influence of these women that is elusive and therefore inescapable. This angle not only reflects a unilinear approach but also a 'top down' approach in which macro developments on an alleged global level effect women on a local level.

Some speak even about the economistic turn among academics specializing in gender and development and find this turn to be ahistorical and ignoring potential socio-political dimensions of restructuring (Marchand 1996:580). Even those who criticize this development as such seem only to want to reproduce the occurrence of globalization as a neo-liberal logic. Within this literature the economic worldwide restructuring in the form of one global capitalism in turn has an often-assumed influence on international governments and on households and families (Connelly et al. 1995; Spike Peterson, 1996:5). We will come back to the supposed character of this influence later.

Here the observation that a link is made between global, national, and local processes will suffice. The question is, however, what the nature of these connections is and what results it has for nations, groups, families, and individuals. The next question is whether the linkages point in the direction of homogenization as a linear process. Many of the globalization thinkers make globalization synonymous with Westernization, either viewed positively from a Utopian standpoint or negatively, critical of cultural imperialism (Appadurai, 1990:295).

We believe the process of interconnectedness as described above moves within the field of tension between homogenization and heterogenization, and thereby follow authors such as Appadurai (1996) and Hannerz (1987). The intellectual exercise needed to go beyond globalization as a homogeneous, unilinear, and macro-process should reflect the changed meaning of space and time as a part of globalization. Flows of capital, commodities, culture, and people are no longer bound to space in the sense of territory. Capital has no loyalty towards its native soil, as Tomlinson so eloquently puts it.[3] The speed with which flows of capital travel across the globe due to digitalization and the shift from trade in commodities to trade in knowledge seems to influence and alter the mechanisms of the market.

Not only are flows of capital no longer bound to territory or time, but flows of culture are also less often bound to time, place, and space. In this respect the concern is not only with time in the sense of speed, but mostly that time in relation to distance is less and less an inhibiting factor. Distance matters ever less, because people can travel more easily.[4] People are also able to be at several places in the world at the same time, in a virtual sense, through video, the Internet, satellites, and other means of communication. Due to intensified migration

---

3. Tomlinson, for example, in his article describes how a powerful financial empire such as that of the Barings Brothers Bank, the oldest trade bank in England (1762), went bankrupt within days due to speculation on the electronic super-highway from Singapore.
4. Although it must always be taken into account that there are different degrees to which this applies to different groups.

and flows of refugees the formation of, for example, the Iranian culture is no longer a matter restricted to Iran, but it also takes place, albeit in different ways, in the USA, the Netherlands, and France (Ghorashi forthcoming; Anderson 1983).

This means that time and space will no longer be a buffer in an exchange of cultures the way it was before. The question that presents itself is whether the disappearance of the buffers of time and space will lead to a slow but steady homogenization of the world. We tend to agree with Appadurai that globalization will result in a continuous field of tension between homogenization and heterogenization, with a multiplying of differences rather than the emergence of a homogeneous world culture. According to Bauman (in Tomlinson 1996:32-33), there is a worldwide (international) spreading of modernization, but not to a universal degree. Even where modernization seems to strike in the form of the often-mentioned McDonaldization, this modernization takes on a more hybrid form on a local level than the growing sales figures of, for example, a product such as the Big Mac seem to indicate.

As far as the reaction to the spreading of modernization is concerned, there are various tendencies to be observed. For example, an acceptance of, resistance to, and creolization of cultural patterns that seem to accompany products like Coca-Cola can be observed. A well-known example of acceptance but not of acculturation can be found with the Mayas in Chiapas in Mexico. They have incorporated Coca-Cola into their religious rituals as a sacred potion. Coca-Cola can be seen as a symbol of modernization on a global level in a dominant Western discourse, but the Mayas have not adapted or recognized this symbolic meaning. In other words, Coca-Cola as a commodity can be found all over the world but it does not have the same connotation everywhere.

An important aspect of this example is that Coca-Cola as a symbol of modernity can also have an entirely different meaning that is virtually unimaginable in a Western discourse. Coca-Cola is a potent symbol of a modern commodity. The Western perspective of global, however, is entirely different from that of the Mayas. And although that perspective was at a safe distance until now, a part of the former colonies, of exotic faraway places, these kinds of perspectives are drawing ever closer due to the continued interconnectedness of the world.

The changes that can be observed under the influence of globalization with respect to time and distance in cultural (and political-economical) differences are breaking away from very set dichotomies within Western thinking about the artificially created cultural other. Memmi (in Hartsock 1987) in his work *The Colonizer and the Colonized* has already eloquently described how time and distance are utilized by the colonizer in creating so-called actual differences between the colonizer and the colonized.[5] The differences between colonizer and

---

5. Compare Nancy Hartsock. She cited Memmi's book to clarify that there is a parallel between how the Western discourse creates the colonized as an artificial other, and the way in which women are created as an artificial other.

colonized were made into absolute and actual differences by the way the colonizer placed the colonized outside the course of history.

The colonized were lazy, backward, and everything that the colonizer was not. These characteristics of the colonized were subsequently made absolute by rooting them in time and geographical distance. The colonized were after all what they were and that would never change. The colonized was subsequently placed outside a possible opportunity of change, evolution, and finally history. Geographically these differences, where possible, were rooted in distance. The distance between the slave quarters and the house of the master on plantations is an example of this. What is in fact a social difference is hence made into a biological and metaphysical difference.[6]

These dichotomous categories are exactly those subject to change due to globalization. These changes not only occur in reality, but also in reflection upon reality, such as in art and science. Where the post-modern crisis of thinking questioned these dichotomies on the level of the scientific discourse these same dichotomies are in practice the subject of discussion due to the large flows of migration, means of virtual communication, and intensification of international flows of capital. The cultural other is no longer far away, different, vague, exotic, backward, repressed and underdeveloped, but a very concrete neighbour. The fact that the distance between people and commodities matters less means that the dividing lines that were considered to be matter-of-fact from an enlightenment and modernization point of view can also be breached in practice. However, this does not mean that people are casting off their historical, cultural, and contextual roots and connections. The connections with culture and history are sometimes apparent from a clinging to dichotomies. In the extreme, religious fundamentalism and nationalism are well-known examples.

To be able to analyse mechanisms of inclusion or exclusion it is necessary to identify on which levels these processes of inclusion and exclusion take place. To grasp global and local flux and closure requires us to dismiss the idea that the world is a collection of nameable groups. As Geschiere and Meyer state: "In order to develop concepts which are suited to grasping flux, social scientists have to struggle hard to get away from the intellectual habit of fixing (…) practices, spaces and countries into a map of static differences" (1998:6). It is the production of differences that is the point here. Thinking in divisions, in other words, the dichotomous way of thinking, that has a prominent place in modernistic thinking is subject to discussion here (cf. Alexander 1994). This means that a different attitude towards differences and the way differences are produced under the influence of globalization is required. But how can we look upon differences differently? We consider it analytically helpful to look at the multidimensionality of the concept of gender and the multidimensionality of difference that is linked directly to it.

---

6. Said likewise describes the European construction of the Orient in his well-known work *Orientalism*.

Three distinct dimensions of gender differences

The discussion about differences, that started with criticism mostly from black women on the white Western middle-class perspective which dominated theories within women's studies, forced feminists to alter their perception of women as belonging to an homogenous category (cf. Lazreg 1988; Mohanty 1991). This was a tough problem for feminism because loyalty between women, considered a fact, came under attack and with it feminism as a political project, as it had been formulated up to that point (Davids and Willemse 1999). An important point of criticism on the Western middle-class perspective was that being a woman was always, but not exclusively, concerned with gender. Gender is also made up of ethnicity, class, religion, and sexual proclivity, to name but a few markers. In order to give these markers a place and to do justice to differences and diversity among women gender is used as a layered concept (Harding 1986; Scott 1989).

Referring to gender in layers is not new within women's studies in the Netherlands, but which layers are being referred to here?[7] As such we prefer the term dimensions to layers or levels. Layers and levels both hold connotations of above and below, higher and lower, which could again lead to statements on dichotomous positions, something that must be avoided. Dimensions of gender may be analytically different, but in practice these are interwoven in a constant dynamic interaction.

To start with, a symbolic dimension may be attributed to this process; the dimension of symbolic order, in which representations of masculinity and femininity obtain their substance, sometimes solidifies into very persistent cultural texts. An example of such a cultural text is that women are more emotional than men and men are more rational than women. This is the dimension of symbols, representations, ideal images, and stereotypes. It is the dimension in which the discursive elements of discourse manifest themselves.[8] Differences between men and women are articulated as absolute differences in this dimension, as differences between *the* man and *the* woman.[9] Dichotomous categories are being articulated here that have a lot more nuance in practice.

The second dimension that can be distinguished within this process is the structural or institutional dimension, the dimension that shapes the symbolic within a socially institutionalized practice, such as the division of labour, educa-

---

7. Scott, Harding, and Hagemann-White each have their own interpretation of the layeredness of gender. Scott refers to four elements, Harding to three layers, and Hagemann-White sees gender as an element of behaviour. Hagemann-White's work is more pedagogical and psychological in nature and is therefore more difficult to include in development studies and anthropological work. Our idea on a multidimensional concept of gender was therefore inspired by Scott and Harding and our own interpretation of it. Cf. Tonkens (1998):42-49.
8. We would like to note that the discourse in our vision envelops the interaction between the three dimensions.
9. Braidotti refers to the multidimensionality of difference instead of the multidimensionality of gender in this case.

tion, health care, and marriage. The representation and ideal of the man as breadwinner is thus shaped within labour divisions, legislation, and institutions such as marriage. This representation creates its own subject position and categories, for example in the Netherlands the category of 'bijstandsmoeder' (mother on social security) where there is no legal category 'bijstandsvader' (father on social security). Within this dimension the structural differences between men and women become apparent. As stated above, it becomes clear within this dimension that men and women differ on the grounds of class, ethnicity, age, sexual proclivity, et cetera. Within this dimension in which the differences of the symbolic dimension presented as absolute obtain meanings in the daily practice of different groups of people, does not suggest that these groups are homogeneous. One 'bijstandsmoeder' is not the same as the next.

This takes us into the third dimension of gender, the dimension of the individual subject. This is the dimension in which individuals shape their identities. Although the second dimension referred to the differences between men and women as well as among men and among women, the third dimension also concerns the differences within men and women. This dimension refers to the process of identification of individuals with the multiple identities or aspects of identities that are handed to them. Notions of the self and the other are also internalized and no longer refer to differences between the self and an actual other, but also to differences within the self. The variation in the way in which individuals assume those subject positions is precisely the result of the space for negotiation that they have. This space for negotiation is not only limited by structural positions and a symbolic attribution of meaning, but also by personal endowments. This space for negotiation is also known as the strategic space or 'room to manoeuvre'.[10] This room to manoeuvre has its limitations in discourses that may have solidified.

The different dimensions of gender are in constant interaction. This means that the actors must always relate to these different dimensions. Within this figurative negotiation is the space that individuals have to exert power and influence upon each other. Although this was referred to as the subversion of the male bastions in the 1970s, this was counteracted by the empowerment of actors and individuals in the 1990s. The concept of empowerment no longer refers to 'liberation' as a reversal of power positions, but to a process. Being able to give direction to one's personal life is central in empowerment. It is in that sense not the power *over* but the power *to*. Power *to* centralize one's own subjectivity as a response to dominant definitions of femininity and masculinity (Davids and van Driel 1999).

The daily living environment is structured by discourses, where claims to truth are no longer questioned. If we are even aware of them, they present themselves as clichés. Constructed truths, but truths nonetheless, or stereotypes in

---

10. Naturally personal experiences and character also influenced this result, but the discussion of it is outside the scope of this article.

this case that, depending on the circumstances, become the dominant way of thinking legitimizing certain practices. Truths that create a certain notion of femininity and actually force women to relate to certain subject positions. This is exactly where the effect of power of the dominant discourse lies. Subjects are not victims of this effect of power, however, but are an active part of it. As Wieringa argues with regard to empowerment, this is one of the major sides where the transformative potential of the empowerment approach should be located. The construction of a collective self for women should enable them to see themselves as vocal subjects, able to define and defend their gender interests in order to critically and creatively reshape their worlds (Wieringa 1994:834). In the next section we will take a closer look at the extent to which the new debate on gender and globalization considers women as vocal subjects.

Globalization and dimensions of gender

The discussion on gender and globalization will here be analysed further using the above-mentioned multidimensional gender model. How do mechanisms of inclusion and exclusion take place in the current scientific debate on feminization of poverty? Which discourses dominate this debate, what are the main scripts, what are the subscripts, and what are the new subscripts?

As has been indicated above, the result that appears on a global level is not the result of a unilinear process: "Global processes are composed of webs of practices that emanate from international, national, regional and local spheres (Villareal 1994:2)." In other words, macro-processes occur in and are transformed into daily life practices. This applies not only to entities such as the state or the market, but also to households and families. The latter two are also constructions that are transformed into living reality by acting subjects who respond to outside changes and impulses. However, what is considered globalization within this process by scientists for the most part consists of the global dimension of this process and only to a lesser extent the interaction with the daily life world. The danger of essentialist generalizations is close in this case.

Generalizations, and especially essentialist generalizations, are in danger of being stereotypical. Differences according to race, class, sexuality, locality, historical background, and age are central elements of deconstruction, as we have stated in the paragraph on gender. The rejection of an essentialist position, however, should not result in the opposite extreme, that is, the perpetual emphasizing of differences among and diversity of women, as a result of which nothing exists but differences. However, generalizations made on the basis of the supposedly common characteristics of the position of women, which are relevant to theory and policy, should be possible and should not be confused with taking an essentialist stance (Martin 1994:644, 646, 648). Generalizations are necessary for a political agenda, for policy, and for a research agenda because otherwise there would only be difference and no possibility of a scientific or political debate (van Driel & Deuss 1997; van Driel 1997).

The debate on the feminization of poverty as a result of globalization does, in our opinion, have essentialist traits on the basis of preconceived generalizations. This occurs especially when the debate on the feminization of poverty focuses on female-headed households as an expression of that same feminization of poverty. The reasoning is as follows: through globalization feminization of poverty takes place[11], this poverty can mostly be found in female-headed households. The step to the claim that households headed by a woman are poor is one that is easily made. The final conclusion in this reasoning, then, is that globalization leads to an increase in the number of poor female-headed households. This reasoning subsequently is used nationally as well as internationally to justify attention to women in policies.

The result is that female-headed households appear as a uniform category and that they are poor and require support. This statement has an implicit economic connotation concerning poverty as well as an implicit and explicit gender connotation. What is implied is that female-headed households are poorer than male-headed households. The question that is not asked, however, is whether women are better off in male-headed households. By making male-headed households the norm important contradictions vanish within these households, and so does the possibly unbalanced economical and social position of women compared to men (cf. Sen 1990). Here female-headed and male-headed households appear as two objective categories placed on opposite sides of a poverty scale. When deconstructing the category of the female-headed household and its assumed poverty the question is whether the above-mentioned statement holds water. This deconstruction is carried out in brief below, and there the relationships between the concepts of globalization, feminization of poverty and female-headed households is central.

Feminization of poverty and female-headed households deconstructed

In one of our researches we took up the task to deconstruct the growth in female-headed households as an expression of the feminization of poverty (van Driel 1994, 1997, see also Mencher & Okongwu 1993 and Chant 1997).[12] In Botswana, where the research took place, the number of female-headed households is currently 50%. The central question of the research was why Botswana has so many female-headed households (and unmarried mothers). The answer to this question is complex and revealed historical aspects and conceptual and methodolog-

---

11. Globalization in the literature on feminization of poverty refers to the impact of Structural Adjustment Policies (SAPs), internationalization of the labour market, and economic restructuring on the position of women.
12. Although in these studies the main emphasis is on developing countries, references are made to developed countries as well.

ical problems. It is the conceptual and methodological problems in particular that arise when assessing the phenomenon of female-headed households. At the conceptual level the definition of households and headship and, thus, of female-headed (or women-headed) households are problematic (van Driel 1994:22-49; see also Chant 1997:4).

To stay with the latter, female-headed households can reveal a highly diversified group of women. Female-headed households mean lone-mother households, comprising a mother and her children. But these households again can differ considerably in marital status (divorced, separated, never married, widowed), stage in the life-course (age, labour burden, access to resources), class position (financial means, social mobility), race (stigmatization, discrimination) and juridical status (*de facto/de jure* status, rights). Female-headed households can also mean female-headed extended households, lone-female households and single-sex/female-only households. Grandmother-headed households and embedded female-headed households can also be distinguished (van Driel 1994; see also Chant 1997:10-26; Rogers 1995). Hence, the concept of female-headed households presents a highly diversified picture.

It might be obvious that these conceptual problems of definition cause methodological problems. Ideological and social aspects influence the data gathered and, thus, the outcome of censuses and surveys. Which households are represented in, for example, census figures and can these figures which are collected in different places at different times be compared? For some regions of the world figures are not available since distinctions between different types of household are not even made. The impact of the period in which we have been studying changes in household/family compositions is of considerable importance, too, as figures on the occurrence of female-headed households in Brazil in the 19th century indicate. In 1802, 45% of all households in São Paulo were headed by women, partly because the sex-ratio was heavily feminine; 75 men to 100 women. In 1836 the percentage was 39, while in the interior of Brazil 25% of the households were estimated to be headed by women. In the 1980s the figures for the whole of Brazil were around 14. 5% (Moore 1994:8; Chant 1997:730). Apart from the conclusion that female-headship is not a recent phenomenon and that problems of definition make data difficult to compare, these data indicate that the numbers of female-headed households can fluctuate over time and that specific causes have to be analysed for different periods.

In the case of Botswana the changes in gender relations and in the composition of households over a period of 100 years were studied. During the pre-colonial time female-headed households were a contradiction in terms: households were, by definition, headed by men. During the colonial time (1885-1966) the phenomenon of the 'femme sole' emerged, which developed after independence into the phenomenon of female-headed households. It was found that due to Christianization changes at the symbolic level emphasized the importance of marriage and women's roles as mothers and housewives and men's roles as breadwinners, supporting their female kin. This ideal of the role of women as housewives and mothers replaced the ideal of the central role of women in agricultural production. At the level of gender structure the sexual division of labour did not change. Women maintained responsibility for subsistence production, whereas men's participation in trade and wage labour gave them access to an independent economic life. As a result, the dominant norms and values at the symbolic level and the actual gender structure clashed at the individual level.

As in the past, women are still food providers, whereas men have been able to escape their economic role. The dominant discourse of women as social minors survived but the ideology of the male breadwinner did not materialize, resulting in diverging interests of men and women, instead of political and economic interdependency between women and men, as in the past. Due to the introduction of wage labour, men no longer need women as food providers to the same extent. Hence, changes at the symbolic level and in both the reproductive and productive sphere have had their own dynamic, but they have also had mutual reinforcing effects, which have produced the category of female-headed households over a period of 100 years (van Driel 1994:204-220). Thus, a direct link between globalization as a recent phenomenon[13] and the increase in the number of female-headed households seems disputable.[14] And although, according to research such as that carried out in Botswana, the number of female-headed households seems to be increasing in certain regions, caution is needed with the interpretation of the data (see also Chant 1997:69-87).

A second important conclusion is that female-headed households are not poor by definition and that poverty in economic terms is not necessarily reflected in social-cultural and psychological terms. An independent position might be preferred or even chosen. In other words, many subject positions are possible in which the meaning of women as the head of a household can fluctuate greatly through time. After all, households are not static units, but change with time, willingly and/or unwillingly. A lower income may even be preferred over a position of dependence and domination.

The research in Botswana has for example shown that female-headed households can be an expression of self-determination; that women can choose a position as a female head. The research also showed that female support networks could be much more important, also in economic terms, both in female-headed and male-headed households. These gender aspects do not however occur in the poverty angle, which is concerned with the economic positions of households, income, and access to resources. Not a trace can then be found of the above-mentioned dimensions of gender. Gender is considered to be one-dimensional, almost an economic calculation.

---

13. Whether globalization is a recent phenomenon or one that goes back a long way is a point of discussion within the globalization debate, which has been noted in the first part of this chapter.
14. See the historical analyses of changed marital and cohabitational patterns by Risseeuw (1988), den Uyl (1995) and van Driel, (1994).

The production of a global discourse

Within the discussion on feminization of poverty a process of exclusion takes place; only economics seem to matter, quantified and objectified. The reproduction of simplifications, especially concerning the feminization of poverty therefore leads to certain clichés that are untrue. This is Marcoux's response to the assumed progress of the feminization of poverty. The author states that no scientific study documents the oft-repeated statement that 70% of the world's poor are women. The author calculates that if adequate data were available, the average proportion of women among the poor would be lower than 55%. Moreover, although women-headed households do seem more vulnerable to poverty than men-headed households, when comparable data are available, the actual difference in poverty incidence is not very great. However, he states that the gender bias in poverty seems to be real and growing, although very unequally across countries and places (Marcoux, 1997:1-8).

Baden and Goetz (1998:23-24) even refer to "Lies, Damned Lies and Gender Statistics" when it concerns the feminization of poverty and female-headed households. They indicate how the above-mentioned statement on women and poverty lacks any foundation. A UN employee stated this under the *assumption* that that was what gender imbalance looked like.[15] Jackson (1998) analyses how women are made into the instrument of the fight against poverty on the basis of such clichés, both nationally and internationally. This means that policy makers and scientists unthinkingly adopt statements on the feminization of poverty, and that they are being reproduced and are thereby given credence that is no longer based on reality.

What is more problematic than this one-dimensional concept of gender in the long run is that the space to act is vanishing. The empowerment of women, which is the concern in most cases, is hereby made into a meaningless slogan. After all, the processes on a macro-level that are said to lead to the feminization of poverty should be reversed and women have no power over that; on the contrary, they are victims of it. An envisaged gender policy is hereby replaced by an anti-poverty policy. The New Poverty Agenda of such multilateral organizations as the World Bank and the UN are also no longer concerned with gender but with how the lives of poor people can be improved in a sustainable way.

This is an implicit reproduction of the ideal of the male breadwinner principle and it is solidified into a cultural text, even in scientific work. The household with the breadwinner father and the domestic and caring mother is the norm.

---

15. In their criticism of the unfounded reproduction of clichés they come across an unexpected ally from the conservative side at the fourth UN women's conference in Beijing. This criticism is utilized to challenge the threat of traditional family values. The religious right sees the traditional family as being undermined by making female-headed households into the target group of policies and by channelling money to this target group. In their article the authors state that an uncritical reproduction of clichés may be harmful to feminist research and possibly discredit it (Baden and Goetz, 1998:23-24).

Female heads of households combine these tasks and this combination then appears as a deviation from the norm. The fact that education and care are also labour is thereby moved into the background (cf. Pearson 1998:178). Female-headed households are not compared to male-headed households in which the male head does not have a partner and takes on the educational and caring tasks. By not questioning this norm it is logical that the thought that female-headed households are not always poor by definition but that they are at a greater risk of being poor takes hold.

Gender is reduced to a problem of poverty within the debate on the feminization of poverty. This also means that the unbalanced position of women is made into a problem of poverty and that gender disappears out of the back door (cf. Jackson 1998). The question here is what is the main script, but the subscripts should also be taken into account, the scripts that are about to be crushed by the force of the main scripts. We would here refer to the above-mentioned argument on the socio-cultural and psychological significance of these households and the implicit norm of the male-headed households. The economic main script not only dwarfs the gender subscript, but even makes it vanish.

Two processes of exclusion take place here. First, the exclusion of gender analyses, which are now apparently unimportant in the fight against poverty. The questions of whether these households are poorer and what the causes of this poverty could be are only addressed in economic terms. As a result, an exclusion of women as acting subjects with their own identities and concerns takes place. Thus the structural and individual dimension of gender falls from view. The definition of female-headed households, produced on a symbolic level, is said to be found in practice; in other words, practice is here being adapted to the symbolic dimension. It then depends on the chosen analytical perspective to which degree women in a specific local and historical context, as in Botswana, relate to this globally produced definition of female-headed households.

What is implied above is that a process of inclusion and exclusion not only takes place on an empirical level but also on the level of production of knowledge. In connecting female-headed households in a linear way to the feminization of poverty and by characterizing the latter as a result of globalization and as a global phenomenon, a semi-global scientific discourse is presented. The result of this global discourse is that female-headed households are defined as poor and thereby as a problem. The infinite diversity of reasons for this fact thereby disappear from sight, while at the same time the demand for the meaning of those households for women themselves also disappears. Female-headed households appear as an objective category of households in which the subject positions of the female head vanishes completely as does the socio-cultural and psychological meaning that their status has for them personally.

What can be learnt from a deconstruction of the link between globalization and feminization of poverty, which was conducted above, is that the old discourse of the male breadwinner as an ideal type is reproduced implicitly, but no less effectively. Moreover, empowerment becomes an impossible task if gender is reduced to a one-dimensional process. If even in the scientific discourse women are victimized, is there still room to develop strategies and policies including the concept of empowerment? This is complicated even further when we have to look simultaneously at the global processes on the one hand and the local processes on the other. Within the debate on the feminization of poverty two processes are unthinkingly reduced to a global phenomenon. When this happens, the global phenomenon only has meaning in terms of a linear way of modernization thinking.

In that sense the debate on the feminization of poverty seems to fall in line with the above-mentioned theoretical positions in which globalization is seen as a homogenizing process. Women who are at the head of a household are thrown together and reduced to a poverty problem and thereby appear as a category on a global level. But, what has happened with women as vocal subjects? In the above approach to the feminization of poverty women seem to have lost their capacity to politicize their interests. An approach that considers women as vocal subjects needs a different angle towards differences and dichotomies. This is further elaborated below.

Differences as the core

Research into the way in which women attempt to politicize their interests will, we consider, require diverse dimensions. These diverse dimensions will be discussed by taking one of our researches into women and political representation in Mexico as an example (Davids forthcoming). In order to fall in line with international democratic principles and global discourses on the empowerment of women, a local process of attribution of meaning takes place and will be deconstructed in the example. This deconstruction highlights that the meaning of motherhood is essentialized to such an extent that the ideal of private motherhood is extended to the public political arena (see also Willemse, forthcoming). From this example it can be concluded that ideas and meanings surrounding motherhood in the Mexican national political context often figure as subtexts in political discourses. Symbolically the image of *La Virgen de Guadalupe*[16] serves as an archetype for motherhood and femininity. Even though the meaning given to this symbol, being a suffering and self-sacrificing mother, is comprehensible all across Mexico different meanings of this symbol of motherhood are articulated differently in the various (party) political discourses. When we look at the struc-

---

16. La Virgen de Guadalupe (now with her own website) is the Mexican apparition of the Virgin Mary. She is a black virgin and a very important symbol in Mexico and in the broader context of Latin America. She is also referred to as *La reina* de Mexico (the queen of Mexico) and is seen as a symbol of the joining of Indian religions and the Catholic religion, and through that for the blending of Spanish ethnicity with the various Indian ethnicities. This blending is usually referred to as *mestizaje*.

tural institutional dimension we, for example, recognize a dominant image of the woman as mother within the right-wing liberal discourse, whereas this image not only has a different meaning within left-wing discourses, but is also articulated with the image of the woman as feminist.

For all of these discourses the definitions of femininity mark the boundaries of 'the accepted' and the matter-of-fact assumptions with reference to femininity on the basis of which women can enter into the political arena. The constructed definitions are then ultimately linked to inclusion and exclusion mechanisms. Within the rightwing liberal discourse for example being a woman is essential-ized into motherhood in a symbolic dimension, and made into *the* difference between man and woman. According to this interpretation women are mothers first and foremost. This idea is elaborated below using an example of how this discourse on femininity is shaped within the rightwing liberal opposition party, the Partido Acción Nacional (PAN).

In their political programme women are not explicitly mentioned: it is much more the family and a woman's role within the family that PAN addresses in its programme pamphlets. PAN promotes itself as the party that guarantees change. It promotes a new nationalism according to a more modern and civi-lized society. It depicts itself as a movement against governmental corruption and a protector of civil rights. The family is looked upon as a breeding-place for moral principles setting the guidelines for the public conduct of civilians. In this way PAN presents its politics, the political always being presented as close to the private, to the personal and domestic sphere. This results in a sharp contrast with the ruling party Partido Revolucionario Institutional (PRI), where the per-sonal life is displaced by public issues (Barrera 1993:89, Massola 1993, Venegas 1993).

To what extent modern and political meanings can be given to the role of the woman as mother depends on the space that each woman is able to create besides motherhood, and without losing the essential function of the mother. Actions by women in the public and political arena are thus justified from the position of women as mothers. Women are expected to be able to combine a pro-fessional and a political career with the essence of their womanhood, that is motherhood. In the literature on Latin America the extrapolation of motherhood from the private sphere to the public sphere is described as the production of the symbol of *supermadres*.[17] This clarifies within a symbolic dimension how women are 'othered'.

One could expect such a discourse in reality to be exclusive rather than inclu-sive for women who aspire to a political career. In practice women are better rep-resented in a right-wing liberal opposition party such as PAN than they are in other parties, especially when looking at high positions. This could be for several reasons that are related to different dimensions of gender. Through a

---

17.   The best-known in this field is the work of Elsa M. Chaney.

symbolic dimension it is clear that a moral, political, and gender discourse come together here. Within the right-wing liberal political discourse these values of femininity are again articulated with a certain morality that is especially formulated in opposition to the governmental party, the PRI. Women are seen as morally purer than men and therefore less capable of corruption because of the values connected with motherhood and on the basis of their symbolic motherhood, as it were. It is especially important to emphasize this for the members of PAN who like to portray themselves as morally pure in contrast with the corrupt members of the PRI.

Another aspect is the space this discourse offers for connecting this image of motherhood with modern meanings, such as professionality and international democratic principles, like a balanced political participation by women, which was briefly touched upon before. This is possible by being a *supermadre*. When we focus on the institutional structural dimension it becomes clear that the opportunities for women to realize this ideal of the *supermadre* is very different for women of different classes and backgrounds. Within an institutional structural dimension it becomes clear that many of the women that are active at a high level within PAN are able to do this because they are part of an elite, highly-educated and financially capable of combining a professional career with the role of motherhood. This therefore constitutes an elite discourse, in a manner of speaking.

However, this does not mean that all women that are active within PAN are mothers or that they use being a mother as a strategy to be a respectable woman as well as a politician. In an individual subject dimension it is possible to identify the different strategies that women develop to create this space for themselves. This is concerned with the way in which women secure a position within this discourse.[18] For example, one of PAN's most successful female members of parliament was not a mother but a single woman who lived alone while she was in office. This is a slightly unusual pattern for Mexico where most women marry from home, even if they have a university degree. Nonetheless the woman was able to develop rhetorical strategies in which she identified with this ideal of the *supermadre*. In her strategy she was able to elevate motherhood to moral motherhood. On that basis she was able to justify her own position within politics and to give her presence as a woman in politics meaning.

Women are therefore not the victims of such a discourse, but are a part of it. This also refers to the dynamics that signifies those discourses. Women are forced to relate to the symbolic dimensions. In that capacity they are forced to negotiate the dominant discourse and in doing so they slightly change its meaning. It is in the dynamics of the interaction between the different dimensions of gender that the possibilities of change lie. The opportunity to determine one's own gender identity critically and creatively also lies therein. When we look at

18. In David's thesis these are referred to in some cases as discursive strategies.

the political participation of Mexican women, and of Latin American women in general, from a historical perspective we notice that women at various points in time have given professional and modern meanings to motherhood in various different ways.[19]

Dimensions of inclusion and exclusion

The discourse on motherhood does not always have to have a repressive or exclusive effect on different groups of women. Women in different Latin American contexts have been able to capitalize, within a gender and moral discourse, on an ideal of motherhood as the original domain of the home and the family. One of the best-known examples from a critical political discourse point of view is that of the mothers of the Plaza de Mayo in Argentina.

What is noteworthy in this case is that motherhood is made essential as it is in many such discourses. This mostly happens in the more politically fundamental discourses. This is not unique to Mexico or Latin America; in Nazi Germany and Nazi Italy this making femininity essential in the role of the mother was also put forward. De Ras (1984) also writes on how the image of Mary as a mother figure was part of the creation of a political fundamentalist movement in Germany at the beginning of the 20th century. Gender is often utilized in these cases as a boundary marker for an ethnic or national identity.

The interesting question is then whether this discourse is comparable as a symbolic dimension to other discourses in which a reaction of closure, of shielding the national, ethnic, or other identity from globalization can be observed. We may then ask ourselves whether such discourses lead to the same strategies on a local level. The conclusion that women may actually be excluded on the basis of this discourse is not one that should be drawn easily; as the example from Mexico shows, some women might be and some might not. Ambiguous meanings are articulated simultaneously within discourses, even when a discourse at first sight seems to exclude women. Globalization then emerges as a struggle for attributing meaning, which may have an entirely different content on a global or a local level. In terms of flow and closure gender can be deployed both globally and locally as a demarcation of a boundary; it is a marking point, as the example of motherhood and women in politics in Mexico shows. Gender then becomes a global and local ingredient of the construction of meaning.

It is important to ascertain how global such discourses are as far as the context and the symbols therein are concerned. How does femininity figure in such discourses? Which contexts are being referred to and which global scale is meant? These questions arise especially when globalization and that which is accredited to globalization, is deconstructed analogously to the concept of

---

19. Compare to the work of Kirkwood (1986) Chuchryk (1994) and Craske (1999).

gender. These questions and the consequences for discussions and research into globalization and gender will be dealt with below.

Dimensions of gender and globalization: concluding remarks

What does this mean for our future research, for the way in which we want to handle the questions on globalization and gender? For our research into 'engendering civil society in a globalizing world'[20] it means that we analyze the processes of change in a deconstructive manner. Globalization is then seen not as an 'out there' process, but as a struggle for attributing meaning that manifests itself on a local and global level. This 'global' aspect can be viewed only from a local context, whether this context envelops a national context, or a village, or family.[21]

The complication with the concept of globalization is that it does and does not exist. It is both virtual and real. The process of globalization can only have meaning and in that sense become real in a certain geographically and historically specific context. As King (1991) also indicates it demarcates a boundary in our thinking, in the sense that the question from which (local) context the global is given meaning must always be asked. In other words, the question "whose global process is meant?" always needs to be asked because this process always takes place within certain constellations of power. As has become clear from the last paragraphs it is more than ever necessary to realize that knowledge must be considered as situated knowledge in discussions on globalization.

Because it was also stated at the start of the article that global is not synonymous with universal it cannot be assumed that there is such a thing as a global phenomenon that has the same meaning everywhere in a local context. As far as the global context is to be seen, it is not homogeneous or universal. There is not just one global context which has the same meaning for all those involved, even if it does cross national boundaries. This meaning is always rooted in national and local history. Where a global context in Mexico is the result of a history of Spanish rule and North-American dominance, this context is more likely to be one of British rule and South-African dominance in the case of Botswana.

In order to gain an insight into the multidimensionality of the so-called global, gender as a multidimensional concept is a useful analytical tool. It is through continued contextualization similar to the multidimensionality of gender that the global and the local are no longer two dichotomous positions, but are inextricably connected. The local remains crucial in the analysis of global processes, but has less of a static meaning. On a local level it not only concerns matters that are linked to a specific time and place, but in the local discourse the

---

20. Cf. Third World Centre, 1999.
21. Our insights with regard to the relation between global and local in relation to the multidimensionality of gender have been sharpened significantly through our discussions with Karin Willemse, for which we extend our gratitude.

global discourse, especially, obtains its own meaning. This meaning is subject to constant change and leads to different realities.

To be able to analyze the floating dynamic of these processes a different way of thinking about differences is necessary. The analytical gender model not only supplies us with ways to connect the global with the local, but also helps us gain an insight into the production of differences. The production of differences indicates how insight into the way in which boundaries are marked is crucial in processes of inclusion and exclusion. This means that one must not only think in terms of global flow and local closure. Flow and closure take place simultaneously on a local as well as a global level. This opens up different perspectives for the scientific debate on gender and globalization. In this chapter, we have attempted to show that the debate on globalization and gender has several pitfalls that can be exposed using the multidimensionality of gender. Furthermore, we hope to have clarified how these pitfalls can be avoided using the multidimensionality of gender.

In this chapter the power of attributing meaning is central in the discussions on gender and globalization. This power of attributing meaning is not limited to the theme of gender. In the debate on globalization, which was discussed in the first part of this chapter, when we refer to the taxonomy of Schuurman we actually come across the power struggle for attributing meaning. The same questions can be asked with reference to the positions mentioned in the taxonomy that were asked in reference to gender and globalization. We would therefore like to use this chapter to stimulate the discussion on the wider applicability of the analytically multidimensional gender concept as a pattern of thought and inspiration for the debate on globalization. This pattern of thought offers openings for a comparison of global processes without falling into the pitfalls of developing new 'grand old theories' implicitly. This hopefully offers the opportunity to think beyond the dichotomies of universality versus particularity and homogeneity versus heterogeneity in the debates on globalization.

References

Afshar, Haleh, Barrientos, Stephanie (1999) "Introduction: Women, Globalization and Fragmentation". In: Afshar, Haleh, and Barrientos, Stehanie (eds) *Women, Globalization and Fragmentation in the Developing World*, London, MacMillan, pp. 1-17.

Albrow, Martin (1997) *Globalization after Modernization: a New Paradigm for Development Studies?* Paper presented at the workshop Globalization and Development Studies, Nijmegen, 30 October – 1 November, 1997.

Alexander, Jeffrey C. (1994) "Modern, Anti, Post and Neo: How Social Theories Have Tried to understand the 'New World' of 'Our Time'", *Zeitschrift für Soziologie*, 23 (3), pp. 165-97.

Anderson, B. (1983) *Imagined Communities: Reflections on the Origin and Spread of Nationalism*, London, Verso.

Appadurai, Arjun (1999) "Disjuncture and Difference in the Global Cultural Economy". In: Featherstone, Mike (ed.) *Global Culture: Nationalism, Globalization and Modernity*, London, Sage, pp.295-310.

Appadurai, Arjun (1996) *Modernity at Large: Cultural Dimensions of Globalization*, Minneapolis, University of Minnesota Press.

Baden, Sally and Goetz, Anne Marie (1998) "Who Needs [SEX] When You Can Have [Gender]? Conflicting Discourses on Gender at Beijing". In: Jackson, Cecile, and Pearson, Ruth (eds) *Feminist Visions of Development, Gender Analysis and Policy*, London, Routledge, pp. 19-38.

Barrera Bassols, D. (1994) "Ser panista: mujeres de las colonias populares de Ciudad Juáres, Chihuahua". In: Massolo, A. (ed.) *Los Medios y los Modos, Participación política y acción colectiva de las mujeres*, El Colegio de México, Mexico D.F., pp. 81-118.

Braidotti, R. (1994) *Nomadic Subjects. Embodiment and Sexual Difference in Contemporary Feminist Thought*, New York, Columbia University Press.

Chant, Sylvia (1997) *Women-Headed Households: Diversity and Dynamics in the Developing World*, London, MacMillan.

Chuchryk, P. (1994) "From dictatorship to democracy: the women's movement in Chile". In: J. Jaquette (ed.), *The women's Movement in Latin AmericaL: participation and democracy.* Boulder, CO: Westview Press, pp. 65-108.

Connelly, M. Patricia, Murray Li, Tania, MacDonald, Martha, and Parpart, Jane L. (1995) "Restructured Worlds/Restructured Debates: Globalization, Development and Gender", *Canadian Journal of Development Studies*, vol. 16, special issue, pp. 17-39.

Craske, N. (1999) *Women and Politics in Latin America.* New Brunswick, New Jersey: Rutgers University Press.

Davids, Tine and Driel, Francien van (1999) "Van vrouwenstrijd wereldwijd naar meerstemmigheid en diversiteit". In: Hoebink, Paul, Haude, Detlev, and Velden, Fons van der (eds) *Doorlopers en breuklijnen: van globalisering, emancipatie en verzet*, Assen, van Gorkum, pp. 406-420.

Davids, Tine, and Willemse, Karin (1993) "Inleiding themanummer: In het lichaam gegrift: feministische antropologen op de grens van kennisoverdracht en representatie", *Tijdschrift voor Genderstudies*, jrg. 2, no. 1, maart, pp. 3-14.

Davids,Tine (Forthcoming) *From Marias to Machas: Gender, Images and Political Representation in Mexico*, PhD Dissertation.

Driel, Francien van (1994) *Poor and Powerful: Female-headed Households and Unmarried Motherhood in Botswana.*, Nijmegen Studies 16, Verlag für Entwicklungspolitik Breitenbach GmbH, Saarbrücken.

Driel, Francien van (1997) *Global Economic Developments and Changing LocalFamily/household Compositions.* Paper presented at the workshop Globalization and Development Studies, Nijmegen, 30 October – 1 November, 1997.

Driel, Francien van, and Deuss, Marleen (1997) "Met vrouwen een andere ontwikkeling? Theorieën, strategieën en verschuivingen in debatten". In: Lieten, Kristoffel and Velden, Fons van der, *Grenzen aan de Hulp, Beleid en effecten van ontwikkelingssamenwerking*, Amsterdam, het Spinhuis, pp. 163-189.

Geschiere, Peter, and Meyer, Birgit (1998) "Globalization and Identity: Dialectics of Flows and Closures, Introduction, Development and Change", 29 (4), pp. 601-615.

Ghorashi, Halleh (Forthcoming) *The Ways to Survive the Battles to Win: Iranian Women Political Activists in Exile*, PhD Dissertation.

Giri, Ananta Kumar (1995) "The Dialectic Between Globalization and Localization: Economic Restructuring, Women and Strategies of Cultural Reproduction". *Dialectical Anthropology*, vol. 20, no.2, 1995, pp. 193-216.

Hannerz, U. (1987) 'The World in Creolization'. *Africa*, 57 (4), pp. 546- 559.

Harding, Sandra (1986) *The Science Question in Feminism*, London, Cornell University Press.

Hartsock, Nancy (1997) "Foucault on Power: A Theory for Women?" In: Leijenaar, Monique et al. (eds) *The Gender of Power*, Leiden, VENA, pp. 98-121.

Jackson, Cecile (1998) "Rescuing Gender from the Poverty Trap". In: Jackson, Cecile, and Parson, Ruth (eds) *Feminist Visions of Development, Gender Analysis and Policy*,London,, Routledge, pp. 39-64.

King, Anthony D. (1991) "Spaces of Culture, Spaces of Knowledge, Introduction". In: King, A. D. (ed.) *Culture, Globalization and the World-System*, London, MacMillan, pp. 1-18.

Kirkwood, J. (1986) *Ser Pollitica en Chile, las Feministas y los Partidos.* Santiago de Chile: FLASCO.

Lazreg. Marnia (1988) "Feminism and Difference: the Perils of Writing as a Woman on Women in Algeria". In: *Feminist Issues*, vol. 14, no.1, pp. 81-107.

Marchand, Marianne H. (1996) "Reconceptualising 'Gender and Development' in an Era of 'Globalisation'". *Millennium*, vol. 32, no. 3, pp. 577-603.

Marcoux, Alain (1997) *The Feminisation of Poverty: Facts, Hypotheses, and the Art of Advocacy*, FAO Population Programme Service, WWW:http://www.undp.org/popin/fao/womnpoor.htm

Martin, Jane R. (1994)'Methodological Essentialism, False Difference, and Other Dangerous Traps'. *Signs*, vol. 19, no. 3, pp. 630-657.

Massolo, A. (1994) "Política y mujeres: una peculiar relación, Introduccion". In: Massolo, A. (ed.) *Los Medios y los Modos, Participación política y acción colectiva de las mujeres*, Mexico D. F., El Colegio de México, pp. 13-40.

Mencher, Joan P. and Okongwu, Anne (1993) *Where Did All the Men Go? Female Headed/Female Supported Households in Cross-Cultural Perspective*, Boulder, Colorado, Westview Press.

Mohanty, Chandra Taipade (1991) "Under Western Eyes: Feminist Scholarship and Colonial Discourses". In: Mohanty, Chandra Taipade, Russo, Ann, and Torres, Lourdes, *Third World Women and the Politics of Feminism*, Bloomington, Indiana University Press, pp. 51-80.

Moore, Henrietta (1994) *Is There a Crisis in the Family?* United Nations Research Institute for Social Development (UNRISD), Geneva.

Pearson, Ruth, and Jackson, Cecile (1998) "Interrogating Development: Feminism, Gender and Policy, Introduction". In: Jackson, Cecile, and Pearson, Ruth (eds) *Feminist Visions of Development: Gender Analysis and Development*, London, Routledge, pp. 1-16.

Peterson, V. Spike (1996) "The Politics of Identification in the Context of Globalization. In: Women's Studies International Forum", vol. 19, nos.1/2, 1996, pp. 5-15.

Ras, Marion de (1984) "Zusterschap voor God en vaderland. De Ordensgemeinschaft Jungdeutscher Schwesternschaften". In: Dresen, Grietje, and Heyst, Annelies van, (eds) *Een Sterke Vrouw...? Over het zoeken van vrouwen naar religieuse identificatie figuren*, Amersfoort, de Horstink, pp. 70-92.

Risseeuw, Carla (1988) *The Fish Don't Talk about the Water. Gender Transformation, Power and Resistance among Women in Sri Lanka*, Leiden, Brill.

Rogers, Beatrice Lorge (1995) 'Alternative Definitions of Female Headship in the Dominican Republic'. *World Development*, vol. 23, no.12, pp. 2033-2039.

Said, E.W. (1978) *Orientalism*, New York, Vintage Books.

Schuurman, Frans (1997) *Emancipatory Spaces in the Global Era*, Paper presented at the workshop Globalization and Development Studies, Nijmegen, 30 October – 1 November, 1997.

Scott, Joan Wallace (1989) "De constructie van gelijkheid versus verschil. De bruikbaarheid van de poststructuralistische theorie voor het feminisme". In: *Tiende jaarboek voor de vrouwengeschiedenis*, Nijmegen, SUN, pp. 96-112.

Sen, A. (1990) "Gender and Cooperative Conflicts". In: I. Tinker (ed.) *Persistent Inequalities: Women and World Development*, New York, Oxford, Oxford University Press, pp. 123-149.

Sen, Gita (1997) 'Globalization, Justice and Equity: A Gender Perspective.' *Development*, vol. 40, no. 2, pp. 21-26.

Third World Centre (1999) *Research Programme 1998-2003, Globalization, Governance and Development: Actors and Structures in Processes of Inclusion and Exclusion*, University of Nijmegen, 12 February.

Tonkens, Evelien (1998) "Gender in welke lagen? Kanttekeningen bij de gelaagde genderconcepten van Scott, Harding en Hagemann-White en hun toepassing in empirisch onderzoek". *Tijdschrift voor Genderstudies*, jrg. 1, no. 1, pp. 42-49.

Tomlinson, John (1996) "Cultural Globalisation: Placing and Displacing the West", *European Journal of Development Research*, 8 (2), pp. 22-36.

Uyl, Marion den (1995) *Invisible Barrier: Gender, Caste and Kinship in a Southern Indian Village*, Utrecht, International Books.

Venagas Aguilera, L. (1994) *Mujeres en la militancia blanquiazul*. In: Massolo, A. (ed.) *Los Medios y los Modos, Participación política y acción colectiva de las mujeres*, Mexico D.F., El Colegio de México, pp. 45-78.

Villarreal, Magdalena (1994) *Wielding and Yielding: Power, Subordination and Gender Identity in the Context of a Mexican Development Project*, Wageningen, PhD dissertation.

Wieringa, Saskia (1994) "Women's Interests and Empowerment: Gender Planning Reconsidered". *Development and Change*, no. 25, pp. 829-848.

Wichterich, Christa (1998) *Die Globalisierte Frau*: Berichte aus der Zukunft der Ungleichheit, RoRoRo Aktuell, Reinbek.

Willemse, Karin (Forthcoming) *One Foot in Haven. Gender, Identity and Islamization in Al-Halla, Darfour, West-Sudan*, PhD Dissertation.

CITIES AND THE GLOBALIZATION OF URBAN DEVELOPMENT POLICY

Ton van Naerssen

Introduction

Rapid urbanization is one of the most remarkable features of today's world. Currently, half of the world's population, around three billion people, lives in cities and their numbers are increasing fast. Since it is expected that the number of people living in the countryside will stay at the same level, all future population growth will occur in urban areas. For this reason, in the year 2025 the percentage of the world's urban population, currently 50, will be more than 60. Around 95% of the growth of the urban population will be realized in cities of the developing world in the South. Its increase will account for more than two billion, from 1,970 billon in the year 2000 to 4,050 billion in 2025 (UNCHS, 1996).

The unequal distribution of urbanization is also to be seen within the South. In Latin America around three-quarters of the population lives in cities, while in most African and Asian countries the urbanized part of the population is still below 40%. Particularly in the latter countries around half of the growth is due to rural-urban migration, which itself is mainly the result of stagnant development in the countryside and the lack of prospects for the younger generation. Even where production and productivity do improve, as in the case of the Green Revolution in Asia, employment opportunities do not appear to increase.

A significant proportion of the world's urban population lives in small market towns and administrative centres. However, more than ever before a high proportion of the urban population lives in large cities of one million or more inhabitants and in *mega-cities* with ten million or more people. The size of many of world's largest cities has also grown considerably. In 1950, the average population of the hundred largest cities was 2.1 million, while in 1990 this figure had already exceeded 5 million. Again the increasing importance of the cities of the South can be distinguished. In 1950, the largest city in the world was New York, with around 12 million inhabitants. The next four largest cities were London, Tokyo, Shanghai, and Paris. Among the 20 largest cities only a few were located in the South. By 2000 the picture is radically different. Mega-cities with ten million inhabitants or more will be predominantly in the South, with Mexico City

(31 million inhabitants), São Paulo (26 million), and Shanghai (24 million) at the top of the list.

It is not only the increase in the size of cities but also their functioning and their interconnections that command our attention. Fast changes are taking place in urban areas all over the world. Technological innovations, in particular regarding information technology, are at the core of these changes. Information technology induces innovation in production processes and the development of new, marketable products. New means of communication, transport technology, and logistics are transforming the world into a 'global village'. Physical distances are becoming less important, thus creating more opportunities for international interaction. A free market ideology reinforces the creation of a single global economy. The World Trade Organization (WTO), the IMF and the World Bank propagate liberalization of trade, the breaking up of tariff and non-tariff barriers, and the free movement of capital around the world. National economies are still identifiable but they are part of regional blocs and strongly connected to the worldwide network of trade and investment. Increasingly, this network is composed of linkages between large urban areas (Scott et al. 1999).

What is the impact of globalization on the growth and development of cities and on city life? What consequences does globalization have for urban policy strategies? These are the two major questions that I will try to answer, in particular with regard to cities in the developing countries. Globalization, of course, is an all encompassing concept. In this contribution I will distinguish the economic, social, and ecological dimensions, and successively indicate their links with urban developments. In the concluding sections I will focus on urban development policies.

Although the importance of small and intermediate cities should not be underestimated, I will focus on large cities with one million or more inhabitants. It is in these cities that globalization processes usually start to make an impact, before disseminating to cities down the urban hierarchy. Moreover, the complexity of large cities requires sophisticated approaches and forms a greater challenge to policy makers than the management of smaller cities.

It is also important to point out that most treatises on globalization and the urban focus solely on the metropolitan areas of the rich countries, which are usually considered as representative of the post-Fordist era. However, leaving the cities of the developing world out of the discussion means neglecting the majority of the world's urban population. Paying explicit attention to developing countries also means that one is aware of the great differences in the economic, social, and spatial aspects of urban areas in the world. In this respect, I uphold the dichotomy between the North (the rich countries) and the South (the poor countries), although I am aware of the fact that in some geographic areas their boundaries are becoming blurred and also that convergent processes can be observed.

The new economies of cities

It has often been remarked that globalization as such is not a new phenomenon. It accompanied the Industrial Revolution and caused a spatial division of work on a global scale. Within this international division of work, the developing countries acted as suppliers of raw materials to the manufacturing industries in the mother countries. Thus an integration of economies on a global scale already existed in the 19th century, and the argument is that only the pace and the intensity of the interactions of the current globalization are new.

However, one can also argue that a qualitative break occurred somewhere at the beginning of the 1970s when transnational companies started to transfer production activities to locations in the developing world where the costs of production, and wages in particular, were less compared to the old production sites. This shift, of course, was possible because the new technology in communication and transport allow for integrated systems of production on a global basis. Nowadays, it goes without saying that transnational companies are constantly searching for new centres of industrial production worldwide (Dicken 1998). Due to the global shift of labour-intensive manufacturing industries, a new spatial division of labour is accompanying globalization. No longer is the South the mere supplier of raw material, it is also producing industrial commodities for the North.

Besides the existence of a new international division of work, the phenomenal growth and power of financial markets worldwide characterize current globalization. In the competition for markets and the search for productive locations, capital moves around the globe, which also affects the distribution of productive capital. With even more speed, financial capital revolves around the globe, to the detriment of the stability of national economies, as has been shown by financial crises in Britain, Mexico, the East Asian economies, Brazil, and Russia during the past decade.

Cities are at the core of generating changes in the geography of production and finance. However, in order to fulfil this function properly they have to meet the requirements of global capital, for example with regard to their labour markets and their infrastructure. Besides that, global competition exists to attract the main agents of change (the factories and offices of transnational companies, internationally operating banks and other finance institutions). As a consequence, cities all over the world are drawn into a continuing process of restructuring to adapt to the changing requirements of capital. Due to the new global economy some cities will lose comparative advantages while others will gain and develop them. Cities are centres for innovation of production and financial processes, and by this they generate changes in the geography of production and finance. Conversely, they have to adapt to the changes they are generating.

One major change concerns the decline in manufacturing industry and the increasing importance of services in the economies of the North. In the United

States, for example, employment in the secondary sector decreased from more than 30% of the total employment in 1950 to less than 20% in 1990. This loss was compensated for by the expansion of the tertiary sector.

Because of the change in the structure of the national economies and the labour markets, the big cities in the North were forced to implement drastic processes of restructuring. Since the 1960s, London has undergone a dramatic process of de-industrialization and lost two thirds of its manufacturing employment. Between 1960 and 1980 New York City lost no less than half a million jobs. The loss has been compensated for by jobs created in the service sector, both highly qualified and specialized services as well as unskilled services. They concern an extension of the financial and production services, consumer services to meet the needs of high-income workers, and small enterprises for lowly-paid production (for example, the sweatshops of the garment industry). There is a need then, not only for a highly skilled, specialized labour force but also for low or unskilled personnel that has to be satisfied with – sometimes illegally paid – low wages: cleaners, office guards and so on (Sassen 1991).

Global cities are those big cities that are strongly integrated into the world economy. These cities are transmission points between the local and the global. On the one hand, they channel local and national resources to the global level, and on the other hand transmit the global back to the national and provincial centres (Knox 1996). Together they form a global urban system with *world cities*, a concept originally conceived by John Friedmann (1986), as key nodal points. World cities are the major sites for the concentration and accumulation of international capital, where the headquarters of the transnational companies and the major financial markets are located. The major global cities are New York, London, and Tokyo. They are the real world cities. A second tier consists of cities with a large influence over macro-regions, such as the European Union or Pacific Asia. Examples are Frankfurt, Amsterdam, San Francisco, and Singapore. A third tier consists of cities with specialized international functions: Milan, Detroit, and Mexico City.

Due to the complexity of the global economy, the headquarters of transnational companies require a great number of specialized services. For this reason, world cities increasingly demand highly skilled, specialized knowledge and information. This concerns in particular R&D laboratories, designers, consultancy firms, transport and other producer services, which are found everywhere in the top cities. The global urban system, however, is a dynamic system from which even the cities at the top cannot escape. Short and Kim (1999) notice that according to such criteria as where the headquarters of the world's hundred largest corporations, global financial centres, and largest banks are located, New York and London are declining in importance compared to Tokyo (for the period 1960-1997).

Lower down the system, cities have to find niches in the global marketplace in order to survive. Losers in this global game can be found in the old industrial regions, where cities were even more affected by the consequences of the restructuring process. The closure of factories started in the 1960s, when new and cheaper resources of energy forced mines to close. Labour-intensive industries, such as textile and shipbuilding, also had to cope with competition from low-income countries. At a later stage the automobile industry also fell on hard times. In the United States, some cities of the Manufacturing Belt, such as Detroit and Pittsburgh, were severely hit. In the U.K. regions and their major cities, for example the North-east and Newcastle, the Midlands and Sheffield and Liverpool, and Scotland and Glasgow, went through a depression. From the early 1990s onwards, when the integration of the world economy started, similar processes occurred in Eastern Europe. In the national states of the former Soviet Union the decline of industrial cities was dramatic and the consequences of this process have been demonstrated in widespread urban poverty. In Germany, Dresden and Leipzig are prominent examples.

Local governments have taken various initiatives to present and restructure their declining cities as areas for new, innovative, and successful industries. For example, Dresden wants to be a new centre for micro-electronics in Germany, and Newcastle presents itself as a centre for culture and entertainment. The well-devised strategies underlining the 'unique' qualities of the cities concerned are of major importance. Image building by way of *city marketing* is crucial, since cities have to compete at both macro-regional and world level. The results of these kinds of restructuring policies are varied; some cities succeed, others fail.

The decline of cities in the old industrial regions is accompanied by the rise of new industrial regions. The Sunbelt in the Southwest of the United States is the most famous example of a large, new industrial region. In the beginning, textile industries and consumer electronics were shifted from the East Coast to this region. Later on, Silicon Valley developed as the core of the Sunbelt. It was largely rural area in the 1950s, but now has 1.5 million inhabitants due to its position as the major high-tech centre of the world. Its existence can be explained by the tendency of big cities to decentralize production sites and relocate to suburban locations or close to highways outside the central areas. In this way offices in the New York Metropolitan Area have been relocated to the suburbs, the *edge cities*. The location of factories in Southeast England was one of the reasons for the de-industrialization of London. Even for professional services, The City is becoming too expensive and a growth in the service sector can be observed in both Inner and Outer London.

Related to this is the changing spatial form of cities that reflects the dynamics of a new *urban network economy*. According to Batten (1995), current globalization shapes a new form of cities and city systems. The global city is multi-nodal and polycentric. It cannot be managed from one bureaucratic centre but needs to be guided from a point which can co-ordinate a flexible network. The same applies at regional and higher levels, where global cities are not mere competitors but also interrelate, since they need each other and are often also complementary.

Thus they need to work together.

The place of the global cities of the South in this global urban system is different from the ones in the North. They, of course, do not shelter headquarters of large corporations or financial institutions, nor do they possess leading stockmarkets: they are integrated in the global system through branch plant economies. Often they are *primate cities*, dominating the national or – in large countries – extensive regional economies. Their markets, especially in such large countries as China, India and Brazil attract foreign banks and branches of transnational companies. Through the creation of Free Trade Zones or Export Processing Zones, they often offer platforms for labour-intensive assembly production.

Cities of established Newly Industrializing Countries (the Four Tigers of Pacific Asia) and of emerging market economies rank at the top of the global cities of the South. Other cities, such as the capital cities of Sub-Saharan Africa and of Central Asia, are weakly integrated in the global urban system. However, it is possible to discern as much dynamism in the urban economy of the South as in the cities of the North. The cities in the South have also been forced to reorient themselves. The urban economy of the primate cities used to be based on their functions as transit ports, government centres, and sites for import-substitution industries geared for the national market. For some decades now, an extensive informal sector has also been part of the urban economy. The primate cities were intermediate between the global cities of the North and the mining towns and centres for the plantation economy. This has been their traditional method of integration into the world economy, and, to a certain extent it still exists today.

For various reasons, such as an underdeveloped transport system and the import substitution policy, the large cities in the South have tended to have a low degree of economic specialization. Now, globalization forces them to specialize. Generally speaking, the growth poles of the urban economy in the South are based on export-based industrialization. Two examples are Penang in Malaysia and Metro Cebu in the Philippines. Both rank as second cities in their countries, behind Kuala Lumpur and Metro Manila respectively, but their growth and development during the past decades is remarkable. Through Export Processing Zones and a blossoming tourist industry, based on beach resorts, golf courses, and the like, they offer specific services and are firmly integrated into the world economy. Penang, for example, is considered the largest centre for the semi-conductor industry in the Pacific. Finally, both cities are, in terms of GRP per capita, relatively better off than the other regions of their countries.

Some cities succeed in going beyond this and develop a broader based international status. Bombay, for example, owed much of its industrialization to the protectionist policies of India. Heavy industry and the textile industry developed behind the tariff walls. Around 1960, manufacturing industry accounted for 40% of the jobs and generated half of the city's income. Bombay could also be considered as the financial capital of India. During the 1980s, however, the city experienced a decline in manufacture, especially in textiles, and a fall in employment in the formal sector. Now, after a restructuring process, the city is recovering with leading economic sectors, such as filmmaking, research, printing and publishing, software programming exports, and medical services (Harris 1995).

Another remarkable example is Singapore, which shows a continuous vitality. During the 1960s, Singapore underwent a transformation from colonial trade centre to platform for labour-intensive export industry. When the goal of full-time employment had been reached, the Singaporean policymakers set about attracting more advanced production processes. An excellent physical infrastructure, investments in education, and deliberate wage increases were instrumental in realizing this aim. Labour-intensive assemblage industry shifted to neighbouring countries and was replaced by highly technological production. Around 1990, Singapore launched the slogan 'Total Business Centre' and announced a change from manufacturing industry to production services, communications, and distribution. More recently, this city-state launched a campaign to stimulate 'creativity' in order to compete in the world market. Singapore is an outstanding example of a city where deliberate policies and efforts by the government shaped, or in the words of Porter (1990) 'invented', comparative advantages.

Similar processes, although to a lesser degree 'socially engineered' than in Singapore, can be observed in such cities as São Paulo, Hong Kong, and Seoul. It is interesting to observe that, in the same way as in the North, decentralization took place in these cities and suburban industrial complexes have been developed. In some regions of the South new industrial cities have come into existence. This happened along the US-Mexican border, when labour-intensive production activities shifted from the U.S. to Mexico. Yet, the cities that are only weakly integrated in the world economy and involved in the new spatial division of labour are still more representative of the urban economy in the South. There are many examples of such cities in South Asia, the Middle East, Latin America, and Sub-Saharan Africa. In these cities employment in the formal sector has barely increased, and it is an extensive informal sector that characterizes the labour market.

Post-modernism and global cities

Global cities are not only sites for the accumulation of capital but also major sites for the creation of a new global culture. It is in these cities, and particularly in the world cities, that new cultural and political identities are being constructed. Globalization and information technology have contributed to a new experience of time and place in what Castells (1996-1998) calls the network society of the 'age of information'. According to him, today we can experience the emergence of a radically transformed, new society, where places lose their importance since the network society is a space of flows.

Other authors do not go that far, but there is general agreement that the current global society is characterized by other ways of thinking and accompanying life-styles, aptly summarized in the notion of 'post-modernism'. Amongst other things, it means that it is not possible to understand today's continuously changing and complex societies through one great ideology or grand theory. Post-modernism emphasizes networking, multiformity, innovation, flexibility, and change. As a consequence, the global cities are *post-modern cities,* full of contradictions and paradoxes, constantly moving and re-structuring (Harvey 1991).

Two outstanding features of global cities are vital to an understanding global culture. In the first place, global cities are receivers of both domestic and international migrants. In the second place, thanks to liberalization and privatization, socio-economic polarization has taken place during recent decades in all global cities, creating new problems. Global cities reflect '...the contradictions of industrial capitalism, among them spatial and class polarisation' (Friedmann 1986). This is where *the new rich,* consisting of the highly educated management and producer classes of transnational companies, as well as the labour force of the producer services live. They can be considered as the leaders and consumers of a sophisticated global culture. However, it is also in the global cities that mass culture has appeared, a process usually referred to as the *McDonaldization* of the world. This suggests the creation of a global culture consisting of two components, more or less parallel to the socio-economic polarization.

However, the picture is more complicated than that. Besides processes contributing to the emergence of an homogeneous world culture, cultural differentiation processes also occur. Local cultures, different from the dominant one, flourish as, for example, in the gay neighbourhoods of San Francisco and *la banlieue* of Paris, where the local ethnic youth culture is represented by North African influenced rap music. The latter relates to what Short and Kim (1998) call the *reterritorialization of cultures,* whereby large groups of migrants maintain their original cultures in other environments and at the same time, since they are not living in their countries of origin will also change their cultures in specific ways. The Jewish population in New York is substantial, Detroit has one of the largest 'Arab' populations outside the Middle East, a large part of London's inhabitants are of South Asian origin, and there are more people from Surinam living in Amsterdam than in Paramaribo, the capital of Surinam. The global city is highly individualized and social relations are fluid. Hence, individuals search for collectivies with whom they can identify, such as groups defending non-material interests (environment), or based on shared images of a larger world (religion) or referring to roots (gender, ethnicity).

It is significant that the cities of the developing countries are left out of nearly all theorizing on the postmodern condition. However, most global cities of the South have already experienced reterritorialization during colonial times, when immigration took place from other regions, e.g. the South Asians in African and the Chinese in Southeast Asian cities. Processes of multi-ethnicity and multiculturalism were often reinforced after independence. Many people from different areas of the national territory flocked to the primate cities. The westernization of the societies of the South can be added to this. Thus, decades before multiculturalism started to be an issue in the North, the inhabitants of the cities of the South were accustomed to constructing their identities from diverse cultural sources.

If cultural differences are representative of global cities, so are striking socioeconomic disparities. We have already seen that there is an increasing demand for a highly skilled specialized labour force and for unskilled personnel. Even where the labour market provides ample opportunities, the contrasts between rich and poor have increased. In the 1980s, the number of well-to-do households in Los Angeles increased from 10 to 25%. During the same years, the percentage of poor households increased from 30 to 40%. The middle classes thus became less important and social polarization occurred. Hence the concept of the *dual city*, the city where a part of the population benefits from the age of information, while other parts experience the disadvantages or are even excluded from the fruits of 'progress'. There is an increasing realization that poverty is not only a of lack of income, it also concerns a matter of social exclusion, that is to say of insufficient access to resources, social networks, and the political process of decision-making (Mingione 1996). Nowadays, this kind of poverty is also prominent in the cities of the North. A striking example are the ghettos of New York, where the life expectancy of the average male is less than that of the average Bangladeshi.

In the developing world, some major changes in the labour market can be observed in countries that are strongly affected by the new international division of labour. In these countries the importance of employment in the private sector, particularly the manufacturing industry, has increased relative to the public sector employment. There is a gender aspect related to this change, since women have entered the secondary sector in great numbers, in particular in unskilled production work in electronics and the clothing industry, but also at a later stage in the tertiary sector, e.g. the finance sector in Singapore. In the South, as in the North, the unemployed are not the only ones who are poor. Due to low wages – a precondition in order to compete in the global market – a new group of working urban poor has come into existence. Women and children figure prominently within this group.

These countries, however, are relatively prosperous compared to those countries left outside the New International Division of Labour, such as the poor African countries. The populations of these countries are among the hardest hit by the Structural Adjustment Programmes (SAPs) of the World Bank and the IMF. The implementation of a SAP entails cuts in the national budget, especially in subsidized social sectors, such as food programmes, education, health, and housing. Private initiatives have to compensate for the loss of the size and quality of these sectors. The principle that services are something that should be paid for naturally means a burden for the poor, simply because they will find it very difficult or impossible to pay. Moreover, the introduction of a SAP usually implies an increase in unemployment, due to redundancies in the public sector and in those parts of the private sector that are not able to cope with import restrictions and international competition. In these countries the major labour market is to be found in the informal sector market of street vendors, market vendors, entertainment workers, small-scale industry, and so on. Moreover, crises and recessions have also contributed to the informalization of the economy.

Social insecurity, instability, and alienation, summarized as 'urban stress', characterize the dark side of life in all cities of the world. Broken families, homelessness, and street children are specific phenomena of global cities. Related problems concern prostitution, drug abuse, alcoholism, and violence. Throughout the whole world, from London to Nairobi and from Rio de Janeiro to New York, the *culture of poverty* (Lewis 1965) is back on the urban agenda.

However, for the poor the global city is not only problematic, it is also perceived as an area offering opportunities to meet their strategies for coping with poverty. Ultimately, that is the main reason why substantial rural-urban migration continues to take place. However, the poor are not passive recipients of urban problems. During the past decades, in many countries it has been demonstrated that the poor are able to organize themselves. Community-based organizations (CBOs) of the urban poor and supportive NGOs have been actively involved in improving the urban environment, especially in the developing countries. In some countries they form umbrella organizations or networks, calling urban social movements into existence (Schuurman and Van Naerssen 1989).

The quest for sustainable global cities

Global cities have to cope both with fast changes in the world economy and substantial socio-economic disparities within their territories. To these, and other related problems, severe ecological problems can be added. In this section, ecology will be discussed in connection with health. In particular the physical environment in global cities of the South, which is having a direct negative impact on the health of the urban population (Bradley 1991). Communal diseases, such as cholera and typhoid, have disappeared in the North, but still occur in the South.

Ecological problems and their solutions can be linked to the concept of 'sustainability', which became popular in 1987 with the publication of the OECD's report 'Our Common Future', the so-called Brundtland Report. In a separate chapter, the report addresses urbanization and its accompanying problems. Some years later, Agenda 21, the result of the 1992 conference on environment and development in Rio de Janeiro, called for action to realize sustainable development; hence, the move towards *sustainable cities*. A sustainable city, however, requires more than ecology; it also calls for a sound economy and the eradication of poverty.

After the Rio conference, around 300 European cities signed the so-called Aalborg Charter and pledged to commit themselves to sustainable urban development. Since then, a number of ideas and initiatives have been developed. There has been the application of energy- saving techniques in housing and building and the internalizing of environmental costs in some consumer prices (the principle of 'the polluter pays'). The separation of solid waste by individual households, and the diminishing of raw materials going into the city and urban waste coming out ('closing the system') have also been started. The latter refers to the concept of the *ecological footprint*, which translates the consumption by territory of population (nation, region, or city) into the amount of land or water area needed to produce the goods and to absorb the waste. For example, it has been calculated that in 1991 the 475,000 inhabitants of of Vancouver consumed and used the equivalent of 2.4 million hectares or 200 times the actual size of the city (IIUE 1997: 90). In closing the system there is an attempt to decrease the ecological footprint. Moreover, one can assume that the global cities in the North have far larger ecological footprints than those in the developing countries of the South. Thus more detailed, comparative research will show how great the existing inequalities between global cities are, and perhaps contribute to a more balanced urban system.

In the global cities of the developing countries both the poverty and the increasing use of energy affect the quality of the cities' physical environment. The second Habitat conference in Istanbul (1996) paid explicit attention to the problems of large cities and the fast urban growth in the South. It was pointed out that poverty in the countryside is being relocated to the urban areas. This creates many serious problems for urban environmental health. Indoor and outdoor air pollution, a lack of safe water and sanitation facilities, and uncollected solid waste are some of the most pressing problems in urban poor areas (see also Hardoy et al. 1992).

Air pollution also creates serious problems. It has been estimated that 1.4 billion people live in cities where annual averages for sulphur dioxide levels and particulate matter exceed WHO health guidelines. Major sources of air pollution are transport, manufacturing industry, and coal or oil-fired power stations. In most urban areas the major culprits are transport and manufacturing industry. Due to the growth of the population and of the urban economy, it is expected that air pollution in the global cities of the South will increase considerably. In a number of large metropolitan areas the problem is aggravated by the surrounding mountains, which restrict air circulation. The morning smog in Mexico City is a case in point. Studies have shown a strong association between air pollution and the incidence of such respiratory infections as chronic cough.

Indoor air pollution is also a matter of serious concern due to the extensive use of biomass fuels for heating, cooking, and lighting. Coal, kerosene, wood, and liquefied petroleum gas are widely used, especially by poorer households. It also increases the risk of fire in the vulnerable built-up neighbourhoods of the urban poor. These fuels burnt in poorly ventilated houses also cause adverse health effects.

The second major problem of the urban environments in the South concerns the provision of safe water and sanitation facilities. Most water supplies are contaminated. Most rivers flowing through the cities of the South are large open drains, containing a mixture of raw sewage and untreated industrial effluent. The rivers are so strongly polluted by organic waste that their oxygen content almost disappears. In the dry season, when the water does not flow, estuaries can be transformed into huge, black, stinking pools. An insufficient supply of clean water, the contamination of water, and inadequate sanitation cause high rates of water-related diseases, such as diarrhoea and schistosomiasis.

Disposal of solid waste is a third problem area. An estimated 30 to 50% of the solid waste generated in urban areas of the South is left uncollected. Solid waste represents a major reservoir of toxic metals in the urban environment. Hazardous industrial waste poses a particular problem as it is currently dumped on open landsites where no provision is made to prevent its exposure to humans. Rubbish heaps build up on streets and open spaces, providing excellent breeding-grounds for rodents and other disease vectors. Children, who often play on wasteland near or on rubbish, are among the first affected.

One example is Dar es Salaam, the capital of Tanzania. The city has a population of around 3 million and an astonishing annual population growth of 7% (implying a doubling of its population within a decade). There is a shortage of clean water. Only 40% of the population have a piped water supply. The water-pipe system is old and dilapidated, with frequent interruptions in the water supply. Only 5% of households are connected to a sewer; the majority of the population using pit latrines. Around 2,000 tons of domestic, solid waste has to be collected each day, but refuse collection rarely takes place. At the end of 1997, there were only 4-15 trucks per day available. In such an environment it comes as no surprise that such diseases as malaria and diarrhoea are rife.

Dar es Salaam is weakly integrated into the global urban system, but this does not imply that people in global cities that are more firmly integrated into the world economy will be better off. Because they usually refer to the average inhabitant, published data will suggest better conditions than actually exist. In global cities socio-economic disparities tend to be great. Therefore, it is not surprising to find that the urban poor are the main victims. They usually live in slum and squatter areas without proper facilities and near polluted rivers and waste dumps. As a consequence, their health status is considerably worse than that of the people who live in the richer residential areas. Such were the findings of several researches, including an international research initiated by the Stockholm Environmental Institute (SEI), comparing Accra, Jakarta, and São Paulo (McGranahan 1991, see also Bradley et al. 1991). In Accra, for example, the overall mortality numbers 5.5 per thousand inhabitants, but varies from 1.3 in the highest income area to 23.3 in one of the urban poor neighbourhoods. Any urban development programme that aims for sustainability must then take into account that ecological conditions, poor health, and poverty are closely interrelated.

Globalization and the new urban policy paradigm

Some trends of convergence between global cities of the North and the South can be observed. The cities of the South have joined those of the North in restructuring programmes to adapt to globalization under free market conditions. The cities in the North have joined those of the South in polarization of social and economic life, multiculturalism, and increasing violence. Further, both in the North and in the South cities have to cope with ecological problems. The challenge of urban development policy consists, then, of three sets of requirements: economic restructuring, a socially balanced environment, and ecological sustainability. Innovative approaches are needed in order to solve the problems, and during the past decade a new policy paradigm has emerged to support such approaches. The new paradigm comprises three interrelated notions: urban governance, community participation, and decentralization.

The UNDP defines *governance* as the exercise of political, economic, and administrative authority to manage a society's affairs. 'This broad concept encompasses the organisational structures and activities of central, regional, and local government; the parliament; the judiciary; and the institutions, organisations, and individuals that constitute civil society and the private sector. The concept of governance stresses the nature and quality of interactions among social actors and between social actors and the state' (UNDP 1997: 4). It is the sharing of decision-making between local state structures, the private sector, and the actors of the *civil society,* the last defending the interest of the civilians.

The concept fits into the general endeavour to limit the role of the government in policies. Government agencies at all three levels (national, regional, and local) are supposed to enable the other actors to act properly. If there are commercial perspectives the private sector will get a chance, while the civil society will take responsibility for social, non-profitmaking activities. Thus there are three major groups of actors in the development process: the state with its governmental agencies; the private business sector; and the civil society represented by non-governmental organizations (NGOs) and community-based organizations (CBOs).

In the global cities, the application of the concept implies greater space for poor communities to participate in urban development processes. By way of participation they can initiate interventions to improve their conditions. Hence, *community participation*, which comprises both the organizations of urban communities and access to decision-making institutions, is another key notion of current urban policies. The more poor communities are organized, the better they can participate in the efforts of local governments to improve the urban environment. By definition community participation is one of the most effective ways to cope with social exclusion. The benefits for the poorer segments of the population can be improved in matters such as housing, public services, and urban violence. Participation means a sharing of responsibility for all kinds of poverty alleviation programmes and thus an enhancement of their sustainability.

Although the notion of participation is broadly accepted, in practice it is often limited to consulting 'the target-groups' of the urban poor. Participation, however, is more than instrumental (Abbott 1996). Real participation demands a political process to get people involved, to mobilize their resources (including social capital), and to strengthen their capacity to participate. This process has to occur at several levels, since the organizational capacity of urban community groups depends on the democratic quality of the national and local governments. They shape the social environment wherein the existence and action of independent CBOs and supportive NGOs can be encouraged.

Participatory processes are difficult to realize in a political climate where democracy is still in its infancy. Enabling governments are a precondition in starting participatory processes at community level. Unfortunately, in many countries it is precisely the socio-political environment that is not yet conducive to effective participation of the urban poor. Latin American countries seem to be ahead in practising participatory processes, while in Sub-Saharan countries effective CBOs are almost non-existent and in many countries of Asia and the Middle East they are controlled by the state.

A third concept of urban development policies concerns *decentralization*. Today, there is a clear tendency to decentralize decision-making and finance from the national to the regional and local – municipal or district – levels. In a centralized system a disproportionate part of the government budget is usually allocated on behalf of the capital city. In giving the secondary and other cities a larger say, it can be guaranteed that they will get a fairer share of the national budget. In addition, the local level is supposed to organize its own income. However, decentralization is more than a technical or administrative matter. It also implies the creation of a local state structure with new, more independent functions. For community initiatives a decentralized system provides new opportunities. It can be expected that bureaucracies are more accessible at local level, so it is at this level that dialogues between government agencies and urban poor communities will start.

The emergence of a new global urban paradigm is strongly related to the spread of democracy within a neo-liberal framework. In this respect one notices a tendency to global homogenization. However, for the time being, different political systems and national ideologies will continue to exist implying that there will be several representations of the same paradigm. Besides, it would be naive to overlook the reality of a huge divergence in resources. The global cities in the South have only limited government budgets at their disposal. For example, while the management of an American city can spend $2,000 per inhabitant, their counterparts in Dhaka or Dar es Salaam have to be satisfied with $2 (UNCHS 1996b: 24-5).

Two urban development programmes

In 1986, the World Bank, the United Nations Development Programme (UNDP) and the United Nations Centre for Human Settlements (UNCHS Habitat) started the *Urban Management Programme* (UMP). Devas and Rakodi (1993: 43) define urban management as local and national governmental interventions in planning, development, and daily operations of a city. In the UMP urban management similarly refers to the whole of urban development policy with both an economic dimension and a spatial planning component. However, the programme underlines both public and private sectors and in doing so does not restrict itself to governmental interventions. Participatory processes are indeed important tools of urban management.

The UMP aims to exploit the economic potentials of cities. The idea is that municipalities must take a leading role in restructuring the city and in providing an attractive investment climate to respond to the needs of potential investors. In addition, urban poverty programmes have to be set up and co-ordinated. Due to – amongst other things – political instability and insufficient financial resources, the global city governments of the developing countries generally lack the capacity to deal with urban problems. Therefore, the major aim of urban management is to strengthen the capacity of governmental institutions, especially at municipal level, and of non-governmental organizations in identifying and implementing policy alternatives. The UMP strongly promotes the idea of urban governance (Cheema 1993).

In due course, the UMPapproach has improved considerably. Nevertheless, the question remains whether the programme can sufficiently deal with the urban problems in developing countries. There are some structural conditions that put limitations on the effectiveness of urban management in general, and onto the UMP in particular. Most global cities in the South will be unable to compete on a global scale, and, among other things, they will find it difficult to attract foreign investors (exceptions are some Latin American cities and the cities of the Asian Pacific Region).

The question of growth and equity is another difficulty, since the objective of urban economic growth and productivity increase can easily frustrate the objective of the eradication of poverty and the creation of employment in small-scale activities. So far, only lip service has been paid to initiatives by the poor: 'The middle and higher classes have until now not been able to accept change in conventional patterns of urban management. They seem unwilling to admit that the poor contribute substantially to both the existence and the prosperity of urban areas' (Oosterhout 1997).

Another programme, which acknowledges the need for consultation, community participation, and decentralization concerns the *Healthy Cities* movement. The movement, which started in the North about a decade ago, is an attempt to implement an integrated approach to urban health. It acknowledges the close interrelationship between health and the urban environment, and it attaches great value to participatory interventions at neighbourhood level. The Healthy Cities movement started in 1986, in the wake of the First International Conference on Promotion of Health, held under the auspices of the WHO in Ottawa. In the declaration of this conference, called the 'Ottawa Charter for Health Promotion', health promotion is defined as 'the process of enabling people to increase control over, and to improve their health'. It also states that health promotion has to work through effective community action. The communities should set priorities, make decisions, plan strategies and implement them to achieve better health. In other words, the core of health promotion is the empowerment of communities, who own and control their own endeavours and destiny (Davies and Kelly 1993: 14 and 56).

Since Healthy Cities is a movement and the idea of it has spread more or less spontaneously to a large number of cities, there is a certain flexibility in what exactly comprises a Healthy City (WHO 1994: 12). Perhaps the simplest definition is to conceive of Healthy Cities as a process for the implementation of the WHO 'Health for All' strategy in urban areas. Such a notion implies that the ultimate aim of Healthy Cities is to reach equity in urban health. The other features of Healthy Cities, such as health promotion, intersectoral co-operation, and community involvement, are meant to serve this aim.

Although the Healthy Cities movement is currently mainly active in the North, it has also spread to cities in the South (Harpham et al. 1998; Van Naerssen and Barten 1999). In 1995, under the umbrella of UNDP/LIFE programme, the WHO started a Healthy Cities programme for five cities in the South: Cox's Bazar (Bangladesh), Dar es Salaam (Tanzania), Al Faiyûm (Egypt), Managua (Nicaragua), and Quetta (Pakistan). Their size, function, and integration into the global system varied substantially (e.g. Al Faiyûm is not really a city). At the end of the programme, in 1999, it turned out that the experiences with the Healthy Cities programme were very different in the five cities, with an ownership of the civil society actors in Managua and state controlled development in Al Faiyûm occupying opposite ends of the spectrum. In the latter case, the programme showed a remarkable lack of innovation and was limited to non-controversial, traditional health issues. This proves that the implementation of one new urban paradigm in global cities will have very different results, according to the circumstances.

Conclusion

Globalization has a strong impact on the worldwide urban system and the functioning and structure of cities. Because of the liberalization of the world economy and the weakening of the nation-state, the global economy becomes increasingly an economy of interrelated city-regions. Global cities are cities that are strongly integrated into the world economy; together they form a system with world cities, the command centres of transnational companies, as centres of a global network. The integration of the developing countries of the South occurs within the framework of branch-plant economies and the new international division of labour. They can therefore be considered peripheral in the global urban system.

Nevertheless, despite their different positions in the urban system, all global cities show similar characteristics. Firstly, in today's global world, cities must compete in the world market and are forced to restructure their social institutions, labour markets, and physical infrastructure accordingly. Secondly, cities all over the world are having to cope with increasing social polarization and imbalances, including urban violence. Thirdly, in order to reach ecological sustainability an holistic approach to tackling urban problems is needed, comprising economic, social, and health aspects of human development.

While cities in the North and South share common problems, the manifestations of their problems and the conditions for their solution are substantially different. Over the coming decades, the huge increase in the world population will mainly take place in urban centres of the developing world. It remains to be seen whether the paradigm of urban governance will be effective in the global cities of the South, since, whatever the institutional changes, they simply lack the financial resources to eradicate poverty and illness. The global urban challenge, therefore, lies mainly in the South.

This article does not pretend to do more than present an overview of the general problems of global cities. It is, however, clear that most of the existing studies on global cities deal with cities in the developed countries of the North. Moreover, it is often denied that global cities exist in the developing countries of the South. Hence, there is a need for research regarding the precise position of the global cities of the South within the global urban network and for studies to be made of individual global cities in the South, their economy, culture, and policy.

References

Abbott, J. (1996) *Sharing the City. Community participation in urban management*, London, Earthscan.

Batten, D.F. (1995) "Network Cities: Creative Urban Agglomerations for the 21st Century". In: *Urban Studies*, vol. 32, no.2, pp. 313-327.

Bradley, D., Caincross, S. et al. (1991) *A Review of Environmental Health Impacts in Developing Country Cities, Washington*, World Bank. Urban Management Programme Paper no. 6.

Castells, M. (1989) *The Informational City: Information Technology, Economic Restructuring, and the Urban-Regional Process*, Oxford, Blackwell.

Castells, M. (1996-1998) *The Information Age: Economy, Society and Culture*, 3 vols., Oxford, Blackwell.

Cheema, G. S. (1993) *Urban Management; Policies and Innovations in Developing Countries*, London, Praeger.

Cohen, M.A. et al. (eds.) (1996) *Preparing for the Urban Future. Global Pressure and Local Forces*, Baltimore, Woodrow Wilson Center Press.

Devas, N. and Rakodi, C. (1993) *Managing Fast Growing Cities. New Approaches to Urban Planning and Management in the Developing World*, Harlow, Longman.

Davies, J.K. and Kelly, M.P. (1993) *Healthy Cities. Research and Practice*, London, Routledge.

Dicken, P. (1998, 3rd.edition) *Global Shift. Transforming the World Economy*, London, Paul Chapman.

Duffy, H. (1995) *Competitive Cities: Succeeding in the Global Economy*, London, E&FN Spon.

Fainstein, S.S., Gordon, I., and Harloe, M. (1992) *Divided Cities, New York and London in the Contemporary World*, Oxford, Blackwell.

Friedmann, J. (1986) "The World City Hypothesis". In: *Development and Change*, vol. 17, pp. 69-83.

Gilbert,A. and J. Gugler (1992, 2nd.edition) *Cities, Poverty and Development*, Oxford, Oxford University Press.

Hall, P. (1996) *Cities of Tomorrow: an Intellectual History of Urban Planning and Design in the 20th Century*, Oxford, Blackwell.

Hardoy, J.E., Mitlin, D., and Satterthwaite, D. (1992) *Environmental Problems in Third World Cities*, London, Earthscan.

Harpham, T., Goldstein, G. et al. (1998) *Healthy Cities in Developing Countries*, London, Earthscan.

Harris, N. (1997) "Cities in a Global Economy: Structural Change and Policy Reactions". In: *Urban Studies*, vol. 34, pp. 1693-1703.

Harris, N. (1995) "Bombay in a Global Economy. Structural Adjustment and the Role of Cities". In: *Cities*, vol. 12, pp. 175-184.

Harvey, D. (1991) *The Condition of Postmodernity*, Oxford, Blackwell.

Hoggart, K. et al. (1992). *A New Metropolitan Geography*, London, Edward Arnold.

International Institute for the Urban Environment (IIUE) (1997) *The Ecological Footprint of Cities*, Amsterdam.

Knox. P.L. (1996) "Globalization and the World City Hypothesis". In: *Scottish Geographical* Magazine, vol. 112, pp. 124-126.

Knox, P.L. and Taylor, P. (eds.) (1995) *World Cities in a World-System*, Cambridge, Cambridge University Press.

LeGates, R.T. and Stout, F. (eds.) (1996) *The City Reader*, London/New York, Routledge.

Lewis, O. (1965) *La Vida. A Puerto Rican Family in the Culture of Poverty*, New York, Vintage Books.

McCarney, P.L. (1996) *Cities and Governance: New Directions in Latin-America, Asia and Africa*, Toronto, Centre for Urban and Community Studies.

McGranahan, G. (1991) *Environmental Problems and the Urban Households in Third World Cities*, Stockholm, Stockholm Environment Institute.

Mingione, E. (ed.) (1996) *Urban Poverty and the Underclass: a Reader*, Oxford, Blackwell.

Naerssen, T. van and Barten, F. (1999) "Healthy Cities in Developing Countries". In: Anders, Narman and Simon, David (eds.) *Development in Theory and Practice*, Harlow, Longman, pp. 230-246.

Oosterhout, F. van (1997) "The Challenge for Urban Management in Developing Countries". In: Naerssen, T. van, et al. (eds.) *The Diversity of Development* Assen, Van Gorcum, pp. 221-227.

Our Global Neighbourhood (1995) The Report of the Commission on Global Governance (1995) Oxford, Oxford University Press.

Porter. M.E. (1990) *The Competitive Advantage of Nations*, New York, Free Press.

Sassen, S. (1991) *The Global City: London, New York, Tokyo*, Princeton, NJ, Princeton University Press.

Sassen, S. (1994) *Cities in a World Economy*, Thousand Oaks (Calif.), Pine Forge Press.

Schuurman, F. and Naerssen, T. van (eds.) (1989) *Urban Social Movements in the Third World*, London, Routledge.

Scott, A.J., Agnew, J., Soja, E., and Storper, M. (1999) *Global City-Regions*. Conference theme paper Global City-Regions Conference, 21-23 September 1999. Los Angeles. UCLA School of Public Policy and Social Research.

Short, J.R. and Yeong-Hyun Kim (1999) *Globalization and the City*, Harlow, Longman.

Smith, M.P. and Feagan, J.R. (eds.) (1987) *The Capitalist City. Global Restructuring and Community Politics*. Oxford, Blackwell.

United Nations Centre for Human Settlements (UNCHS/Habitat) (1996) *An Urbanizing World*. Global report on human settlements, 1996, Oxford, Oxford University Press.

United Nations Development Programme (UNDP) (1997) *Reconceptualising Governance*. Discussion paper 2, Management Development and Governance Division, Bureau for Policy and Programme Support, New York.

World Commission on Environment and Development (1987) *Our Common Future*, Oxford, Oxford University Press.

World Health Organization (WHO) (1993) *The Urban Health Crisis. Strategies for Health* for *All in the Face of Rapid Urbanization*, Geneva.

World Health Organization (WHO) (1995) *Building a Healthy City: a Practitioners' Guide*. Prepared by Unit of Environmental Health, Office of Operational Support, Geneva.

NOTES ON CONTRIBUTORS

Martin Albrow is Research Professor in the Social Sciences at Roehampton Institute London. His books include *Max Weber's Construction of Social Theory* (MacMillan, 1990) and *The Global Age* (Polity Press, 1996). He is founding editor of *International Sociology*, and an Honorary Vice-President of the British Sociological Association.

Tine Davids is a cultural anthropologist and attached as lecturer to the Institute of Development Studies at the University of Nijmegen, the Netherlands. She is currently writing her Ph.D. thesis on women and politics in Mexico. Since 1998 she has run a consultancy agency, Genderconsult.

Francien van Driel is a lecturer at the Institute of Development Studies at the University of Nijmegen. Her teaching and research focus is on gender theories and the links with general development theories. Her regional specialization is sub-Saharan Africa. She is author of the book *Poor and Powerful: Female-Headed Households and Unmarried Motherhood in Botswana*, (Breitenbach, 1994) and she has written several articles on gender and development theories and policies. Her current research focuses on family support networks, household compositions, social capital, and women's empowerment in Southern Africa.

Detlev Haude, an anthropologist by training, has been working since 1980 as Development Economist at the Institute of Development Studies at the University of Nijmegen. His teaching and research topics include the political economy of development, the history of economic development thinking, and processes of industrialization. He is a member of the editorial board of the development journal *Peripherie*. Most recently he has broadened his field of work into the area of social economics.

Reinhart Kössler is attached as Professor to the Department of Sociology of Münster University in Germany. He has also taught at the universities of Bremen, Oldenburg, Hanover, Dar es Salaam, Frankfurt-on-Main, and Bayreuth. He has published widely on current development issues - primarily concerning Southern Africa, Eastern Europe, and East Asia - industrial relations, nationalism, and ethnicity, as well as wider aspects of social theory and international politics. He has been a founding editor of *Peripherie, Zeitschrift für Politik und Ökonomie in der Dritten Welt* since 1980 and a corresponding editor of *International Review of Social History* since 1995.

Kristoffel Lieten is at the Amsterdam School of Social Science Research and teaches at the Faculty of Social Sciences at the University of Amsterdam, where he is in charge of Development Sociology. He is also the chairperson of a Child Labour Research Foundation. Most of his books relate to theoretical issues in development, supported by extensive fieldwork. He has published extensively on the effect of land reforms in Kerala and West Bengal, on rural development in northern India and Pakistan, on multinational corporations and development, and on political issues in their historical and social context, particularly related to South Asia.

Marianne H. Marchand is Senior Lecturer in International Political Economy, and Gender and Development, at the University of Amsterdam. She has contributed to Stubbs and Underhill, *Political Economy and the Changing Global Order* (1994), and the special Third World Quarterly issue on *The South in the New World (Dis)order*. With Jane Parpart she is co-editor of *Feminism/ Postmodernism/Development* (1995). She is currently working on gender, regionalism, and development in Latin America.

Anton van Naerssen is a human geographer and physical planner with a special interest in urban poverty alleviation and participatory processes in urban and regional planning. He is Senior Lecturer at the School of Environmental Studies of the University of Nijmegen, the Netherlands.

Arie de Ruijter has been , since 1983, Professor in Cultural and Social Anthropology at Utrecht University (the Netherlands) and Scientific Director of the Dutch national research school CERES. He has published extensively on structural anthropology and methodology of the social sciences. Recently his research activities have been focused on identity formation, citizenship, and ethnicity. His recent publications include 'Cultural Pluralism and Citizenship' (*Cultural Dynamics* 7, 1995), 'The Era of Glocalisation', in: T. van Naerssen, M. Rutten & A. Zoomers (eds), *The Diversity of Development*, Assen, van Gorcum, 1997), and 'Ambivalences and Complexities in European Identity Formation', in: M. Gastelaars & A. de Ruijter (eds), *A United Europe. A Quest for a Multifaceted Identity*, Shaker Publ. Maastricht, 1998).

Anne Sisson Runyan is Director of Women's Studies and Associate Professor of Political Science at Wright State University, Ohio, USA. She is co-author (with V. Spike Peterson) of the first and second editions of *Global Gender Issues* (Westview Press, 1993 and 1999) and co-editor (with Marianne H. Marchand) of *Gender and Global Restructuring: Shifting Sightings, Sites and Resistances* (Routledge, 2000).

M.A. Mohamed Salih is Professor of Politics of Development at the Institute of Social Studies, The Hague in the Netherlands. He has published widely on environmental issues. His books include *Ecology and Politics: Environment Stress and Security in Africa* (Scandinavian Institute of African Studies, 1989); *Environmental Liberation and Politics in Contemporary Africa* (Kluwer Academic Publishers, 1999); and *Environmental Planning, Policies and Politics in Eastern and Southern Africa* (MacMillan and St. Martins Press, 1999).

Frans J. Schuurman is a senior lecturer at the Institute of Development Studies at the University of Nijmegen, the Netherlands. He has edited a number of volumes on development issues including *Urban Social Movements in the Third World* (with Van Naerssen; Routledge, 1989), *Beyond the Impasse* (Zed, 1993), and *Current Issues in Development Studies* (Breitenbach, 1994). His current research interests focus on the role of civil society and forms of co-management in the development process.

John Tomlinson is Professor of the Sociology of Culture, and Director of the Centre for Research in International Communication and Culture (CRICC) at Nottingham Trent University in the UK. He is the author of *Cultural Imperialism* (Pinter, 1991) and *Globalization and Culture* (Polity Press, 1999). He is an associate editor of the journal *Theory, Culture and Society,* and a managing editor of the Sage/CRICC book series Global Power/Cultural Spaces.

INDEX

INDEX